D0786958

TALKING BACK

TALKING BACK

Native Women and the Making of the Early South

ALEJANDRA DUBCOVSKY

Yale
UNIVERSITY
PRESS
New Haven and London

Published with assistance from the Annie Burr Lewis Fund.
Published with assistance from the Louis Stern Memorial Fund.

Yale University Press books may be purchased in quantity for educational, business, or promotional use. For information, please e-mail sales.press@yale.edu (U.S. office) or sales@yaleup.co.uk (U.K. office).

Set in Janson type by IDS Infotech, Ltd.
Printed in the United States of America.

Library of Congress Control Number: 2022942806
ISBN 978-0-300-26612-2 (hardcover : alk. paper)

A catalogue record for this book is available from the British Library.

This paper meets the requirements of ANSI/NISO Z39.48-1992 (Permanence of Paper).

10 9 8 7 6 5 4 3 2 1

Para Mami

Contents

Acknowledgments

THIS BOOK TRULY BECAME a book after a "Mid-Career Book Manuscript Workshop" organized with generous funding from the University of California Humanities Research Institute (UCHRI). Susan Amussen, Lisa Brooks, Brian DeLay, Aisha Finch, Rebecca Kugel, and Ann Little read a full manuscript draft. They gave me incredibly wise, incisive, and generative suggestions. As I worked through these ideas, several obliging colleagues read drafts of the project. I want to especially thank Ademide Adelusi-Adeluyi, Emily Berquist, Denise Bossy, Verónica Castillo-Muñoz, and Elizabeth Ellis. Jane Landers met with me to discuss sources and share resources. Aubrey Lauersdorf graciously discussed the region and its history with me. Brooke Bauer and I shared manuscripts and the joys (and struggles!) of this kind of work. Brianna Leavitt-Alcantara came to the rescue when I thought I had lost all my images in Seville. Peter Mancall answered every question; his kindness and knowledge cannot be overstated. Aaron Broadwell, a friend and collaborator, has fueled my love for the Timucua language.

Throughout the many years this project developed, I had the opportunity to workshop and present at several venues. Juliana Barr, Amy Braden, Leila K. Blackbird, Sharon Block, Jorge Cañizares-Esguerra, Jessica Cattelino, Megan Cherry, Andrew Devereux, Bradley Dixon, Kathleen DuVal, Robbie Ethridge, Nicole Eustace, Hannah Farber, Michael Francis, Barbara Fuchs, Glenda Goodman, Steve Hackel, Ellen Hartigan-O'Connor, Carrie Heitman, D. Andrew

Johnson, Matthew Kruer, Karen Kupperman, Peter Mancall, Ernesto Mercado Montero, Hayley Negrin, Lindsay O'Neil, Tawny Paul, Tanya Peres, Nathan Perl-Rosenthal, Carla Pestana, Josh Piker, Steve Pincus, Guadalupe Pinzón, Jenny Pulsipher, Cynthia Radding, Julie Reed, Roy Ritchie, Sarah Rivett, Carol Shammas, Susanah Shaw Romney, Christina Snyder, Terri Snyder, Jessica Stern, Dana Velasco Murillo, Gregory Waselkov, Judy Wu, and so many more asked questions, offered suggestions, and made critiques that have made my work and my thinking sharper.

I was incredibly fortunate to receive one of the initial UCR–Huntington Library Advancement of the Humanities Fellowships. This extraordinary fellowship gave me the precious gift of time—time to think, to write, and to interact with many wonderful scholars. I want to especially thank Steve Hindle and my fellow fellows: Allison Bigelow, Verónica Castillo-Muñoz, Elizabeth Dillion, Andrew Lipman, Mary Mendoza, Katie Moore, Michele Navakas, Dan Richter, and James Sidbury.

At the University of California, Riverside, Allison Palmer, Michael Austin, and Veronica Ibarra provided invaluable support. Cliff Trafzer offered unyielding encouragement and kindness. Dana Simmons organized a writing retreat that allowed me to put on paper some of the earliest ideas of the project. Lucille Chia, Kim Yi Dionne, Jonathan Eacott, Steve Hackel, Randy Head, Rebecca Kugel, and Kiril Tomoff have kindly shared their insights at critical junctures. I also participated in an interdisciplinary working group at the Center of Ideas and Society, and I benefited greatly from conversations with Covadonga Lamar Prieto, Susan Laxton, Margaret Nash, Victoria Reyes, and the undergraduate and graduate student participants.

As the book took shape, I relied on the marvelous editing services of Audra Wolfe and Beth Sherouse. And at Yale University Press, Adina Berk proved a model editor in every way. Ash Lago, her assistant, was also incredibly helpful. Elizabeth Casey, who did the copyediting, proved a careful and caring reader. I also want to thank the two anonymous readers of my manuscript, who provided thoughtful suggestions and made this project better in every way. Much thanks also to Bill Nelson for the maps. Finally, a big thank you to the artists and writers who corresponded with me and allowed me to feature their powerful pieces. These contemporary artists tend to work far from the regions and time periods covered in this book; but in their distinct, locally rooted, culturally specific, and thought-provoking representations, these pieces evoke a shared argument about the endurance, resilience, and power of Native women.

My friends and family kept me going. Piali ran all the miles with me. Becca, Monica, Caroline, Kim and Ann, and Chung-Hay were always there. My B'nai Mitzvah crew and the congregation of Temple Beth El helped more than they will know. Katie, Chuck, Patrick, Megan, and my beloved niece and nephew, Emilia and Aiden, kept me smiling. Martín and Alyssa are simply awesome. Y el apoyo y amor de mis papis, Laura and Jorge, es infinito.

COVID-19 and the global pandemic affected my family in ways that now seem routine. Ryan and I stumbled and struggled to find time, balance, and some semblance of normality, and though we never found any of that, we found much in each other. Joaquín and Santiago helped with their love, endless curiosity, fabulous adventures, and questionable decision-making skills. Through each hurdle, with much whiskey and even more running, we made it through each day. Ryan, Joaqui, and Santi, you remain, still and always, the best part of every day.

Glossary

buhío	council house
cacica	female Native chief
cacique	male Native chief
compadrazgo	godparenting
Criollo/a	person of Spanish descent born in the Americas
entrada	expedition
holata	Timucua title, usually meaning chief
junta	council
junta de guerra	war council
legajo	bundle of documents
madrina/padrino	godparent
mujer/es	woman/women
principal	Native leader
real/reales	Spanish coin
repartimiento	system of forced labor
testigo	witness
sabana	field
visita	survey
visitador	surveyor

Introduction

Native Women in the Early South

THERE WERE SO MANY BOSSY women in Florida. Friar Francisco Pareja complained about them in his 1627 rendition of the Adam and Eve parable, which he concluded by stating, "and thus women retained their desire to be bossy, as I saw they were in Florida."[1] Pareja railed against Native women and their excessive freedoms. They were just like Eve, greedy, prideful, and sinful. They corrupted men and defiled the very institutions that kept order in society. These Native *mujeres mandonas* (bossy women) could tell men where to live, when to come home (or not), and when their marriage was over.[2] Spanish secular and religious officials found Native women and their power unsettling.

Native women's bossiness had little to do with Spanish men or their concerns, however. They were not bossy because of them, nor in spite of them. Native women played important and clearly recognized roles in the early South, as Timucua Eve makes perfectly clear. Timucua Eve appears in the Timucua translation of Pareja's Adam and Eve story. Timucua, a Native language spoken by hundreds of thousands of people in what is now northern Florida and southern Georgia, has no reliable grammar or dictionary, so it has taken decades of interdisciplinary, collaborative, and communal work to begin reading and properly translating the Timucua portions of this religious text. Meaning that the Adam and Eve parable Pareja preached to his Native congregants can now be read as it was written by Timucua authors, rather than through the Spanish translation alone.[3] In the Timucua version Timucua Eve has a powerful voice, and she has a lot to say.

> Porque Eua auiendo tomado la mançana para comella no fue á su marido antes de prouarla, y le hizo algun comedimiento, para q̃ el comiese primero, sino que antes de comunicarlo con Adam abrió la boca, y se la comió. A lo qual responde en el 1 libro de Paradiso, que como el Demonio la auia prometido, que comiendo aquella fruta seria como Dios, amóse á si antes que á su marido, y que á nadie, y quiso ser ella primero como Dios, que no el, y por algun rato ser siquiera superior á su marido. (After Eve had taken the apple, why did she not go to her husband and give him some food? Why did she eat it first, without telling Adam; instead, she opened her mouth and ate it up. The first book of Paradise explains that the Devil had promised her that if she ate the fruit, she would be like God. She loved herself more than her husband or anyone; she wanted to be like God and didn't want [Adam] to be first, and so in order to be superior to her husband she ate it first.)
>
> Caqi, isinima, ofuenonco, cumepalinolehabele, hachaquenta, Euamano mine inihimima belenotiqua henihaue masinotiqua, hono michu macota hebi? R. Nanacu hiti hebuanonco hohota hetanaqeno. Dios intamaqui, chinibohabele masibiqe, naquana, Diosintamaqui, lesiromanta, mine hubuasosiquana inihimima, napaqeqe, hubuasosino toroqua, mancotaheqi, ofuenoma, inihimima, oho anano, vquaqua hoqua anoyayileta, nia parucusi yayinecheta, hachibueno inemi, nahiabanecheta, cume mandasotelahacu, Adam inihimima viroyayi norocoma Rey holataleta, intelahacu, mineno anopequatalesta nipatafilesta intaqe, hoqua habitimatiqua, lehani manta viromima chitolesiro manta, macota, hetechulaha. (After saying this, one

> should consider why did Eve take and eat food without calling her husband and saying, "Let's eat"? Because the Devil's words had been, "after you both eat, you will be like Gods," and wanting to be like God without delay, she forgot her beloved spouse; without loving him, she thought, "If I give it to him after I eat it, I will be a woman war-chief [parucusi], knower of all things. My heart wants this. [But] if Adam, my husband, who is already a strong man, a king, a chief, does this [eats first], then I will be his servant." [Eve] thought, "I will not waste time"; she wanted to be the boss of her husband. She took it [the apple] and ate it.)[4]

Though both the Spanish and Timucua versions describe how Eve took the forbidden fruit, they are strikingly different. The Spanish account is moralistic, judging Eve (and solely Eve) for her transgression; the Timucua translation instead shows a paradise thrown off balance, in which Adam and Eve were pitted against each other. Timucua Eve "loved her spouse," but she did not want "to serve him" for the rest of her days. She wanted more. She wanted to be a *nia parucusi* (a woman war-chief) and *hachibueno inemi nahiabanecheta* (knower of all things). Although tone is hard to decipher in these texts, there is something comical about a Franciscan friar with limited control of the Timucua language intending to preach about Eve's weakness and wickedness, who instead ends-up describing a Native woman telling her husband, "No, I am the boss!" Timucua humor disrupted, even destabilized Franciscan teachings. It was a powerful tool that spoke of a living, breathing, functioning Native world—a world of bossy women.[5]

Finding Timucua Eve might seem tricky at first. She only appears in the Timucua version of the text, which means that uncovering her story, reading her version of events, and understanding her perspective requires working with Native language sources that have not been read in their original form for hundreds of years.[6] But she is also right there. Timucua Eve is not some secret, hidden away in a lost manuscript. She appears in a published seventeenth-century catechism, the exact type of source historians are supposed to read and analyze. The problem with finding Timucua Eve is that she is *not* missing, not really. It is her presence, resolve, and power that actually leave us nonplussed, calling into question the sources we validate and value as well as the harmful narratives of erasure and declension we tell about Native women. Timucua Eve insists that we frame our understanding of the past differently.

Native women are rarely the main focus of colonial documents. Their inclusion often appears accidental or as nothing more than happenstance; in one instance, for example, Spanish officials hired an Indian spy to discover the whereabouts of English traders but instead they received a lengthy report about the shifting locations of towns, changing demography, and inter-tribal politics that hinged on the marriage of a particular kinswoman.[7] What seems like a frustrating comedy of errors—in which Spanish officials asked a straightforward question but received a roundabout answer detailing the actions of a woman—was nothing of the sort. To obtain the intel they desired, Spaniards had to heed the inner workings of a Native world that held Native women—as well as their knowledge, labor, and power—in great esteem.

But Spaniards often failed to recognize or even see the value of Native women. As Theda Perdue tells us in her groundbreaking work on Cherokee women, "Native women exist in the historical shadows," dismissed or even outright disregarded by European sources.[8] Timucua Eve shows that the problem goes beyond the limited number of accounts by and about Native women, and extends also to the limited ways historians situate Native women in the colonial past. Consider Álvar Núñez Cabeza de Vaca, who produced perhaps the best known, frequently cited, and most often taught narrative about the early Southeast. His account hardly mentions women.[9] But this omission does not mean that Native women were missing or unimportant in the early South; it merely points to Cabeza de Vaca's narrow understanding of and access to the Native world he was traversing.

Spanish officials were not good at owning their shortcomings, however, and, as it turns out, historians are not that good at it either. The Timucua language sources clearly illustrate the point; they have been used and often quoted, but by not attempting to work with Native language materials or think through the Timucua language, scholars have created an incomplete story that favors

Spanish perspectives and priorities. We must stop ignoring sources written in non-European languages.[10] Early Spanish sources often downplay the roles and importance of Native women, and the histories that rely on these sources replicate the absences of the archive. A vicious cycle then ensues that naturalizes an unnatural silence, for obviously Native women were there, and they did (and do) matter.

Fortunately, there is a growing literature on Native women's history—with some exceptionally poignant works by Native women themselves—that seeks to reverse an erasure that began at the moment of source creation and was further compounded by a historiography complicit in the archive's many silences.[11] Much of the new scholarship on Native women tends to be contemporary and glosses rather quickly through the colonial era, where sources are hard to access and written in languages other than English. This takes us back to Timucua Eve. Her story undermines a common assumption: control over Native women (or most women for that matter) was so complete as to render them irrelevant to the structures and processes that shaped the colonial world. Timucua Eve stands apart from this totalizing power. Centering Native women not only helps question the completeness of colonial control but also inserts contingency to the subservience historians have assumed of other women.

Attempts to narrate women's historical voices and life stories have taken many forms, from biographies to critical explorations of the expectations, cultural contexts, and norms that governed the lives of women and men.[12] As they are in other parts of Spanish America, these stories of, with, and by women in Florida are scattered among other accounts—official reports, correspondence, judicial cases, commercial dealings, edicts, religious doctrine, and a slew of other materials that, on the surface, have little to do with women or their inner struggles. Women are often everywhere and nowhere in the Spanish records; they are most legible in moments when colonial institutions, such as the church, tried to exert control over their bodies and souls.

Unlike other parts of Spanish America, however, in Florida the stories of women have been little explored. Native, Spanish, Criolla, and African women left records documenting their daily lives, revealing stories we have never heard, and creating a different archive of the early South. In their variety, difference, and level of detail, these Florida sources help fill a gap left by English documents from this period, which only contain fleeting references to women until the mid-eighteenth century—basically until women's own diaries, letters, and accounts allowed them to speak for themselves.

La Florida was a Spanish colony, but Spanish institutions proved relatively weak. The *cabildo*, the main structure the Spanish Crown used to establish government and rule in its overseas empire, seems to be missing in La Florida.[13] There was no separate judicial branch, so the governor also sat as judge. The military, the largest employer in the colony, remained understaffed and undersupplied for the duration of the Spanish occupation in the region. Even the Catholic Church struggled. Although the Florida friars maintained the largest European presence away from the coast, they hardly received visits from bishops or other high-ranking officials; the Inquisition, which spread throughout the Americas in the sixteenth and seventeenth centuries, failed to reach the colony.[14] There are no inquisitorial trials or records from the region, and hence there are no witches in La Florida, or none that the Spanish dared to prosecute.

It is easy to assume that when Pedro Menéndez de Avilés, the first governor of La Florida, reached the area in 1565 and established a permanent settlement, everything changed, as if all that had been suddenly stopped and something new started.[15] But the sociopolitical practices that Native people developed over centuries—traditions that allowed them to maneuver through conflict and violence and that offered a clear path for governance—did not abruptly end with the arrival of Spanish colonists. On the contrary, it was their endurance, rather than their abandonment, that is worth noting.

Timucua Eve is a case in point. As she declared her intention to become a "war chief," she found herself in good company. Early Spanish *conquistadores* frequently remarked on Native women in positions of power; they encountered female chieftainesses, *micas*, and *cacicas* (female chiefs) all throughout the Southeast.[16] And though much changed in the region with the invasion of European newcomers, the practice of appointing women chiefs continued well after the Timucua version of the Adam and Eve parable was published.[17] A 1634 petition by two exiled Timucua men poignantly recalled how their cacica had organized an ambush against Spanish officials. "She was the *cacica* of said place [San Juan del Puerto] having seen the Spanish take her brother prisoner. . . . [S]he got angry and blocked the path for the Spanish, and we being young men and subjects of her . . . we had to help."[18] Although the exiles' brief petition was recorded almost a decade after the incident in an attempt to secure a pardon from the crown, the power of the cacica in their account was unmistakable. During the mid-1650s, when Timucua towns organized a well-coordinated military attack against the Spanish, several cacicas led the charge, including the cacica of Nicaya, who was responsible for preparing her people for the coming war and erecting a palisade around her town; María, cacica of San Juan Ebanjelista, who was repeatedly identified as the one in charge of her town; and several other female leaders from smaller towns, including Molina, cacica of San Juan de Guacara, and two unnamed female leaders from Santa Ana.[19] Unlike Timucua Eve, these Native leaders did not simply express a desire to be nia parucusi; they already *were* women war chiefs. As Native women continued to serve in powerful positions through most of the colonial period in La Florida, Native understanding of gender and gender norms also continued to frame Timucua society.

This book begins in the 1690s, almost as if starting midsentence. By then, the Spanish colonial project in the region was well underway. And while the findings of anthropologists, literary scholars, and linguists have been indispensable, this book remains rooted in an Indigenous archive forged within a Spanish one. Included are sources ranging from formal Native testimonies and appeals to brief comments and jokes. There are manuscripts and sometimes printed accounts authored and dictated by Indian actors. These are complicated and negotiated texts, which are nonetheless teeming with untold stories and histories. It is mostly through Spanish accounts, *visitas* (surveys), *residencias* (performance reviews), reports, letters, and legal documents that we get to see and hear Native people. Unsurprisingly, then, it is a Spanish and colonial perspective that repeatedly plays out in these sources. For example, we learn more about how much the colonists wanted a fort in San

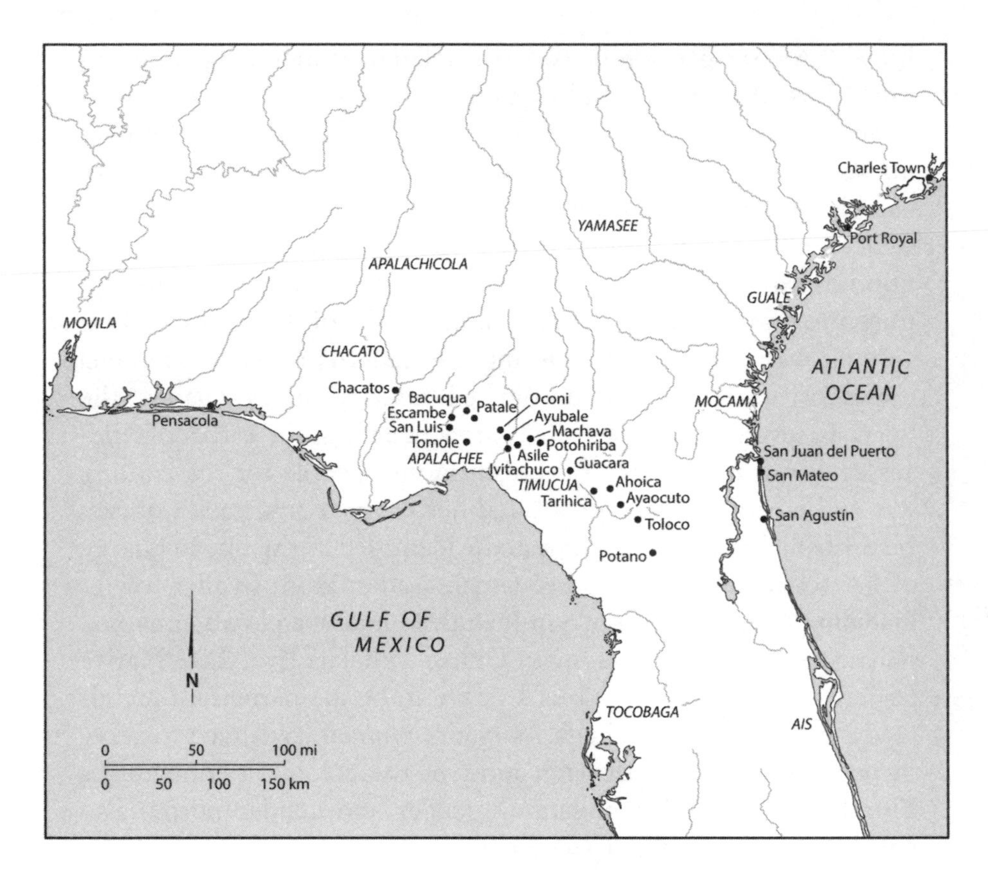

1. *Early South, 1670–1700s (Map by Bill Nelson)*

Agustín than about the hundreds of Native laborers who helped build it. This distorted emphasis keeps our attention on a tiny and at times inconsequential outpost, rather than the much larger and more significant Indigenous world.[20]

So, we must constantly readjust our approach to colonial history. This calls for an attentiveness that on the surface seems quite simple. After all, how hard is it to say that Native women lived? That Native women worked? That Native women effected change? It turns out that those statements are quite difficult to make because they require a careful and continual refusal of an entrenched, even seductive colonial narrative built on the disappearance and dismissal of Native women.[21] We must read colonial texts while listening to Native women.

To center Native women's stories, along with their struggles, words, and triumphs, we must place them within the Indigenous contexts that they both inhabited and shaped. In Marilou Awiakta's beautiful and personal exploration of Selu, the Corn-Mother, she writes:

> Weaving begins at the center. The base is tightly woven to hold the ribs in balance. The weaving may become slightly more relaxed as the basket takes shape . . . over . . . under . . . over . . . under . . . until it is finished. From the simplest baskets to the most complex . . . this principle is the same: *the ribs must be centered and held in balance.*[22]

Native women, as Timucua Eve could attest, were those ribs; they held their world in balance.

This book is, in many ways, an effort to reckon with Timucua Eve and the Spanish Eve that accompanied her in translation. It explores the lives, spaces, and accounts of women, mostly Native, but also Spanish, Criolla, and of African descent. Centering these women in the story of early America offers more than new voices and perspectives. It challenges what is unknown and unknowable, transforming both colonial narratives and colonial archival practices by showing that Native women were a central force in the early Southeast.[23]

That simple statement, which demands little more than a basic recognition of the subjectivity of Native women, changes everything. A world where the safety and livelihood of Native women was a given proves radically different from the South that would come into being after the American Revolution. This region changed from a place that valued the leadership, skills, and knowledge of Native women into a space that tolerated, even promoted, their indiscriminate murder and enslavement.[24]

Colonialism, disease, and slavery transformed the region into something that most of its inhabitants would have found unrecognizable at the start of the sixteenth century. But what is crucial to understand is that Native women were not bystanders to these changes; they were not accidental casualties of the warfare and violence that engulfed the region; they were at the eye of the storm.

Native women were the ones who kept the region fed, improved the lands surrounding the towns, defined territoriality and safety, and shaped the fight against colonial intrusions. Their adaptability allowed them to respond to the stresses, ecological as well as political, that challenged their world.

This book is about women. It is also about war, slavery, loss, and remembrance; but Native women, mostly from the Timucua, Apalachee, Chacato, and Guale nations, and Spanish, Criolla, and African-descent women, mostly living in San Agustín and San Luis, the two main Spanish hubs in colonial Florida, are the focus and frame of the narrative. It takes place in what are now the states of Florida and Georgia, spilling over at times into South Carolina and Alabama. And it chronicles a relatively short period of time, from the 1690s to the 1710s, when the bulk of the fighting of the War of Spanish Succession (1702–1713), known as Queen Anne's War in the English-speaking colonies, consumed the region.

The history of the War of Spanish Succession, much like the Nine Years' War (1688–1697) that preceded it, has been mostly understood as a struggle for power in Europe, and it is a largely uncontroversial subject of historiographical inquiry. This war, which lasted a little over a decade and ended with the 1713 Treaty of Utrecht, is seen as part of a larger cycle of violence and conflict caused by the expansion of France under Louis XIV. The decision of Carlos II, king of Spain, to name the Duke of Anjou (grandson of Louis XIV) as his heir to the Spanish throne is commonly understood as the trigger for war. The budding alliance between France and Spain threatened the political balance in Europe. English and Dutch rulers saw their continental and overseas enterprises jeopardized by Franco-Spanish unity.

Though the War of Spanish Succession was one of the first wars that were fundamentally about empires—their boundaries, roles, and obligations—there have been only a handful of studies on the American fronts of this conflict, and even fewer of these works have explored regions south of New England. This book's two parts detail the lead-up and the conflict of Queen Anne's War in the American South, but they do not tell a standard military history.[25]

The first chapter uses the 1695 murder case of a Chacato woman to introduce both the early South and the evolving role of women and gender in the region. Her murder trial reframes well-trodden narratives of Spanish colonization, English incursions, Indian slavery, population decline, and land loss through the perspective of a Native woman. The chapter that follows expands on the powerful endurance of this Native world. It uses three case studies—a dispute over succession in the town of Santa Elena de Machava, a supposed rebellion against Franciscan incursions into Native life, and the 1695 survey on Apalachee towns—to show the centrality of Native women in their respective communities. The last chapter in this section takes this story into a colonial context, exploring how Native and Black women lived in Spanish Florida and worked to protect their bodies, livelihoods, and communities. A personal and in many ways an intimate fight, these women's struggles outline the limits of colonial power.

The second part of the book examines women in war. It opens with the 1702 siege of San Agustín and shows how women's wartime experiences shaped discourses of war, fighting, and victory. The next chapter picks up in the aftermath of this attack, as many Spanish and Criolla women in Florida petitioned the Spanish Crown for monetary support. These petitions provide some of the only firsthand accounts of the conflict's front lines and reveal the many and taxing roles women took on during wartime; but they also demonstrate the highly racial and gendered ways colonial officials understood suffering and distributed aid.[26] The final chapter explores the aftermath of the war and uses the life and personal account of Doña Juana de Florencia, an elite Criolla woman, to illustrate how Spanish officials remembered and documented their massive defeat. Then it turns to Native accounts to disrupt Doña Juana's and Spanish renditions of events, creating a different archive of the war, one that privileges Native narratives of strength and resilience.

What follows is an account of the early South populated and shaped by women. Their experiences not only offer new and sometimes surprising stories, but they also call into question what we know about the past and how we came to know it. Native women, in their absence as well as in their sometimes small, other times audacious, often fleeting, yet still lasting presence, show us how to unravel colonial narratives and weave instead stories of family, love, longing, danger, pain, violence, land, and death. Some of these threads can be quite familiar; others take us to places, times, and people that are hard to recognize, even though many have been right there, in plain sight. Native women urge us to look once again. To see them. To hear their stories. For they are talking back, revealing a different kind of colonial past, one that demands and celebrates a Native future.

PART I
The Land of Women

CHAPTER ONE

An Yndia Chacata Guide

In 1695, a Chacato woman was killed in northern Florida. Maybe. There was a body, a culprit, and a set of suspicious circumstances. The murderer even admitted to a crime, except that he confessed to killing a slave raider instead of a hapless woman who had somehow found herself alone and far away from home and kin. Few things were clear, and many details remained unknown. Who was this woman? Where did she come from? How had she traveled so far? Why was she killed? The only certainty in her story seemed to be her death, and even that repeatedly came into question. The Yndia Chacata, as the trial documents refer to her, enters into historical view simply to die. Her name is not recorded; neither is her age, height, nor any other descriptive feature. Lost also are the material and immaterial things that gave meaning to her life: the songs she sang, the dances she danced, the clothes she weaved and decorated, the pottery she made, the fields she planted, the meals she prepared, the aunties who joked and gossiped with her, the sisters and cousins who helped her pass the time, and the mother who imparted more than everyday wisdom to help her make sense of the difficult world into which she was born. To make matters worse, the few words she uttered, or rather the few that Spanish officials chronicling the murder trial deemed important enough to record, come to us ventriloquized by testimonies of men—men who did not even speak the same language she did.[1]

The 1695 murder trial is thus not about the woman who was murdered. It is about the man who might have killed her and the men who might have saved her, as well as their motivations, geopolitical realities, and struggles. The trial begins with a dead Native woman but quickly leaves her behind. It becomes, instead, a political struggle among rival Native leaders in Timucua and Apalachee towns, Indian settlements in what is now northern Florida. Timucuas and Apalachees were two of the largest Native nations in northern Florida, and though they shared many commonalities, they had distinct languages, political structures, and cosmologies. Western Timucua towns and eastern Apalachee towns met in an uneasy border near present-day Tallahassee. The drama that unfolds in the trial revolves around this contested space and proves riveting. There are betrayals, complicated backstories, and hidden contests over land and influence. The intriguing tale spun by the trial documents is hard to resist, and the scant information about the murdered Yndia Chacata hardly seems important.

After all, what matters more: a nameless Native woman found dead on the side of the road, or politics and power? Politics and power! Or that is what the trial suggests over and over again, and that answer seems right, or at least it seems bigger and weightier. In reality, however, this opposition—the value of a woman's life or the structures and mechanisms of power—proves a false dichotomy. The Native woman, both dead and briefly alive, had everything to do with politics and power in colonial Florida. Nearly a century later, Nanye'hi, a well-respected Cherokee leader, spoke of the dangers in dismissing women's voices. "You know that women are always looked upon as nothing," Nanye'hi began her statements during the 1781 treaty negotiations with the newly formed United States, "but we are your mothers; you are our sons. Our cry is all for peace. . . . Let your women's sons be ours; our sons be yours. Let your women hear our words."[2] Native women and their stories deserved to be heard. Their "cries" were everyone's cries, Nanye'hi insisted; their universality had enormous potential.

Many seventeenth- and eighteenth-century Spanish sources in La Florida left that potential untapped. Most Spanish officials served in administrative or military roles and remained firmly rooted in San Agustín, the main Spanish outpost in La Florida since the 1560s. Florida had seen some of the earliest and most disastrous Spanish colonial *entradas* (expeditions), and unlike México and Peru, where tremendous wealth had been discovered, Florida had proven a sinkhole that devoured Spanish investments. There was little incentive for the Spanish Crown to devote many resources or men to Florida, especially since other colonies in the Americas proved more lucrative and far safer ventures.

As a Spanish colony, La Florida was routinely understaffed and poorly supplied. Government and military officials complained repeatedly about the limited power they exerted over the region. Franciscan friars, responsible for the evangelization and conversion of Native people, operated in a slightly larger jurisdiction. They ventured into Native towns and established missions along what is now northern Florida and coastal Georgia, but they did so in relatively small numbers. In 1695, over a century after the Spanish Crown had declared its control over La Florida, none of the Timucua and Apalachee towns involved in the trial of the murdered Chacata woman had any permanent Spanish residents. This Native land was under Native control.[3]

Spanish officials in San Agustín struggled with this reality. The vast majority of documents they produced downplayed Native power and instead prioritized Spanish military activities, Spanish proselytizing and missionary endeavors, and matters that reflected Spanish needs, fears, and desires. Spaniards were not just the authors of our main source of information about life in seventeenth-century Florida; they were the protagonists. Even so, no amount of declaring themselves important or placing themselves at the core of the story could stabilize their precarious hold over the region.

The 1695 trial that records the death of the Yndia Chacata emphasizes that precarity. It is shoved at the end of a larger *legajo* (document bundle) that also included two official *visitas* (surveys) of Native towns in Timucua, Apalachee, and Guale, along the coast of what is now Georgia; an inquiry into the actions of Diego de Jaén, the Lieutenant of Guale, who was accused of abusing both his power and Guale people; and another case about two Apalachee Indians caught making and using counterfeit coins.[4] Although Spanish officials organized the proceedings of the 1695 murder trial, collected the evidence, and interrogated the witnesses, the resulting testimonies offer a rare glimpse into Native lives and actions. A complex Indian world emerges, in which the histories and alliances among Native towns matter more than some distant and small Spanish population in San Agustín. Timucua, Chacato, Apalachee, and Apalachicola actors populate the story and dominate its narrative, entangling the inquiry into a single act of violence within the sinews of Indian politics. Yet the stories that the 1695 trial prioritizes—tales of conflict, power, and violence—are all by and about men.

The Yndia Chacata, then, is a surprising and at times unreliable guide through the contested colonial world she both inhabited and helped shape. She disappears as quickly as she appears in discussions about community, social breakdown, order, balance, and family. She offers an intimate, at times even tactile, understanding of the interpersonal relationships that defined her life, which unfolded in the simultaneity of empire building and colonial conflict. In allowing the Yndia Chacata to tell her story we must rely on the available colonial documents but refuse to let them dictate the terms of historical engagement. Her violent death, the trial that followed, and the many uncertainties that surrounded both events center the experiences and struggles of Native women and show how far their adaptability could stretch, as well as where and how it snapped.

Native stories do not always start at the beginning. In one of the many Creek stories about the origin of corn, a woman "of the Tāmālgi clan" repeatedly "fed her neighbors and friends" a "delicious" meal made from corn, but when "they noticed that she washed her feet in water and rubbed them, whereupon what came from her feet was corn," they refused to eat. The woman understood their apprehension and offered a solution: "Build a corncrib, put me inside and fasten the door. Don't disturb me, but keep me there for four days, and at the end of the fourth day you can let me out." They did exactly as she told them, and when they opened the door on the fourth day, the crib was filled with corn. The woman then "instructed them how to plant grains of corn from what she had produced. They did so, the corn grew and reproduced, and they have had corn ever since."[5] This marvelous Creek story has many similarities to those told in the Cherokee, Choctaw, and Chickasaw traditions, which all describe women as the providers or producers of corn and the keepers of agricultural knowledge. Communities openly acknowledged their dependence on women's skills and expertise, for what Native women did was nothing short of miraculous: they cultivated a food source that fed a continent.[6]

Most of these origin stories begin with a world already in motion. Unlike the Judeo-Christian creation story in the book of Genesis, which finds Adam and Eve in Paradise, in a perfect state of harmony, these Native stories begin in a state of chaos searching for balance. Clans are working to make their town prosper; neighbors are hosting neighbors in order to share in their wealth; men and women are surviving, though not quite thriving without corn. Thomas King, a renowned Cherokee and Creek author, explains how Native stories take place in "a world that is complex and complete."[7] In the Creek corn story, the women of the Tāmālgi clan enter this world radiating knowledge and power, but the story includes almost no other information about them. In her important work on Selu, the Cherokee Corn-Mother, Marilou Awiakta writes, "The Corn-Mother came into the world as a mystery, and she remains a mystery in many ways. . . . Just as you think you know something about her, you realize it's only a beginning."[8] Selu might be elusive, but she makes herself legible in her enduring lessons, in the relationships she forged and required, and in the transformed world she helped make.

The Yndia Chacata is the same. Her story did not begin when she comes into view in the Spanish archive; and although it might seem obvious that she did not simply appear and disappear when the archival sources say so, her own experiences and history are hard to trace. She "remains a mystery in many ways." She collides with the contested world of Timucua and Apalachee border towns like a meteor entering the atmosphere, leaving only bright, scattered glimpses of what once composed her whole. These pieces do not appear in order and seem to lead everywhere and nowhere at the same time. The Yndia Chacata thus tells many stories, some geographical and some interpersonal, but all about relationships and balance, or rather about the growing imbalances that threatened her relationships and thus her very existence.

Hers is a Native story about a Native world, but it is folded inside a European source and archive trying to tell a different narrative. The trial seeks to solve a crime by finding the man responsible for the woman's murder; it is not interested in who the woman was. The singularity of the Spanish source and the plurality of the Yndia Chacata's narrative are in constant struggle. "The truth about stories is that that's all we are. . . . So you have to be careful about the stories you tell. And you have to watch out for the stories that you are told," warns King. The trial speaks of violence and unrest; the woman speaks of family and homelands; and though both are tightly entwined, they do not share a common narrative or starting point.[9] We thus meet the Yndia Chacata not only mid-story, but amid many stories.

The first and perhaps most obvious story the Yndia Chacata tells is of her own untimely death. It begins with violence, pain, and fear—or it must have, for the archive records none of it. Instead, the Yndia Chacata starts the story already dead, as an unmoving and silent cadaver unceremoniously left on the ground. Her mangled body seems proof of a life violently ended and of little else.[10] She makes her first appearance, then, not as a full-fledged (or even partly fledged) actor, but as a body part—a scalp, likely hers, carried into San Pedro de Potohiriba by Santiago, a Timucua man from that town. The story also begins with a lie. The fifty-eight-year-old man said nothing of a woman and instead recounted how he had killed an Apalachicola slave raider intent on capturing and enslaving Timucuas.[11] Outnumbered and outgunned, Santiago had nonetheless overpowered the enemy, carrying the scalp back home as proof of both the dangers posed by slave raiders and his ability to defend his town.

San Pedro de Potohiriba was abuzz with talk of Santiago, slave raiders, and the scalp. In the 1690s, slave raids against Timucua towns were not yet commonplace, and killings, even in self-defense, were no small matters. Santiago was from the Ustacan-speaking towns at the western-most edge of Timucua, meaning that his town was far closer to the Apalachee territory and the main Apalachee town of Ivitachuco than to Santa Fé, where Spanish forces and officials charged with supervising Timucua usually resided (see figure 2). News of Santiago's exploits had thus reached Don Patricio, the *cacique* (chief) of the leading Apalachee town of Ivitachuco, well before any Spanish officials learned what had happened. Don Patricio found

Santiago's story unconvincing and decided to launch his own investigation.[12] Eager to learn more about Santiago's deadly skirmish, parties of Apalachee and Timucua Indians raced each other to see if they could find any of the remaining members of the Apalachicola slave party and locate the cadaver of the man Santiago had killed and scalped. Santiago had claimed that the confrontation occurred near Asile Chua. The search parties found no immediate trace of the raiders, which at first was not too surprising considering slaving parties moved quickly through the region and the one Santiago met was not likely to stick around after being discovered and suffering a loss. But the problem was that there was also no trace of the dead Apalachicola; and to make matters worse, Santiago refused to guide anyone to the site of the supposed confrontation.[13]

It was during this unsuccessful geographical search that the first outlines of the Yndia Chacata emerge. She was in the doubt cast on Santiago's claims and in the questions Diego, a leading Timucua man from the town of San Matheo, and three of his kinsmen began formulating after they followed Santiago's instructions but found no body "in the area that was indicated."[14] Had Santiago lied about *where* the attack had taken place? Why would someone who had proudly showcased the scalp at the town council misrepresent the incident's location? The Yndia Chacata was the (yet unknown) answer to the questions raised by the Timucua and Apalachee search parties.

Diego and the rest of the San Matheo scouting party had only searched for a short while in the area Santiago had indicated before giving up and turning west toward their hometown. They had not traveled long when a group of San Pedro men, perhaps relatives and neighbors of Santiago, approached them. The San Pedro Timucuas entreated them to lie. They implored Diego that "he should return and that he should tell them in his place of San Matheo that he had seen the traces" of the body.[15] Shocked by the request, Diego refused. After a tense back-and-forth, the San Matheo party continued their journey home. It was then that Diego and his men made a surprising discovery in an unexpected place: they found a corpse near a stream called Ygiuiura Yvita. The San Matheo Timucua Indians had inadvertently located the body they had been sent to find, but it was "not in the spot that Santiago . . . was saying."[16] In this moment, the search for the body of an

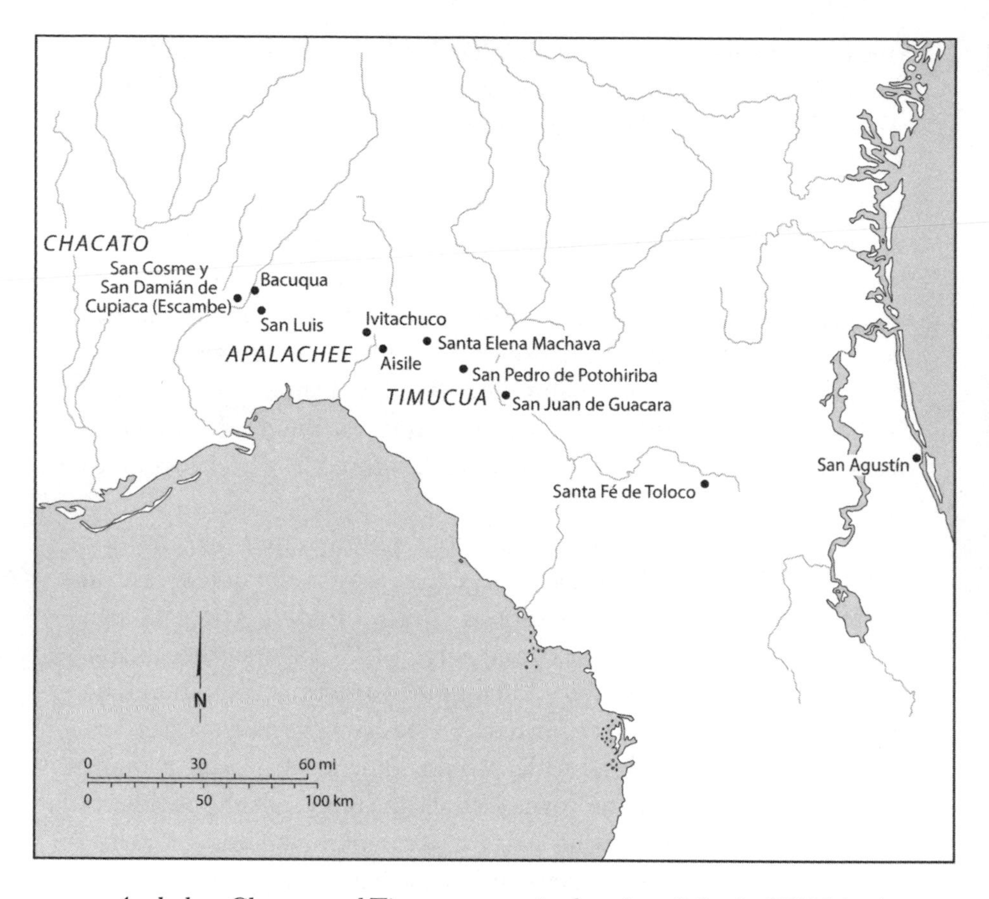

2. *Apalachee, Chacato, and Timucua towns in the 1690s (Map by Bill Nelson)*

Apalachicola slave raider became a murder investigation of someone else entirely.

The witnesses first describe the Yndia Chacata by what she was not. She was not a man. She was not in the right place. She was not readily identifiable. She was not named. She was not the default, but the alternative to a story that did not add up. As such, the importance of her body and scattered hair clippings, discovered by chance, was how both Native leaders and Spanish officials complicated Santiago's claims. She remained an elusive figure in the trial, quickly fading into the background of the colonial documents trying to make sense of her death. Her murder might have sparked the court case, but Spanish officials were far more preoccupied with understanding or, at the very least, documenting the political motivations and decisions in the case than in reckoning with her death. What had happened to her? How had she died? Who had killed her and why? Her encounter with Santiago, her purported murderer, is entirely absent from the document. There are no records of what occurred, when they met, or the sequence of events that led to her untimely death. Everything relating to her actual murder happens off the page.

The Yndia Chacata's last sighting offers some of the only hints of what transpired in the final days of her life. She had met a man named Chucuta Antonio, an Apalachee Indian from the town of Ivitachuco who had taken up residence just outside San Pedro's city limits. It is unclear if he had chosen to live outside the town limits or if the San Pedro council had not given him permission to stay within the town. Regardless, he had erected his home in a very strategic place: along the path that connected the current town of San Pedro to the town's former site. This path, no longer used by Spaniards, was clearly still open and important to Apalachee and Timucua peoples, who engaged with each other in trade, diplomacy, and military campaigns in ways that did not involve Spaniards. Chucuta Antonio's proximity to, but separateness from, San Pedro is an important reminder of how Native people negotiated and appropriated spaces nominally claimed and demarcated by colonial powers. This Ivitachuco man's life outside San Pedro reveals a vibrant world operating just a short walk away from Spanish influence.[17]

In his testimony, Chucuta Antonio tried to reduce the intimacy of his encounter with the Yndia Chacata. He described how he had merely tried to aid a person in need. He "told her that she should sleep there; that in the morning he would bring her to the place of San Pedro; that is where he had come out from and that there would be Mass."[18] There is no indication that the woman agreed to this proposition or that Chucuta Antonio's insistence that she "sleep there" was optional. The evidence suggests she had little desire to stay with Chucuta Antonio. After sharing a meager meal and heading to bed, Chucuta Antonio woke to find her gone. He recalled how he "awakened at midnight, at which time the said Chacata had already gone; and that while he tried to imagine where she could have gone to, he heard the barking of dogs in the place

3. *Mikayla Patton*, With Love *(2020). The San Matheo Indians describe "clippings, as it were, from cut long hair" near the body of the Yndia Chacata. Patton's powerful work evokes both the violence and possibility of their finding. (Photopolymer Intaglio on Repurposed handmade paper. Courtesy of the artist)*

[of San Pedro] and it appeared to him that she had arrived there."[19] The low howls in the distance seemed to calm Chucuta Antonio's imagination and, realizing she had likely reached San Pedro, he quickly went back to sleep. In his testimony, he carefully decontextualized her decision to leave. The Yndia Chacata's sudden desire to continue her journey unaccompanied and under the cover of night had nothing to do with him. Instead, her actions appear ill-advised, placing her on the same path as Santiago, her murderer.

The Chacata Yndia might not have stayed with Chucuta Antonio by choice, but she had willingly left him. Her actions might have been foolish, but they were also rooted in her desire to get away from a man she did not know or trust. The Yndia Chacata had realized Chucuta Antonio posed a threat the moment she saw him. When she spotted him along the trail, she made an effort to "cover her nakedness with a little skin and a little bit of Spanish moss." At the sight of Chucuta Antonio she tried to make her body less exposed.[20] The panic she felt as she crouched to the ground and grabbed what was near to conceal "sus carnes" (her naked flesh) is palpable. Something clearly happened that night, and though the testimony makes no mention of sexual assault, the Yndia Chacata's sudden disappearance from Chucuta Antonio's bedside suggests that her initial fear was justified. But no one asked. Spanish officials did not question why she had left the supposed safety of a man who had vowed to help her, walked away from a home and shelter, and chose to head into the complete darkness of night. Instead of following her, Spanish officials followed Chucuta Antonio, Santiago, and the other men who might have crossed her path. The trial became a power struggle between Timucua Indians from San Pedro and Apalachee Indians from Ivitachuco.

Apalachees and Timucuas had a long, complicated history of interaction that predated European incursions in the region. At their height, Timucuas had thirty-five separate chiefdoms with shared social, cultural, and political practices; but they had never consolidated into one cohesive unit. Disease and war had taken their toll on Timucua populations. By the mid-seventeenth century, less than thirteen thousand of the quarter million Timucuas who had once resided in La Florida remained. Apalachees had also experienced a sharp population decline, but the six to eight thousand Apalachees who continued living on the ancestral lands were better positioned than their eastern neighbors. With access to large, arable land tracts that grew maize, Apalachees saw Spanish interest turn in their favor. In the mid-1650s, Florida officials began bypassing their older Timucua allies, whose lands had never produced as much yield and whose dwindling numbers made it increasingly difficult for Timucua chiefs to find enough men to fulfill the *repartimiento*, the labor draft expected by San Agustín. Spanish officials were eager to trade for Apalachee grain that could help sustain the struggling Spanish colony; they disregarded Timucua requests while furnishing Apalachees with more gifts and goods. Timucua resentment grew toward both Spanish officials and their Apalachee neighbors. In 1656, violence finally broke out. Timucuas fought against a small contingency of men from San Agustín and a large company of Apalachee warriors; the latter proved decisive to subduing Timucua fighters and dissuading other Native groups from joining the cause. Spanish officials then removed much of the Timucua leadership and forced the remaining Timucua towns to relocate along the *Camino Real*, the main Spanish road through Florida. By the start of the eighteenth century, what had once been a tense but relatively balanced arrangement between Timucuas and Apalachees was now clearly asymmetrical.[21]

The Yndia Chacata died and lived in this world. Yet recognizing her subjectivity requires working against a colonial archive that undermines that recognition at every turn. She enters into the trial as nothing more than a mutilated body—a piece of evidence intended to convict Santiago. Contextualizing her death and life becomes an exercise not merely in working through (or against) a male gaze, but in grappling with an account that introduces her through naturalized violence. Although the interpretive and speculative work needed to reconstruct her life will never render her story complete, merely acquiescing to the inadequacies of historical documentation is a dangerous enterprise. To simply ignore the Chacato woman in Santiago's trial is to reproduce the profound silences created, perpetuated, and maintained by men eager to prove and preserve their own power through and in her death. By pushing the story of the trial just a little back in time, the Yndia Chacata gains focus. She appears not as a casualty but as a young woman walking a land she knew well.

The Chacata woman "was there." Her presence was most unexpected for Chucuta Antonio, an Apalachee Indian from Ivitachuco who had gone to Saturday night mass in the Timucua town of San Pedro de Potohiriba. He "was a short distance out from Saturday prayers with his torch, [and] he reached the spot where there was a woman of the Chacato Nation."[22] The Yndia Chacata was there and Chucuta Antonio did not know what to make of her. He called to her. Maybe he tried speaking in Timucua first; after all, he was on Timucua lands and had just returned from a Timucua town. But he struggled with the language and may have quickly switched to Apalachee, his native tongue.[23] Chucuta Antonio was probably more successful then, since the Chacato and Apalachee languages had enough commonalities to allow for a certain degree of mutual intelligibility.[24] After a few words, Chucuta Antonio moved slowly toward the Chacata woman. She clearly looked uneasy, and to prevent her from running away Chucuta Antonio quickly decided to communicate his friendly intentions by offering some food. He held up his "tolocono," a traveler's meal, and signaled his desire to share it.[25] As they ate, Chucuta Antonio inquired about her movements. He was most curious about how "a woman of the Chacato nation" had gotten there.[26]

The Yndia Chacata said nothing about her physical flight. She did not give any details about her trek in the depths of winter. Her journey had been long, as she was far from home. She had startled Chucuta Antonio, but she was clearly following a path and did not appear lost. It seemed to Chucuta Antonio that she was heading south, following routes and waterways she likely knew by name.

The first mentions of Chacato Indians (sometimes called Chatot) appear in Spanish sources in the late 1630s. They were then living between the Chipola and Choctawhatchee rivers—Choctawhatchee literally means "Choctaw River," but in earlier representations, the name was spelled Chata Hooche, possibly meaning "Chacato River."[27] But Chacatos had not stayed there long. By the early 1670s, they had moved near the Apalachicola, Chattahoochee, and Flint rivers.[28] Within a couple of years, Chacatos were on the move again, and most Chacato towns were now closer to present-day Pensacola. Tracking Chacato movements requires reading omissions as well as mentions. A clear example comes from the

Chacato towns that appear in the 1683 Manuel de Solana map; these towns are missing from the reports produced three years later, and though it is possible that Spanish officials simply failed to include them, it is also possible that the Chacatos had chosen to move their towns once again. In the 1690s, there are new references to Chacato towns, this time farther north than in the past.[29] By the winter of 1695, when the Yndia Chacata surprised Chucuta Antonio along the trail, relocation and travel were nothing new for the Chacatos. She had been on the move her entire life.

The Yndia Chacata knew the land through motion. She had traveled, lived, heard stories about, and studied its main waterways. Like most Native women, the Yndia Chacata had a daily, practical relationship with water as well, as she was responsible for bringing water to her town.[30] The Yndia Chacata then used the water to cook and prepare meals for her community.[31] She would have made a wide variety of dishes but relied on durable meals to feed her family through the cold months of winter. Corn hominy was an easy favorite; it was nourishing and lasted for a long time. The watery top part became fermented and could be drunk throughout the day; the thick bottom part mixed and became more flavorful as the week wore on. The Yndia Chacata's knowledge of the land and waterways had nourished her community through its many relocations; now these skills helped her survive a perilous trek.

The Yndia Chacata knew how to find sustenance, even in the months when options were limited. Chucuta Antonio had greeted her with food, but he mentioned that she was carrying "a *tocalito*" or travel sack filled with nuts, perhaps American groundnuts, chestnuts, or possibly hickory nuts, though these were mostly used to make nut oils and flour. The Yndia Chacata had kept an eye out for the seeds of the American lotus, an aquatic plant abundant in the region's waterways, which has highly visible seedpods. Its plentiful seeds are rich in protein and can be eaten raw like nuts. She could have also dug up and boiled, grilled, or even just gnawed on some cattail root. Cattails were relatively easy to find and, as the Yndia Chacata knew, the bitter-tasting roots were best in the winter months.[32]

The Yndia Chacata also used the rivers and streams for food. She had to fish and gather freshwater mussels with care, since the water was cold this time of year and she had limited protection from the elements. She might have set up a simple fish trap by the shore.[33] Chacato men and women both practiced fishing; in fact, one of the final comments Chucuta Antonio made about the Yndia Chacata alluded to her fishing skills. Even though he firmly insisted that she had left him in the middle of the night to reach San Pedro, at one point he briefly entertained an alternative: "the said Chacata Indian had left, going out to fish."[34] There was no hint of surprise in Chucuta Antonio's remarks; fishing and perhaps even trapping small prey like birds had sustained the Yndia Chacata as she walked the land.[35]

When asked about her travels, the Yndia Chacata offered only an indirect answer. She told Chucuta Antonio "de donde venía," where she was coming from, rather than "a donde yba," where she was going. This slight shift was perhaps an attempt to conceal information she did not want to share or, conversely, it might have been a way for her to communicate only what she wanted to disclose about herself. She simply stated: "she was fleeing from the enemy."[36] In a second retelling of this same exchange, her answer became slightly more specific: "she was coming fleeing the Yamasees, who had imprisoned her and she had fled from them."[37]

In one terse sentence she made sense of everything—the reason for her surreptitious travel, her lack of companions, and even her need of shelter and protection. But her enslavement was the start of another story, not the ending. Unraveling this part of the Yndia Chacata's complex history requires pushing further back in her story and even further away from Spanish documents, because before "she was there" in front of Chucuta Antonio in the Timucua-Apalachee border—before she walked alone for miles—the Yndia Chacata was forcibly taken from her home. She was an Indian slave.[38]

We don't know who took her and we don't know where, but we do know that the Yndia Chacata fled her captors and thus shifted the narrative of her enslavement. There are very few sources about Southeastern Native people's firsthand experiences in bondage, let alone their escape from captivity.[39] Captured Timucuas, Apalachees, Chacatos, Mocamas, Guales, and Apalachicolas tend to become simply "Indian slave" or "Spanish/Florida Indian slaves" in English sources. Their names, nations, towns, and numbers are underreported or simply absent.[40] The archival stories of captured Native people seem to end abruptly once they reach English lands. As if that were it. Once enslaved, once captured, their stories are over. Conversely, records dealing with slavers and traders abound. The Indian slave trade emerges from the English archive as a story about English expansion and growth, about "the rise of the English empire in the American South," as the subtitle of Alan Gallay's classic study on the Indian slave trade argues. It is a story about Indians, without any Indians.

Thomas Nairne, a leading trader and promoter of South Carolina, perfectly summarized how English colonists saw the Indian slave trade:

> These Expeditions have added very much to our Strength and Safety; First, by reducing the *Spanish* Power in *Florida* so low, that they are altogether uncapable [sic] of ever hurting us; then by training our Indians Subjects in the Use of Arms, and Knowledge of War, which would be of great service to us, in case of any Invasion from an Enemy; and what is yet more considerable, by drawing over to our Side, or destroying, all the Indians within 700 miles of Charleston, This makes it impracticable for any *European* Nation to settle on that Coast.[41]

Indian slavery gave the English "Strength and Safety." It removed "all the Indians" near Charles Town, opening up vast tracks of land and opportunity with its violence. It made Indian allies dependent on South Carolina, and it helped eliminate the threat of "Spanish Power in Florida."

The Yndia Chacata was then a byproduct, not an actor, in this history of Indian slavery, which went something like this: English traders tapped into existing Native practices of slave raiding and captivity, but by exchanging guns and other European commodities for Native slaves, South Carolina traders shifted the parameters and the stakes of captivity. Groups like the Westos, followed by the Savannas, Yamasees, Apalachicolas, and Creeks, formed trade partnerships with South Carolina traders and officials, attacking and enslaving first their rivals and then their neighbors to acquire weapons. A vicious and violent cycle soon spiraled out of control, making Native people without weapons particularly vulnerable and compelling those with guns to engage more aggressively in the slave trade in order to obtain more guns to protect their communities.[42] The Native world shattered under the pressures of Indian slavery, and a new colonial order took place. The Yndia Chacata proves hard to find within this story, in large part because it is not about her.[43] It is about South Carolina and how this southern English colony grew to prominence.

At a quick glance, Spanish accounts offer another side of the story. Instead of touting a profitable expansion fueled by the Indian slave trade, Spanish reports, letters, censuses, and surveys all detail the massive devastation caused by slave raids. The slave trade made Spanish Florida increasingly unsafe. The Spaniards found themselves surrounded by hostile and armed Native neighbors. If the captured Yndia Chacata added a piece to the growing English empire in South Carolina, her enslavement further weakened Spanish claims to Florida. Yet these competing English and Spanish accounts of sprawling violence said little of the Yndia Chacata and her experiences.

Even so, the Yndia Chacata was much more than an unwitting player in Anglo-Spanish rivalry. She was part of a longer and larger history of Native captivity and enslavement in the region, of Native alliances and conflicts, and of Chacato resistance and adaptation to colonial pressures. She was part of a history that centered neither English growth nor Spanish loss, but Native perspectives and understating. Her desire for freedom and her struggle for safety challenged Indian slavery as well as the caustic histories of its power.

The attack that took the Yndia Chacata from her home might have come at night. Slaving parties, comprised of a small number of well-armed Native men, depended on the element of surprise. Slave raiders had to travel fast and far. Their simple goal was to take as many people as they could manage while avoiding casualties. After all, slave raiders then had to carry and transport the enslaved many miles to where they could be sold. Though there are records of slave raids that captured thousands, most attacks proved small and tended to target towns with limited access to European weapons. While the violence of the slave trade could and did prove overwhelming, it was not arbitrary. Not every town was attacked. Not every community faced the risk of enslavement. In other words, there were reasons why slavers raided specific towns.[44]

The 1704 Apalachicola attack on the Apalachee town of Ayubale offers a case in point. Ayubale was the first town attacked during two devastating waves of slaving raids that razed Apalachee. It was not the biggest town, nor the one closest to the border, nor even the most defenseless, so at first glance the Apalachicola decision to attack Ayubale is hard to understand. But the Apalachicolas had specifically selected Ayubale. They were looking for a small group of Chacatos who had been living in the Apalachee town for several years and had been involved in a brazen attack against an Apalachicola hunting party years earlier.[45] A dispute about stolen hides might seem inconsequential—especially compared to the trans-Atlantic, imperial war that had prompted South Carolina to sponsor the 1704 Apalachicola attack on Ayubale. Yet it was this inter-Indian conflict that determined where, how, and who participated in this slaving raid. Often narrated as examples of English thirst for power or Spanish weakness, slaving raids like the ones that destroyed Ayubale also offer evidence of a different struggle, one rooted in Native priorities and concerned with who controlled the land and how borders were demarcated and enforced.[46]

Though the specifics of the Yndia Chacata's captivity are hard to recreate, her enslavement was a deeply gendered experience. Once taken, she found herself in the hyper-masculine and violent space of slave raiders. Those marching her away from her home were all men, while most of the people who walked alongside her were women.[47] In terms of her company, captivity differed little from home. Her daily activities, from cooking to weaving, from making pots to gossiping, would have occurred surrounded by her female kinfolk. The Yndia Chacata was used to laboring alongside other women. But men, especially armed men, had no place in her day-to-day life. They terrified her. They had removed her from all she knew and forced her to walk for days. Chucuta Antonio mentioned some bruising around her wrists, suggesting that her captors had kept her hands bound for quite some time. Maybe she had marched tied to rope beside other women in a similar condition, or maybe the slave raiders only bound her at night to prevent her from escaping.

There is no way of knowing with any degree of certainty which Chacato town the Yndia Chacata had called home. The many silences and uncertainties surrounding the Chacatos were not merely the consequence of deficient Spanish knowledge or archival practices; Chacatos had purposefully established their towns far away from the prying eyes of Spanish officials.[48] Governor Laureano de Torres y Ayala wrote that the Chacato had "the most outlying mission post and curacy of his Majesty in this region."[49] But the Chacatos' effort to live connected to, yet independent from, one set of colonial pressures had left them exposed to another: Indian slave raids.[50]

Several months before the Yndia Chacata found her way into the Spanish archive, English-armed Indians, possibly Yamasees, Apalachicolas, Sabacola, and/or Tiquepache, had attacked the towns of San Nicolás de los Chacatos and San Carlos de Sabacola, near the confluence of the Chattahoochee and Flint rivers. The Spanish reported that "the enemy" had taken at least "forty-two Christian people" to Charles Town, mostly women and children.[51] The Yndia Chacata might have been one of those forty-two, but she also could have been captured in a different attack, one that failed to register in either the Spanish or English archives.

The Yndia Chacata, with her surprising presence and equally confounding absence, was more than the victim of a terrible crime. Mishuana Goeman argues, "The bodies of Native women are dangerous because they produce knowledge and demand accountability, whether at the scale of their individual bodily integrity, or their communities' ability to remain on their bodies of land and water."[52] The Yndia Chacata helped produce dangerous knowledge: Indian slave raids were spreading deep into Apalachee and Timucua territory; Timucuas and Apalachees could not properly protect their people or keep safe the lands they tensely shared. The Yndia Chacata demanded, with her death and silence, accountability. Who could walk safely in these lands? Who actually controlled the land between Timucua and Apalachee? What did that control look like? And how would it be enforced?

The slave trade was like a violent cartographer, redrawing the region's geopolitical terrain and connections. For the Chacatos, Indian slavery had forced them to make and remake difficult decisions about who they were, where they lived, and what that meant. Slaving raids against the Chacato towns of San Carlos and San Nicolás in the mid-1670s show this process in action. Chiscas (and, in all likelihood, some misidentified Yamasees) launched a series of coordinated attacks along the Chipola River, the main tributary of the Apalachicola River. The raids at first affected only small communities, like the Chacatos who had set up towns farther north, along the confluences of Cowarts and Marshall creeks. Empowered by their success, the slave raiders moved south and targeted the outlying settlements of the much larger Apalachee nation. Apalachees moving between towns were particularly vulnerable; this exposure could include traders, diplomats, and hunters, but it mainly endangered those who traveled unarmed and had to leave the safety of the town to tend fields, collect water, and gather nuts and roots. In other words, women and children became common targets. By the summer of 1675, Ivitachuco, one of the most important and the most eastern Apalachee town, was on high alert. There were reports of slave raiders roaming the area and, in what was likely a failed slave raid attempt, several Apalachee people had been killed.[53]

Chiscas and Yamasees had spent the year systematically testing the potential reach of their attacks. They wanted to see how far east they could carry out their slaving expeditions and how much military pushback they would receive. But in targeting Ivitachuco, they overextended and became exposed. Recalling these early attacks, an Apalachee explained that "for many years Christians have been attacked and killed on the royal roads, without our knowing [who] . . . carried off men, women, and children as slaves until last year . . . because of the deaths they made in Huistachuco we learned that they [the attackers] were Chiscas."[54] Now that the Chisca culprits had been identified, Apalachee leadership mobilized. Matheo Chuba, Juan Mendoza, Don Bernardo Hinachuba, and Bentura asked for permission to lead an attack against the Chiscas.[55] "We have no peace," the Apalachee leaders protested. "They are constantly killing our relatives." Carrying a banner displaying Our Lady of the Rosary on one side and a crucifix on the other, they vowed certain victory because "as Christians, God will favor us."[56] Seeking to recover the women who had been taken or, at the very least, hoping to intimidate Chisca raiders, the Apalachees flew the image of the Virgin as a warning of war, not peace.

Chacatos had adopted a different strategy for dealing with slavery. They were a much smaller group than the Apalachees, whose population remained in the tens of thousands and who lived in a large network of interconnected towns. Chacatos had no more than a thousand people in their nation. They lived in a small cluster of towns and depended on support and kinship relations with non-Chacato peoples, including the Pensacolas, Chines, Tawasa, and Amacanos.[57] Notably, Chacatos sought alliances with groups of similar size and influence, and, at first, they chose to move away from larger and more powerful nations, like the Apalachees and Apalachicolas.[58]

Since Chacatos could not openly fight slave raiders, they had to find safety by relocating. In 1675, as the Apalachee marched against the Chiscas, they were surprised to learn that the Chacatos had moved once again. The Apalachee war party had hoped to find food and welcome in Chacato towns as they made their way to Chisca territory. But when the Apalachee reached the Chipola River, they made an unpleasant discovery: the recently raided Chacato towns of San Carlos and San Nicolás were now uninhabited, and their surviving populations had clearly moved elsewhere.[59] Though historians have demonstrated that movement and mobility could be a source of Native agency and power, often unexplored is the gendered nature of slavery and the mobility it provoked.[60] After all, the Chisca and Yamasee raiders had not likely captured more than thirty or forty individuals. The towns of San Carlos and San Nicolás were affected, but they still had sizeable populations. So, why had they left? Why had Chacatos chosen to relocate their entire towns?

The problem was *who* the raids targeted, not merely how many people the slavers had taken. "And what hurts the most," explained the exasperated Apalachee leaders as they surveyed the bare Chacato lands, "is the slaves they carry off and what they are doing with the young women."[61] By targeting Chacato women, Indian slavers had done irreparable damage to these Chacato towns. Chacatos lived in towns of around two to four hundred people. Though most slave raids managed to take twenty to thirty individuals, if the majority of those captured were women, Indian slavery had the potential of eliminating the autonomy and reproductive capability of these matrilocal communities in which women not only determined succession lines but also kept their communities populated and fed, had a say in where their husbands lived and worked, and made their towns' well-being and future viable.

Native women's abrupt and forced departure thus profoundly destabilized the Chacato community. If twenty women were taken from a town of two hundred, that town's future was seriously jeopardized. The Chacato chiefs' decision to abandon San Carlos and San Nicolás makes more sense in the context of women's value and the centrality of gender. Chacato relocation prioritized the safety of their remaining "young women" and the future of their entire communities. Without young women, Chacatos could not survive, and so they moved.[62]

Slavery and movement went together. The Yndia Chacata likely knew that well. If she was older than twenty, she had survived the Chisca attacks on her towns; if she was older than twelve, she had moved with her community at least twice seeking safety from other waves of slave raiding; and if she was older than nine, she had traveled to the confluence of the Chattahoochee and Flint rivers seeking safety. Even if the Yndia Chacata had not physically endured earlier slaving raids, she had grown up constantly on the move. She repeatedly heard stories, cautionary as well as didactic, about slavery. Her aunties would have warned her about walking alone; her mother would have asked her to stay on known trails and streams as she fulfilled her chores; and she likely knew people who had gone missing.

Stories about Indian slavery are hard to come by, but one account about a Hitchi woman targeted by Yamasees speaks to the trauma of this violence:[63]

> It is said that there was once a woman belonging to the Tcikote clan who dwelt at some distance from her town. . . . The woman had two children living with her. One night the Yamasee came to her house, surrounded it, and at daybreak made an attack upon it. That woman had a gun with her

> which she seized, and she shot at them. They would run away, and, when they came on again, she would shoot again. She put the older boy outdoors and made him run away, saying to him, "Run and tell the people at the town." While she continued to shoot, she took the second boy, who was very small, on her arm and ran off with him. As they continued to pursue her, she laid the boy beside a log when she jumped over it. But they came up, discovered the child, killed him and returned with his scalp. Upon this the woman reached the town and told what had happened. While she was running away she shot one of the Yamasee and killed him, dragged him back and laid him close to the door, after which she ran off. . . . She thought, "While I was fighting I was whooping," but she was only crying. This is how the story goes.[64]

The Hitchi woman in this story lived away from the relative safety of town. She was without male protection. Maybe she was a widow. Maybe her brothers and uncles were out hunting or fighting. Maybe she was a stand-in for all the women left and made vulnerable by the slave trade. She was not defenseless, however. The Hitchi woman shot at her attackers and thwarted their repeated attempts to take her. Her quick thinking managed to save her older child, but her infant was not so lucky. Her desperation after her younger son's death is unmistakable. She screams, whoops, and charges at the slave raiders, killing one and forcing the other to flee. But in the end, her ferocity becomes engulfed in a profound sadness. She thought she was " 'whooping,' but she was only crying."

The Yndia Chacata experienced the pain and violence of slavery long before she came face to face with her own enslavers. She had spent a lifetime relocating with her kin, making and remaking "multiple homes."[65] As Daniel Justice argues, "Indigenousness doesn't always require an eternal presence in a particular location: though not elastic, the relational principle of people is adaptable to multiple spirits and sacred landscapes."[66] Only glimpses of these movements and adaptations are visible in the colonial archive. But these willing and sometimes forced relocations were central to Chacato survival—central to how the Yndia Chacata and Chacatos envisioned their future.[67]

The story of the Yndia Chacata has so far unraveled backward, exploring the events and processes that led to her sudden appearance in the Spanish archive. There was her travel into Timucua-Apalachee border towns, her escape from Indian slave raiders, and her capture and forced march away from her town. But before we unwind the thread completely and take the story all the way back to her home, where her journey started, we should consider where she was going. Her intended and never-reached destination was more than just a future taken away from her; it was a link to her past and her homelands.

Chucuta Antonio was convinced that the Yndia Chacata was headed toward a Spanish town, though she never said as much. The most important components of her journey remain vague, for she had never provided a clear point of origin nor an intended destination. Chucuta Antonio had simply deduced her travel plans from her experience in slavery. If she was indeed "fleeing the enemy," then her town had been attacked and was likely gone. Her community had failed to keep her safe, and so the Yndia Chacata had limited options when she fled her captors. She had decided to run toward Spanish care, a haven that could ensure her protection and keep her safe from slavery, or so Chucuta Antonio concluded. It was a rather convenient reading of the Yndia Chacata and her movements, considering that Spanish officials were listening and recording Chucuta Antonio's testimony.

Maybe the Yndia Chacata had other goals entirely. Maybe she was not trying to reach San Pedro or any other mission towns. Maybe she had trekked all those miles looking for her people. Before her capture, Chacato leaders had been talking for months about relocating once again. They had lived east, south, and north of the main Spanish mission towns in Apalachee, but as slave raiding intensified, the Chacatos began discussing a new strategy: moving their towns within Apalachee territory or, more specifically, moving away from the main slaving corridors—nearby communities, like Hitchi and Apalachicola, were also facing similar predicaments. Chacatos had long resisted this option. Although they were not hostile to the Apalachees, they were not Apalachees themselves. They had long lived autonomously, deciding when and where they interacted with their neighbors. Slave raids changed all that. After a series of raids targeted the recently established Chacato towns on the Chattahoochee and Flint rivers in 1694–1695, many of the surviving Chacatos relocated to the Apalachee town of Escambé.

Apalachees welcomed their once distant neighbors but made it perfectly clear that protection from slavery would come at a price. Chacatos signed a treaty with the Apalachees agreeing to a tributary and subservient relationship in exchange for safety. Apalachees placed specific prohibitions on the hunting rights of the Chacatos now incorporated into their lands. Chacatos could not kill bears, panthers, *pájaros blancos* (white birds), and other protected game. "If the case arises that they [Chacatos] hunt it, they are to bring it and present it at the council house of this place of San Luis."[68] The Chacatos agreed to trade part of their autonomy to keep slave raiders at a distance, "having come there [Apalachee] on account of the harassment, injuries, and persecutions that the heathen Indians were inflicting on them."[69] Chacato refugees complained about their new living arrangements in Apalachee, but though many Chacatos "reported . . . the discomfort in which they were living and the affliction they were experiencing," Apalachee harassment was preferable to the devastation of slaving raids.[70]

It is unlikely that Yndia Chacata knew about the treaty or the new living conditions Chacatos faced in Apalachee towns. But she did know that her people were likely to relocate their town rather than rebuild it after a slave raid, especially if women and children composed the majority of those taken.[71] As her captors carried her north, she might have concluded that the Chacato who had survived the attack had moved south into the towns of their more powerful Apalachee neighbors, as they had long discussed. Her journey toward a Spanish mission town, then, might not have had anything to do with wanting Spanish protection, as Chucuta Antonio had posited, and everything to do with finding her own people.[72]

In her search for safety, the Yndia Chacata also searched for home. Her travel, captivity, and flight—all of her movements—captured the immediate and almost complete attention of Chucuta Antonio and the Spanish officials recording her story. But these movements were only part of the story, and maybe not even the part she most cared about. Left unspoken was her intended or even imagined destination. The Yndia Chacata was living in the shadows of her people's many removals, trying to get herself back to the light. She was now part of a larger story, one she had heard (and possibly lived through) many times before. It was a story about Chacato movement and relocation—not movement for movement's sake, but movement to obtain protection, preserve family, and survive.[73]

The 1695 trial could barely make sense of the Yndia Chacata's dead body, let alone imagine what she did when she was alive. But the Yndia Chacata once had a home, or more specifically, many homes as the Chacatos relocated their towns to avoid slave raids and Spanish incursions. In Chacato towns, the Yndia Chacata worked, sang, danced, laughed, cooked, farmed, and lived. In Chacato towns, she was a person, with a name and a history repeatedly denied her by the sole colonial source documenting her story. The Yndia Chacata simply being in her homelands is then an act of resistance. She saw these moving and changing lands as *hers*. Matrilineal societies conveyed property through women, and though it is unclear if Chacatos allowed women to serve as chiefs, women exercised political clout by appointing their clan leaders, participating in council discussions, serving as the only permanent members of their households, and providing their children's identity. Native women had clear and recognized power in Chacato towns. Before her captivity and murder, the Yndia Chacata had never been a man's property nor subject to patriarchal hierarchy.

Gender mattered for the Chacatos. It was prescribed in their divisions of labor and the distinct tasks men and women performed. Though there were always exceptions, men and women had separate roles.[74] These arrangements meant that Chacato society was not gender neutral or gender equal. On the contrary, it had clear gender norms and expectations. The Yndia Chacata knew that well. Her tasks, obligations, and choices reflected Chacato gender arrangements: she prepared food that men had brought her; she lived with her mother's family in a house that her uncles and father had built; she kept the family, and men kept them all safe. But for Chacatos, the distinctions between men and women were far less important than the ways their roles and duties complemented one another. Balance, rather than division or hierarchy, was at the core of Chacato society.

Chacato efforts to find balance in the ever-shifting colonial world refocus the struggles of the Yndia Chacata. She was one case, one story, but she shines a light on Native women and the importance of their labor, knowledge, and duties in their communities. Her movements echo the many relocations Chacatos endured to keep their towns safe and conserve their kinship ties. Her enslavement reveals the often-unrecorded slave raids that devastated the region. The Yndia Chacata speaks to the violence ripping Chacatos apart, but also to the unmistakable forces binding them together.

The Yndia Chacata was a nameless murder victim in the colonial Spanish documents. In her homelands, the Yndia Chacata becomes much more. She has power—spiritual, political, and economic power—and, though Spanish officials would have most likely failed to recognize the valued roles she played, her community would not have failed her in this way. Perhaps then it is better to end her story at the beginning, in her homelands. This inversion not only challenges the narratives that treat Native worlds as mere precursors to a supposedly more interesting—or at least better documented—colonial story, but also prioritizes Chacatos, their homelands, and their struggle for an increasingly elusive gender balance.

CHAPTER TWO

Standing in Place, Not Standing Still

It seemed that everyone was hungry in Santa María, the main town of Guale, in what is now the southeastern coast of Georgia. The winter had been long, food reserves were running low, and tensions were high. Compounding the town's dire situation were Indian slave raids. These attacks struck with terrifying relentlessness and made any movement in and out of the town dangerous. The people in Santa María thus faced an impossible dilemma: leave town to gather food but risk getting captured and enslaved or stay within the town and face starvation. Every choice seemed to lead to death. As John Worth has explained, "The overall picture provided by the available historical and archeological data is one of dramatic demographic collapse."[1] Slave raiding, the *repartimiento* (Spanish labor draft), forced labor in colonial towns, and the strains of mission life—which included sporadic but truly ravaging outbreaks of epidemic disease—not only drastically decreased the Indigenous population of the region but also prompted an out-migration from Florida.

This bleak "overall picture," however, focuses on the disorientation and loss caused by colonialism rather than on Native responses to that violence. Like most metanarratives of colonial conflict, it amplifies European voices while silencing Native ones. But Native people had much to say. Their stories, council meetings, and petitions do more than unsettle the violence embedded in colonial narratives; they present alternatives. Native communities and leadership worked actively to oppose the multiple, moving fronts of empire. Native chiefs and *principales* (leaders) spoke about the loss of life in their communities without ever assuming that their concerns were a foregone conclusion. There was nothing inevitable about slave raiding, the repartimiento, or even the exodus of people out of their towns; Native communities could and did maneuver this turbulent wake. But it was not easy, especially when Spanish officials like Diego Jaén, the Spanish lieutenant governor of Guale, made the situation worse. He had "ordered . . . the said Juan Chicasle [chief of Santa María] to send women of this said place out to the woods alone to search for roots of *ache* [a starchy root] for the soldiery."[2] The Spanish prioritized the need for food over the well-being of Native women; the Guales disagreed, insisting that the choice was a false one since Native women and food provisioning could not be disaggregated from one another.

Chief Juan Chicasle refused Jaén's order. He understood the precarity of the situation but could not comprehend why Jaén's proposed course of action seemed almost intent on hurting Native women. Chicasle explained:

> To send the women of this said place out to the woods . . . was not advisable and that they [the women] should not go. . . . [I]n order to find them [roots], it was necessary to go away very far, where, going alone and without men, some misfortune could happen to them should they encounter some bandit pagan Indians who roam about on the mainland. . . . [I]t would be better and more secure that the men go search for the said roots.[3]

Chicasle agreed that the town needed food, proposing that the men go gather roots instead or, at the very least, accompany the women. The danger posed by "bandit pagan Indians who roam about on the mainland"—that is, slave raiders—was very real. Santa María women traveling alone and "very far" from home could prove easy targets.[4]

Native women had always been the ones in their communities who had gathered roots, nuts, and other nourishment to supplement the harvest; they had always been the ones who kept Guale fed. Jaén claimed that he had to allow them to perform this important activity, or otherwise "all the women were [soon] going to come to ask me . . . [to] give them permission to go to mainland to search for *ache*."[5] According to the lieutenant, Native women were unyielding, and he could not stop them from going out of town. It was a strange argument to make, considering it required Jaén to appear powerless in response to the demands of Native women—or at least the hypothetical demands of Native women, since no Santa María Native actually approached the lieutenant for permission to leave town.

Gathering roots was, then, the premise, not the point of this contentious exchange.[6] The real question was who would protect the people of Guale and how. Jaén posited that it was only the Spanish militia that gave Santa María a fighting chance; he was willing to risk the lives of a few Native women because his men needed to be fed and ready for action. Santa María was "facing the closest settlements of the English and of other nations of Indians allied to them[;] from moment to moment . . . [the town] must be ready for some hostile act."[7] Chief Chicasle thought the lieutenant had missed the point entirely by fixating on the English threat. The Spanish lieutenant was treating Native women as nothing more than a means to an end, a way to feed the soldiers who "were dying of hunger."[8] But Chicasle insisted that without Native women—without their labor, bodies, and knowledge—Santa María would not survive the rest of the winter. Endangering Native women to feed Spanish soldiers, whose main task after all was to protect Guale, seemed like a terrible contradiction to Chicasle. He prioritized Native women's safety because he both valued and needed their labor and expertise. Unlike Spanish officials, Chicasle did not express a need to protect women because they were weak or inferior; on the contrary, Native women were for him the key to Guale's survival and future. The chief's simple refusal showed the different and at times competing ideas of gender held by Native and Spanish peoples.

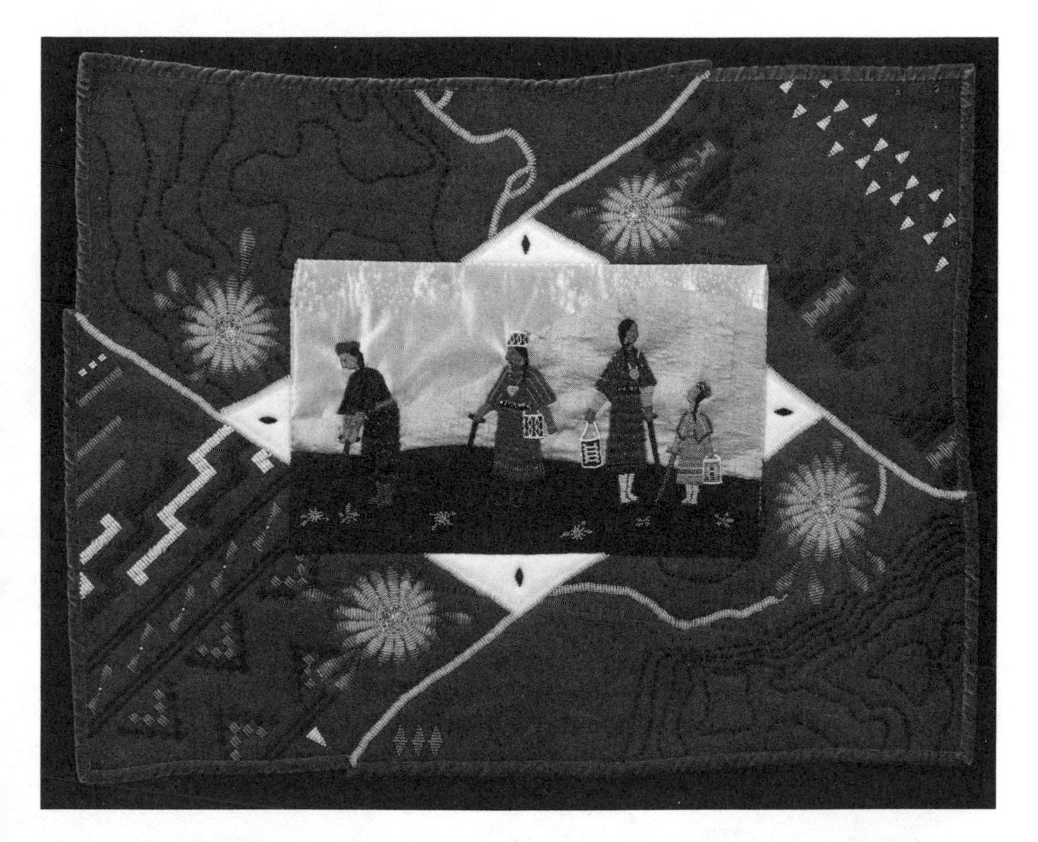

4. *Molly Murphy Adams,* And Still They Come to Dig Bitterroot *(2009). Beadwork on silk, microsuede, and hand-dyed wool. Molly Murphy Adams's careful beadwork on wool, silk, and suede was based on historic photographs of Salish people digging bitterroot plants near what is now the University of Montana campus. This piece shows the connection, both historic and enduring, between Native people and the lands they inhabited. Murphy argues that Native people continued their practices even as colonial narratives tried to erase and remove them. Although Guale and Timucua women dug in a very different environment and followed other traditions, they also deployed their environmental knowledge to survive both within and beyond Spanish colonial efforts. (Courtesy of the artist)*

No one asked the Native women if they wanted to leave town and search for ache. In his "Memorial to the King of Spain," Alonso de Leturiondo likened ache to other starchy roots, explaining, "ache yields a flour whiter than that from wheat; and by pounding it in a hand mortar and throwing water on it, the pungency and poison are removed and it is possible to make everything from the dough that can be made from wheat." Ache made good bread, but acquiring and processing the root were both labor-intensive activities; it grew in swampy areas that required women to wade knee-deep in water while carrying heavy baskets on their shoulders.[9] Had Guale women begged Jaén to allow them to leave the relative safety of their homes and go into the swamps without protection? It seems unlikely. Had Jaén compelled them to go? Quite possibly. Perhaps the truth rests somewhere in between. Native women knew leaving was not safe, but ache offered the best of the available choices: it was a durable source of nourishment, and it grew in places slave raiders tended to avoid.

Native women left little evidence of how they felt about having to adapt to new, circumscribed realities. Spanish sources, on the other hand, had much to say about Native women, rarely any of it good. Native women repeatedly enter the Spanish archive in the context of loss. They lose their family, land, home, kin, and even themselves to the region's enveloping violence. In the last decades of the seventeenth century, Spanish officials mostly held English slave traders and their Indian allies responsible for this destructive violence, but they also acknowledged, sometimes begrudgingly, that their own *colonos* (settlers) were not entirely blameless. Inquiries, court cases, and even visitas shed light on abusive Spanish policies and individuals. These concomitant forces—slavery and colonialism—wreaked havoc on the fundamental structures of Native life in Florida and made Native women particularly vulnerable, or so Spanish sources contended.[10]

Native people told their own stories. Enslavement, abuse, and fear all had a role, but so did Native women. Native women responded to and negotiated the growing violence around them and, in doing so, forged possibilities and even different futures for themselves and their communities. Their safety—their ability to grow food, move about the region, and support their families—offered the clearest demarcation of the limits of Spanish encroachment and Indian slavery. Native women were central to the stability and endurance of their communities. Simply put, where and when Native women were safe, Indigenous power was tangible and consequential.[11]

Benito demanded his town back. Santa Elena de Machava was a small western Timucua town, located near the much larger and influential town of San Pedro de Potohiriba. Benito's claims rested on a complicated family history that spanned back over four decades.

> Señor Benito, principal Indian and *cacique* of the town of Santa Elena de Machava and its lands, and natural lord of them, in the provinces of Florida. He says he is the legitimate son of María Magdalena, who was niece of Lorenzo, legitimate cacique of the said town, and that being thus that on account of the death of his said mother and uncle, the said chiefdom pertained legitimately to him.[12]

The current chief of Machava was Pedro Meléndez, who had risen to power in the aftermath of the so-called Timucua Rebellion. In the early days of 1656, Timucua leaders had rallied against Spanish officials and ranchers, demanding the end of abusive labor policies and practices against their people.[13] The first Timucua attacks had caught the Spaniards off guard, but within weeks Spanish officials were ready to retaliate in full force, even convincing a powerful Apalachee force to join their ranks rather than support their Native neighbors. Timucuas found themselves quickly outmanned and outgunned by the Spanish-Apalachee coalition. After capturing and killing the leading Timucuas, Florida governor Diego de Rebolledo developed a campaign of subjugation, relocating all Timucua towns to the Camino Real (the main road connecting San Agustín to Timucua) and replacing any Timucua leader considered disloyal. Pedro Meléndez had assumed a leadership role at Machava during this time, supported and endorsed by Spanish officials seeking to undo the effects of the violent unrest in Timucua.

Benito's claims to the chiefdom of Santa Elena de Machava predated the reorganization of the Timucua towns, the rise of Pedro Meléndez, or the political upheaval in Timucua. Benito was the eldest son of María Magdalena, who was in turn the eldest daughter of Chief Lorenzo's eldest sister. María Magdalena had been born to power, but fate had other plans. Her mother had died in childbirth, leaving both an infant without a mother, "she was a girl and alone," and a chief without the counsel of a beloved sister.[14] Benito claimed that in this moment of tragedy for his family, Pedro Meléndez saw an opportunity: "on account of their [lineage] being few [in number compared to] those of the lineage of Pedro Meléndez, who at the present is the principal cacique of the said town of Santa Elena de Machava, [he] took it away from them and treated them badly with all violence in time past."[15] It is unclear if Pedro Meléndez's family was indeed significantly bigger than Benito's, but it was clear that the death of Lorenzo's sister had put in jeopardy the stability of Machava's ruling family. In other words, María Magdalena's mother had occupied an integral position in her town, even if the Spanish record could not be bothered to include her name.

María Magdalena knew her name. She had grown, married, and formed a family during this time of tremendous loss. It did not matter to her whether Lorenzo had given up his power willingly or Pedro Meléndez had taken it by force; she had taught her daughters and sons that Santa Elena de Machava was rightfully their land. Through their mother's resilience, Benito and his brother Gregorio had developed the tools to fight. They had learned their family history. They had found both elders and young men who supported their mother's story. They had made allies of the town principales of San Matheo de Tolapatafi, San Francisco de Arapaha, Ybichua, Ybiuro, San Juan Ebanjelista de Arapaha, and San Pablo. As Spanish surveyors came to the town, María Magdalena's sons had repeatedly tried to secure an audience with them, and, when that failed, they had petitioned for permission to travel to San Agustín and present their case directly to the Spanish governor—though Pedro Meléndez, intent on keeping his claims over Machava, denied all their requests. In recounting all these efforts, Benito mentions he had "written many letters, all of them seized by the opposition."[16] This throwaway line in his 1670 petition merits a pause.

Benito wrote many letters. Were they written in Timucua or Spanish? Was he the only one of his siblings who could write?[17] The record gives no insight into these epistolary exchanges, only that this Timucua family took to the pen several times and thought it a viable venue to communicate their complaints. These letters hint at a large and vibrant world of Timucua literacy and writings hidden in plain sight. Timucuas wrote, with frequency, elegance, and anger. An often-cited quote from Francisco Pareja, a Franciscan friar devoted to learning and documenting the Timucua language, reveals Timucuan proclivity and interest in the written word. "Many Indian men and women have learned to read in less than six months," explained the friar; but in the same breath he bemoaned that "they write letters to one another in their own language."[18] Pareja had hoped to tie Timucua literacy to Catholic teachings, conversion, and mission activity, but it was clear from the earliest Franciscan dealings in Timucua at the eve of the seventeenth century that reading and writing were not just tools of empire. Timucua writers recorded their stories and histories within colonial texts; they used the written word to protest Spanish abuses and demands; and they wrote about internal conflicts, local concerns, and one another.

The letters Benito sent articulated his matrilineal claim to Santa Elena de Machava. Although he was writing to a Spanish audience in a colonial context, his appeal rested on both recognizing and validating the Timucua line of succession. His lineage and that of his mother helped undo the misguided Spanish interference that had allowed Pedro Meléndez to remain in charge for so many years. Perhaps what is most remarkable about Benito's epistles is how unremarkable they were. No one seemed surprised by Benito's letters. No one questioned the validity of his requests. Timucua and Spanish officials both recognized his claim to Santa Elena de Machava as legitimate because of his mother and her history. There was debate as to how Chief Lorenzo had lost control of his chiefdom; there were questions about what would happen to Pedro Meléndez if Benito assumed power; there were even larger discussions about the proper relationship between the town of Santa Elena de Machava and its more powerful neighbor San Pedro de Potohiriba. But there was no question that Benito, the eldest son of María Magdalena, was the legitimate heir and true ruler of Machava.

On March 20, 1670, Benito made and subsequently won his case in a general *junta* (meeting) in San Pedro de Potohiriba. His

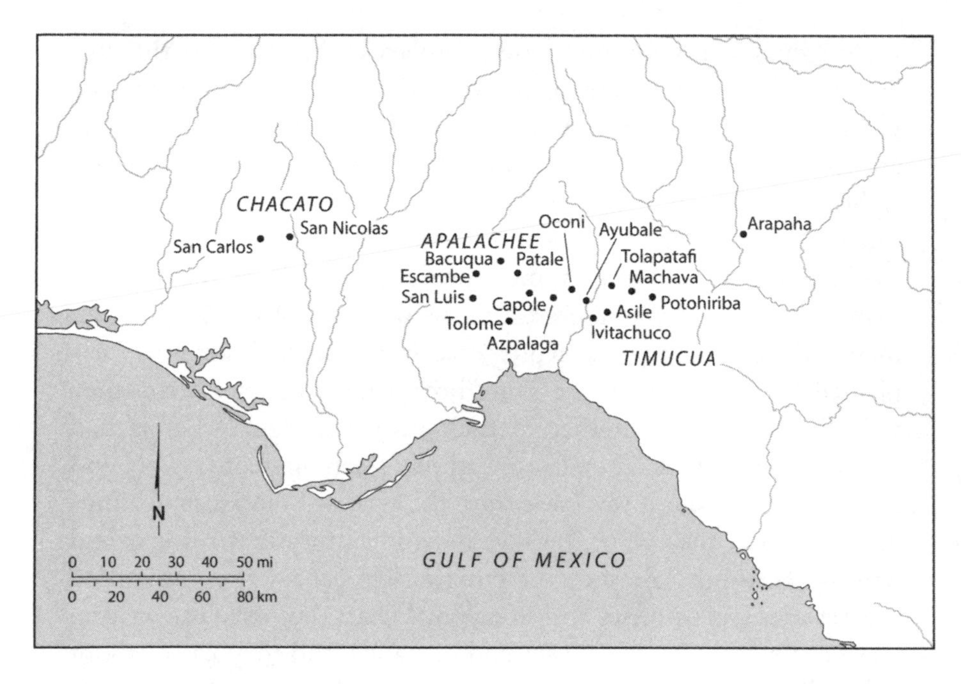

5. *Main towns in western Timucua and Apalachee, 1670–1700s (Map by Bill Nelson)*

victory came at a difficult time for Timucua. Slave raids had battered the safety and stability of many Timucua towns. Some communities had been unable to counter this violence and found themselves displaced. Florida officials offered a sympathetic ear but continued sending most of their goods and supplies farther west, trying to secure the friendship of Apalachee Indians. Moreover, they continued to demand that Timucua chiefs send men to San Agustín to fulfill the repartimiento.[19] Benito knew the fragility of his new appointment, which is why he asked for more than just what was owed to him. In a letter expressing approval, Lieutenant Governor and Captain General Pedro Benedit Horruitiner concluded "that they ought to restore to the said Benito . . . the said chiefdom of Santa Helena de Machava and its land with all his rights, and as such he was commanding and commanded that he be seated in the principal barbacoa [beds/seats] of this council house of San Pedro [de Potohiriba]."[20] Benito had requested that his position as chief be reinstated in Machava, which it was, and then he had made an even bigger ask: a seat at the main council house in Potohiriba (see figure 5). Santa Elena de Machava had its own council house, but this newly appointed chief and his principales also wanted to participate in the larger political discussions held in San Pedro de Potohiriba.

The relations among Timucua towns are hard to explain, especially since each functioned with relative autonomy and it often took a colonial mandate, an outside attack, the outbreak of a devastating epidemic, or a combination of those factors to compel towns to come together. The Timucua people shared a common language and many sociopolitical practices, but they never coalesced under a common ruler. Benito's dual request, for Machava and for a seat in Potohiriba's council, thus affords a closer look at how Timucua worked. During the 1670 junta, Benito made clear that securing his place as chief of Machava would not be enough to ensure his or his town's success. Machava was a small, independent town that was nonetheless beholden to the decisions made around San Pedro de Potohiriba's main council fire. After all, the council that convened to hear Benito's case met in Potohiriba, not Machava; rather than a slight to Machava, the selected meeting place signaled the importance of both Benito's requests and their resolution.

Council houses were large, circular buildings prominently located at the center of town. They were a microcosm of Timucua society; their architecture, sitting arrangements, and select participation replicated gendered social norms and affirmed principles of balance. These important buildings allowed men to socialize, make weapons, and rest; diplomatic talks between Spanish officials and Native leaders took place there; important visitors to the town rested and ate at the council house; and they were opened up to the community during dances and festivals.[21] Predominantly but not exclusively male spaces, the "community house, which they call Buhío . . . [has] its seats placed around with great order and arrangement, with the one belonging to the principal chief being the best and highest. . . . Those of the remaining leading men follow after this seat, without there being any confusion in it, while also having seats for the remaining common people."[22] The council houses were a physical embodiment of the Timucua political structure, which had clearly demarcated hierarchies, but operated on the basis of persuasion and consensus, rather than competition.

San Pedro's *buhío* was the heart of western Timucua, but Benito knew that it was matrilineality that made its heart beat. During the junta of 1670 he turned not to his newfound allies or his steadfast supporters to claim a seat at the council house, but to his mother and grandmother. His political savvy and connections amounted to little without his family's matriarchs. They were the foundation of his appeal and the reason for its success. María Magdalena and her mother had died by the time Benito reclaimed the chiefdom that had once belonged to his family. Their roles in the story are easy to miss. The junta of 1670 shines a spotlight on Benito and his sophisticated knowledge of both the Timucua and Spanish political systems. It shows how Native towns dealt with one another and negotiated hierarchies of power within Timucua. All the people who attended the 1670 junta were men; all the chiefs mentioned by name were also men. But succession, the very thing debated and fought over during this meeting, worked through Native women. Though no woman physically participated in this council, women's existence was central to the process.

Recognizing this dynamic is not about creating false equivalences—arguing that Native men and women played similar roles in the junta—but about understanding that Timucua was a matrilineal society in practice, not just in theory. Benito's many appeals culminating in the 1670 junta showed how that matrilineality worked. Benito's mother and grandmother were the link to his and Machava's past; they were also, and perhaps more importantly, the key to their shared future.

Benito was hardly the only Native leader who appealed to have his power reinstated through matrilineal claims. In the last decades of the seventeenth century, Spanish officials heard many similar requests; they proved generally sympathetic as long as questions about succession came from a Native man. Native women also fought for their lands and their rights to govern them. They also framed their requests through their matrilineal lineages, but unlike Benito, they faced skeptical Spanish officials who repeatedly questioned their ability to lead. Native women not only had to prove that they were the rightful heirs of their titles and lands but also that, as women, their power would be recognized and validated by their communities.

Juana Meléndez experienced Spanish resistance to her leadership firsthand. She was the Native cacica of San Juan del Puerto, in the provinces of Guale and Mocama, or what is now the southeastern coast of Georgia. Women had held political positions in Guale towns as far back as the Spanish could remember.[23] Juana Meléndez had risen to power during a time when Spanish officials needed her help as much or even more than she needed them. In 1665, she became chief of San Juan del Puerto when Chief Bernal, an important Spanish ally, died. At the time, she was in charge of the much smaller town of Santa María, and Spanish officials worried that her authority would not be respected. But the Guales did not share their concerns; as Florida officials surveyed the region, they found that everyone agreed she was "la más principal," literally meaning "the most prominent person."[24]

In 1678, after serving almost a decade as a chief, the cacica Juana Meléndez wished her niece to assume power. In her petition, "Juana Meléndez stated that she was very old" and ready to cede command to the next generation: "the said chieftainship . . . she was renouncing and renounced it in favor of a woman called Merenciana, her niece."[25] Juana Meléndez wanted to enjoy the last years of her life in a more peaceful manner, but she made it clear that she would only step down once her handpicked successor was approved. The leading men of San Juan del Puerto readily agreed to her terms, confirming that the chiefhood would now "belong to her [Merenciana] legitimately." Spanish officials once again seemed reluctant. "After they all had said she was the legitimate heir, the said señor and visitor asked them a first and third time to give it a good consideration." But the people of San Juan del Puerto explained that they had little to think over. Merenciana was "entering as she was entering"; in other words, she was the rightful heir and rightful ruler of their town.[26]

Matrilineal practices were a load-bearing pillar of Native society. In the century since the Spanish had established a permanent outpost in Florida, Native people had faced challenges so enormous and profound that they often defied description: drastic population loss, abusive labor practices, disease, violent attacks, enslavement, and usurpation of their lands. But the junta of 1670 flips the narrative: it reveals not simply turmoil but also what remained. Historians often cite 1670 as a notable year in the region since it marks when settlers founded Charles Town, the southernmost English town in North America. Most books on the early South mention Charles Town, but not San Pedro de Potohiriba. And who can blame them? A small gathering in an Indian town cannot compare to the founding of a new colonial settlement that would utterly reshape the region's geopolitics. By looking ahead to what was to come, however, we often miss what was. Amid change and colonial pressures that would only increase after English settlement, matrilineal traditions provided stability, structure, and possibility for Timucua and other Native groups in the Southeast. Sarah Deer, a Native scholar and activist working to end violence against women, writes about the ongoing importance of "matrilineal descent," which, she argues, "may be one of the salient gender characteristics that has survived over the centuries. . . . Many Native people may not know much about their language or precolonial government structures, but still retain a strong connection to their clan and matrilineal ancestry."[27] Benito made a similar argument in 1670. Spanish and Native leaders both would come to accept his claims and acknowledge him as chief of Machava; matrilineality had not only supported but also ensured his rise to power.

In a truly peculiar passage of the Timucuan Catechism—often called the Movilla Catechism because Friar Gregorio de Movilla helped compile it (1635)—the priest accused Timucuas of using their own kinship terms incorrectly.

> Caqi ano malesisinomano heca istanaqe quimonoletela manetiquani maca, hoistanaqua Christiano inemi istamonimaqui, monolehauela. (Many of these kinship terms you should not understand them in the way that you do, but how I and all the Christians call them.)[28]

Movilla criticized Timucuas for using terms like father, grandfather, grandmother, son, and daughter all wrong.[29] He was more concerned with correcting the misguided and unchristian practices of Timucuas than understanding how Native people actually represented their own relationships. Like most Franciscan friars, Movilla worked to insert Catholic and patriarchal practices into Native communities; and though he boasted huge success in converting Timucua people, he discovered that when it came to gender norms and social structures, Native people had little desire to engage, let alone change. These ideas were foundational to how Timucuas saw themselves and their society.[30]

Timucuas had no singular word for family or kinship. In the Catechism, Timucuas translated the Spanish word *parentesco*, meaning relationship and/or lineage, as *anomale*, likely meaning "relative."[31] *Anomale* was a vague word, and Timucuas most often relied on other, far more specific terms to explain the nature of their familial relationships. John Reed Swanton recorded over forty different Timucua family terms. Some, like *nebana* (maternal uncle) or *nibe* (paternal aunt), described individual relationships; others, like *poi* (what sisters called their older brother) or *pacanoqua* (a child born between others), accounted for connections among people; and terms like *yacho pacano* (a mother who has lost a child) or *yachema* (a mother whose daughter has reached maturity) spoke to the evolving nature of those connections and allowed for change in a person's situation. Timucua familial terms provided details about the person described as well as the person using them, including age, sex, and whether the relationship came through the father's or mother's side, the latter being more important because in matrilineal societies maternal relationships implied a shared clan. Terms like *anomale*, which were broad and ill-defined, might have meant little in the everyday Timucua experience, especially since most Timucuas lived in relatively small towns of several hundred people where most inhabitants were related to one another in some way. It is no surprise that Spanish officials struggled to understand what a Timucua family entailed or who it included. But lack of understanding never impeded Spanish interference with Native life.

Reducción is a horrible colonial term; it refers to an Indigenous community fully brought into Catholicism, requiring not simply the conversion of a people's belief system but also changes to their economic practices, clothing, language, traditions, and social norms. This term most commonly refers to the Jesuit missions established in Paraguay at the same time Franciscans endeavored to Christianize the Native populations of Florida. Paraguay's thirty or so reducciones of the Guaraní people were in operation for well over a century, had an average population of 50,000, and produced impressive church structures now recognized as world heritage sites.[32] Florida had no such equivalent. At the height of missionization activity in Florida, there were seventy Franciscans serving thirty-five scattered mission sites, none that could boast structures as prominent as those in Paraguay or the ones that would dot California's coastline a century later—and none that had that many converts.

Florida missions did not look much like missions, or at least not like the Spanish missions of Hollywood movies or romanticized postcards depicting a bygone Spanish past. Florida missions did not have brick façades, archways, or imposing structures. Most churches in Florida were small, round, and likely Native buildings quickly readapted to meet Franciscans' needs. A makeshift cross outside a doorway might have served as the distinguishing feature between a Catholic structure and a Native one. Native interaction with Catholic churches and practices thus varied widely. San Agustín and San Luis, the two main hubs in Spanish Florida, were the exception to the rule. They both had church buildings that were large and easily recognizable by their Spanish architecture. Their size and shape made them a bit of an anomaly when compared to the smaller mission structures in Guale, Timucua, and Apalachee.[33] It is important to remember, however, that most Native people in Florida did not encounter Catholicism, Franciscans, or the church in these large, rectangular settings. They likely went to the churches in their own towns. They did not share the pews with Spanish or Criollo congregants, and the friar was likely the only European for tens of miles. Florida missions were firmly rooted in a Native world, and the Franciscans knew that as well.[34]

Franciscan success depended on Native welcome and support. Rather than reducciones, the missions in Florida, at most, managed to open a dialogue—one that Native people maintained in their own language and, despite Friar Movilla's reprimands, on their own terms.[35] If Franciscans tried to shift this arrangement or overextend their reach, Native people pushed back. In 1675 this is exactly what happened in the main Chacato towns. Franciscan intrusions on

Chacato marriages, sexual practices, and family life led to violence. Spanish officials would go on to call the events in Chacato "a rebellion," "a controversy," and "throwing off the obedience . . . given to his Majesty."[36] All these descriptions suggest Chacato acknowledgment of, even agreement to, Spanish jurisdiction.

Chacatos would surely have been surprised by the implications of these terms, for it was the friars who had sparked the controversy and disrespected established norms and authority. The Chacatos had not rebelled; they had simply removed from their homelands the Catholic troublemakers who had sought to upend Chacato gender roles and behaviors. It was not the first time Franciscan missionaries had meddled with Native gender norms or found themselves expelled from a Native community in Florida, nor would it be the last.[37] The events in Chacato in 1675, like those during the 1670 junta in San Pedro de Potohiriba, showed the centrality of gender in the making and unmaking of colonial-Native relations, as the incident placed Native women as integral to Chacato society, order, and the maintenance of both.

For years Franciscan missionaries and Spanish officials had wanted to expand mission activities west of Apalachee. Most of these efforts amounted to little until, in 1674, the Spaniards caught a break.[38] Although Spanish officials never questioned why the Chacatos reversed their policies and suddenly welcomed the Franciscans—merely assuming that it was in the interest of every Native person to want conversion and a closer relationship with Spanish Florida—it was clear that changing geopolitical circumstances and the growing need for allies prompted the Chacatos to rethink their arrangements with Spanish forces. Chacatos agreed to let friars into their towns and build two missions, which would each have a friar in residency.

Within months of their arrival, Miguel de Valverde and Rodrigo de la Barrera claimed to have converted more than three hundred Chacatos, an impressive number considering the towns they served had small populations. San Nicolás, located west of the confluence of the Chattahoochee and Flint rivers, had about one hundred people. San Carlos, a town farther west, had about four hundred.[39] Franciscan success in Chacato seemed predicated more on force and violence than on Chacato interest, and despite often boasting of their many converts, Valverde and Barrera required constant military presence to support their endeavors.

Violence and missionization went together. Though Valverde and Barrera did not have much power in Chacato and though they were in Chacato homelands at the invitation and discretion of Native people, the colonial policies that the Franciscans helped buttress sought to redefine how Native people farmed, worked, prayed, celebrated, dressed, and lived their lives.[40] Franciscans were not intent on helping Native people "transition to the new colonial world"; instead, they were part of an imperial regime violently imposing its own norms and power.[41] Valverde and Barrera followed the paternalistic script laid out by Friar Movilla in his 1635 Catechism, positing that Chacato notions of "family" and "marriage" were not just incorrect but amoral. They publicly reprimanded several Native men and women for following Chacato practices in Chacato towns, all the while urging them to abandon their customary norms and behaviors. The friars were asking Chacatos to change what they most sought to preserve.

The "Chacato Revolt" was not about a Native group resisting European encroachment; it was about a tiny handful of Franciscans trying to interfere with Native gender conventions but failing in that effort. The trouble took shape when Friar Valverde and Friar Barrera went after Juan Fernández de Diocsale. He was the principal chief of San Carlos de Achercatane, and he had four wives. Polygamy, though not common for Chacatos, was a sign of status and power.[42] The Franciscans, already upset with Diocsale over his irregular mass attendance, decided to make an example of him. Without warning, they took three of Diocsale's four wives away, leaving him with the one allowed by Christian law.

No one asked the Chacato women if they wanted to go. Their desires and rights were simply disregarded. Though the Spanish argued that they were protecting these women by removing them from the residence of an adulterer, Valverde and Barrera were actually taking them away from *their* home, since Native women owned and controlled this property. Diocsale lived in their dwelling, not the other way around. Although we know almost nothing about these women, the fact that they all lived together hints at shared familial ties. "Practicality encouraged men [who wanted multiple wives] to marry women of the same lineage, often sisters," argues Theda Perdue. "That way, he only had to reside in one household rather than divide his time between the lineages of unrelated wives."[43] There is no evidence to suggest Diocsale had married sisters, but there is also no evidence to suggest he resided in more than one home. Diocsale's wives ran this household; they fed, clothed, and housed the leader, but more importantly they provided him with the family connections that affirmed his leadership.[44]

The very norms and behaviors Diocsale regarded as foundational to his survival were the ones Franciscans opposed. Though he wanted the friars gone and would eventually rally a force against them, Diocsale's first order of business was reconnecting his familial ties. Chacatos were a small nation, and many of its leadership had personal, political, and fictive connections with multiple communities.[45] Diocsale's wives were Chacatos, but with them gone, he needed the support of his matrilineal kin. Diocsale's mother was not Chacato, but Chisca. Chiscas were a Native neighbor and sometimes ally of the Chacatos who had long resisted Spanish missionization. As chief, Diocsale had repeatedly leveraged his position between the Chacato and Chisca people, and when Valverde and Barrera upended his personal life he turned to his matrilineal kinship ties for help. Chisca support strengthened his resolve against the Spanish. Historians are often keen to see Native ambitions—especially Native male ambitions—as connected to state power. Native (male) decisions and actions then become commensurable with those of Europeans and fit together in a shared colonial narrative. But Diocsale prioritized his family and his matrilineal ties; he did not view the Franciscans as equal players. Valverde and Barrera had done little to recommend themselves; they were only a small, inconvenient part of his narrative, which otherwise centered Native priorities and people.[46]

Chacatos left almost no records of their marriage or sexual practices, but across the Southeast, Native marriages were a family undertaking, requiring the involvement of parents and other relatives to bless the union. Consent among all parties was crucial. In the 1613 Timucua *Confessionario*, Friar Francisco Pareja sought to insert Spanish priests into the Indigenous notion of marriage. "Have you arranged that someone be married according to the Indian way without giving notice to the parish priest?" the Spanish text anxiously inquired. But the Timucua translation, written by Timucua authors, asked something totally different: "Anopira comeleta niamate nata hibuasi mota viroma nacunata hibuasomata mosobi cho?" (Did you advise that the Indians should act voluntarily and that the woman should speak [her consent] and then that the man should speak [his consent]?)[47] For Timucuas, getting married had little to do with the Spanish *Diosi* (God) and instead required that a woman and a man (in that order) express interest in marrying one another. Both parties had to agree. Both parties had to want it. Timucua marriage, like most Native marriages in the Southeast, was not about the subjugation of women under their husbands' authority. It was about family, consent, and love.[48]

Native people could marry whom they pleased, though unions within the same clan were frowned upon. Many Native stories contain expressions of joy and desire, "a wish to marry," when describing someone's future partner. Polygamy, as Diocsale showed, was practiced but usually reserved for elite, male members of society. While Native women did not have multiple spouses, they could and did leave their husbands. Divorce required Native men to vacate their homes, which belonged to their wives. After the marriage ended, divorced men returned to the house of their mother or sister. In a Cherokee story, for example, an owl tricked a Cherokee woman into marrying him, but when his deception was uncovered, the woman ended the marriage and "drove him from the house."[49]

The Franciscans viewed Native women's marital agency with suspicion. Luis Ubabesa, a Chacato military leader from San Nicolás, had just begun his Catholic instruction when the Franciscans publicly shamed him for having extramarital relations with an Apalachee woman: "The said priest on a feastday punished the woman in the church and reprimanded the said Ubabesa."[50] It is interesting to note that Valverde and Barrera reserved the physical punishment exclusively for the Apalachee woman. She got the beating; he got the talking to. Neither Ubabesa nor his Apalachee partner thought they had done anything wrong. Their relationship was consensual and willing. And although the Franciscans described the Apalachee woman as wedded, the fact that her husband was no longer living at her house perhaps indicated a change in her marital status. Valverde and Barrera never bothered to learn the specifics, however; they simply disciplined them both. As with the removal of Diocsale's wives, Franciscan efforts to redefine Chacato marriage and family norms met stiff resistance.

Chacatos had received the Franciscans, allowing and even aiding in the construction of missions, and some Chacatos had readily embraced Catholicism. But when it came to gender practices and norms, most Chacatos would not budge—rather they would fight. Support for expelling the Franciscans gained momentum quickly throughout Chacato towns.[51] Diocsale even threatened those who opposed his plan, "saying that the Chiscas were going to kill anyone who would not follow them."[52] In the end, the Chiscas did not come, and Barreda, the only Franciscan left in a Chacato town in 1675, had discovered the "plans to take my life" and fled.[53] Barreda had not traveled far when one of the two guides who had vowed to take him to safety turned on him and struck him with a hatchet. In shock and in terrible pain, Barreda somehow managed to grab his musket, shoot his assailant, and flee with his life. Believing the priest dead, Chacato leaders in San Carlos began celebrating their success.

Diocsale heard of the priest's auspicious escape from Elena, his daughter-in-law. Elena was married to Carlos, son of Diocsale, who had opposed his father's plot to kill the friars. Diocsale had boastfully approached Elena's house, taunting her with his victory and her husband's folly in opposing his plan. Elena seems to have been more than just his son's wife; she was knowledgeable, well-connected, and actively involved in her community's struggle and survival, much like a "Beloved woman," a term used for Native women who held prominent and respected roles in their communities.[54] She immediately rebuffed Diocsale's assertions: "He said to her that they have already killed the priest, and . . . she told him that instead the priest had killed the Indian who had wanted to kill him."[55] Elena knew of Diocsale's failure before he did. In her testimony before Spanish officials, she describes Diocsale as losing his temper, yelling about the ineptitude of his followers and bemoaning "that he was to have done it . . . and that from the blow that he would have given him [the friar], he would have split him open like a pumpkin, and then he began to yell like a Chisca."[56] Diocsale had used his matrilineal ties to the Chiscas to demand respect and solidify his power.

Elena turned that logic on its head, using the term *Chisca* almost like an insult.[57]

The Franciscans both won and lost against Diocsale. After hearing from the injured but miraculously alive Friar Barreda, Spanish and Apalachee soldiers moved into Chacato towns and any further talk of killing friars quieted abruptly.[58] Diocsale and the other Chacato leaders were promptly imprisoned.[59] But the Franciscans never returned to Chacato towns, their access indefinitely rescinded. Chacato gender norms and behaviors, while not impervious to colonial pressures, had remained very much in play. The 1670 junta in San Pedro de Potohiriba had shown the importance of matrilineality, and the so-called Chacato Revolt of 1674–1676 had revealed how far Native people would go to protect and defend the gendered foundations of their communities.

In 1695, the Spaniards conducted a series of visitas of their Florida missions. The *visitador* (surveyor) for Timucua, Apalachee, and Chacato was Joaquín de Florencia, who belonged to a powerful family that controlled much of the Spaniards' economic activities and many political posts in Apalachee. Unsurprisingly, most Indian leaders mistrusted his intentions and said nothing when asked "whether anything occurred to them that they would ask for, denounce, or report."[60] In the Apalachee towns of San Cosme and San Damián de Escabí, "The cacique Don Bicente and the rest of the leading men replied that they did not have anything to petition or to present either for or against any person . . . because they found themselves all in unanimity, and of one mind and with a good heart, peaceful and calm without having any grievance to report."[61] All was well in Apalachee, the chiefs insisted.

All was well except the women. The one complaint Apalachees did make before the powerful visitador came on behalf of the Native women.

> The only point that the said cacique don Bicente raised was that for three years an Indian named Tomás has been absent from this place, who is in the quarries of . . . the presidio of San Agustín . . . [and] that he is married and that his wife finds herself suffering [in] great need because of the said absence.[62]

Tomás's wife wanted her husband back. It was a perfectly ordinary request. It was also the only one that Native men who spoke before the visitador made. They did not mention disease, violence, or slavery. They instead expressed concern about a Native woman. When asked about the most pressing problem in his town, Don Bicente's answer came in the form of an unnamed Apalachee woman, identified only by her relationship to her husband and her suffering. Perhaps ventriloquizing the woman's plea was a political tactic. Don Bicente knew that a paternalistic request, which portrayed Native women as helpless without their husbands and Native men as incapable of protecting them without the aid of Spanish officials, would fold perfectly into Spanish ideas of family, marriage, and gender obligations. Perhaps it was a safe complaint to make. The chief could use talk of Native women and family to indirectly admonish Spanish policies and labor practices—after all, the Native women were missing their husbands because these men were away from home due to the repartimiento that forced them to labor in Spanish haciendas and government projects.

But perhaps we should take Don Bicente at his word. The cacique was not saying that Native women were the *only* issue in San Cosme and San Damián de Escabí; he was saying that they were the one concern he wanted the visitador to know about.[63] Native women emphasized the importance of family and gender for the stability of Apalachee society. The very structures that Friar Movilla had argued Native people failed to properly understand had actually kept Apalachee strong. But as Native men left their towns, some willingly and many more by force, Apalachee women faced new demands on their time and bodies as well as new threats to their lives and livelihoods. Native women's sensitivity to these adverse conditions, coupled with their willingness and even resolve to testify before the visitador, made them useful indicators of how their communities dealt with such pressures. Don Bicente, like most Apalachee caciques, viewed the deterioration in women's well-being as a warning of more problems to come. It was quite simple really—if Native women were in trouble, then Apalachee was in trouble.

"She is suffering" was perhaps the most repeated phrase in these requests by and about Native women.[64] What did that sentimental note mean? The vague and all-encompassing quality of the Spanish word *sufriendo* leaves many questions unanswered. When speaking in Apalachee or Timucua, the caciques could have used a variety of terms and phrases, including *calamo*, meaning suffering from hunger, cold, or discomfort. In fact, the way the Spanish translation is written seems to imply that the "suffering" the women endured came from the additional labor, such as having to clear the fields themselves or find additional ways to supplement their diets in their husbands' absence.

The caciques might have used an entirely different term to communicate suffering. Though very little Apalachee language text survives, in Timucua, for which there is a robust record of the language, the chiefs could have said the words *isticobo*, *tarisa*, *chacabuo*, or even *malutimo*.[65] These verbs also imply suffering, but they speak to the spiritual and even mental nature of the women's struggles. The most common form of the word *suffering* found in Timucua language texts, which mostly come from translations of Catholic doctrine, is "isticobo iso," meaning "undergo torment." Native women sustained constant torment from foreign slavers and Spanish officials, who could kidnap them or their children at any time. The Spanish language text hints at the physical nature of the women's travails without their husbands. The Timucua might have also spoken to the emotional and mental toll for Native women living in these violently uncertain times.

Don Patricio, the cacique of the leading Apalachee town of Ivitachuco, agreed. After claiming that everything was in order—"nothing occurred to them to petition for relative to their government or their village"—he then listed the names of nine married men who were compelled to find work away from Ivitachuco. He explained how Native women from his town "beg of his excellency that he, for his part, use his authority so that they may come back to resume the aforesaid marital life and to dwell in their village."[66] Once again, Native women articulated and were used to articulate the need to preserve Apalachee families and kinship ties. Ivitachuco women also reminded both Don Patricio and the Spanish visitador that they expected their husbands to "dwell in *their* village," and while Florencia probably interpreted this to mean that the women wanted their husbands back in Ivitachuco, the women were probably also speaking literally. According to matrilocal practices, men went to live with their wives, who in turn influenced where their husbands dwelled. Native women were thus critical in shaping both colonial rule and Native autonomy. Don Patricio glossed over such implications and appealed instead to the patriarchal sensibility of the visitador. Emphasizing the forlorn women of Ivitachuco who were "in great need" without their husbands, the chief managed to sidestep the role Spanish officials had played in the removal of these men.

Other Native leaders took a more direct approach. Hinachuba Adrian, cacique of the much smaller town of Santa Cruz de Capole, spoke candidly about the disappearing population of his town. He repeated some of the earlier demands that Apalachee women had made and asked for the return "of four married Indians. . . . Who are Chuguta Marcelo, Chinocossa Jucepe, Abaiaga Axnd, and Vicente Abaiaga, who are married and who, in addition to being missed by their wives, are missed also by the village because it has no more than twenty men and of these some are elderly."[67] Santa Cruz de Capole was losing people rapidly, a pattern that repeated itself across Apalachee. Hinachuba Adrian used the demands of the women in his town not only to identify and communicate this decline but also, and perhaps more importantly, to rally against it. Native women were key to the survival of Apalachee society.

The leading men of San Martín de Tolomi also tried to explain the stakes of Native women's demands. After stating that nothing of consequence was happening in their town, they reported: "There were four married men at the presidio [in San Agustín], who are: Paslali Alonso, Pansaca Juan Mendosa, Pansacola Julian, and Ocolasli Baltassar . . . and because of their absence a field is not planted . . . and they [their wives] and their children find themselves perishing."[68] Native women did not simply want their husbands back—they needed them back. Tolomi women and children were "perishing" without them, and "[in] their absence a field is not planted." But how could that be? Apalachee men were not the farmers. Planting the fields was women's labor and responsibility.[69] Moreover, Native men had always spent time away from their towns, in order to hunt, fight, or engage in diplomacy. Their absence had not impeded the planting of fields in the past. What had changed?

The answer was clear: Native women could not do their work safely anymore. Without Native men to patrol the fields and towns, Apalachee women had become more vulnerable to both Spanish violence and external threats, particularly slave raids. Without Native men, Native women could not perform their work with as much ease or productivity. Moreover, Native men were gone for longer stretches of time and, when they returned, they did not bring back food or goods to supplement the harvest Native women had produced. The women of Tolomi needed to be allowed to plant without harassment or fear, and though the harvesting of one field would not remedy all the town's problems, it would improve the situation. That was the contingency Native women introduced; this pattern of loss could be stopped if women were protected, prioritized, and heard.

Severe food shortages only aggravated these problems and pushed questions of labor and gender to the forefront of many Apalachee communities. The Timucua towns of San Francisco de Potano, San Diego de Salamototo, and San Pedro de Potohiriba also reported dangerously low harvests in the 1690s.[70] In Guale, the sharp population decline had already made the labor associated with food production a tense issue. In 1681, Captain Francisco Fuentes, a leading Spanish officer in Guale, chastised Friar Juan de Uzeda for forcing Guale women to work overtime to provide additional crops for the mission. The friar, worried about the food stock, had ordered the women to stay after mass and "shell corn," but Fuentes had "told the indias [sic] to go home, that this was not a workday." The captain feared that this specifically gendered abusive behavior would only drive the remaining Guales away.[71]

The Guales demanded Native women receive better treatment. Don Joseph de la Cruz Tunaque, a cacique of Guale, wrote a letter to the governor complaining about the labor his daughter and other women were forced to perform to keep Friar Juan de Uzeda fed.[72] The chief argued that the gendered extraction of Native labor was not merely offensive but also untenable. Tunaque explained that, if these labor practices continued, he would be compelled to move to "this presidio [San Agustín] with all my family, even though I should lose my planted fields."[73] Tunaque was doing more than complaining. He was threatening Florida's governor with the most powerful weapon at his disposal: his "planted fields." If Native women were not better protected, the chief would abandon the crops, leaving behind much-needed food reserves and forcing San Agustín to accommodate even more hungry mouths.

In his travels through Timucua and Apalachee, the visitador Florencia identified over fifty Apalachee men living away from their spouses and communities. That meant more than fifty Native women were forced to maintain their households without their husbands and an untold number of sisters, mothers, aunts, daughters, and grandmothers had to perform extra labor to keep their communities together and functioning. Their demands spoke to Native women's political consciousness. For Native women, the familial had always been political and the political had an integral place in their home—an expansive space that extended far beyond their wattle and daub walls.[74]

These complaints were not new. The repartimiento had long pulled Native men from their homes to work on colonial projects, and though Spanish law had supposedly exempted married men from working away from their towns for prolonged periods of time, the reality proved less accommodating.[75] Caravans of Apalachee men marching with goods and supplies died of exhaustion along the trails; weeks of service in San Agustín could turn into months and years; and the promised payments would often fail to arrive or proved far less than expected.[76] Native men were typically the sole focus of the repartimiento. They were the ones selected to serve and fulfill the labor draft requirement. And they were the ones who protested its conditions. But while Native men were drawn into the repartimiento, Native women became trapped in different yet nonetheless exploitative labor arrangements.

Chuguta Francisca, an Apalachee woman from Our Lady of la Candelaria, provides a chilling example. She was from a small town within a day's walk from San Luis, the main Spanish hub in Apalachee. Chuguta Francisca had worked for some time in the household of Diego Ximénez, a Spanish officer in the region. As she spoke before the council and the visitador, it became clear that her long employment in his house was not entirely of her own making. Ximénez had likely taken her away from her kin and town by force. But when Chuguta Francisca spoke, she focused on her needs and her future, not on what had transpired:

> They request that his excellency deign to order that the Spaniards who dwell in these provinces are not [to] take away the women with violence or carry them off against their will for their service. And likewise that an Indian woman from this place, named Chuguta Francisca, had been serving the adjutant Diego Ximénez and assisting him in the preparing [of] the food on his hacienda, and he dismissed her without paying her anything.[77]

Chuguta Francisca wanted payment for her time and labor on Ximénez's hacienda. She wanted "to make him compensate for her work." Chuguta Francisca knew that being dismissed without payment was not only unfair but also illegal. She thus demanded "that he apply the remedy that is appropriate so *they* will not be afflicted with similar injuries and annoyance." Chuguta Francisca as well as the town leaders presenting her request were rather vague about who "*they*" referred to. Was it the people in Our Lady of la Candelaria? Was it other vulnerable Native women? The record does not state, but the visitador understood perfectly the urgency of the case and "replied that they could rest assure[d] that the matter would be rectified completely."[78]

But why hadn't Chuguta Francisca just left the hacienda? If Ximénez had forced her to work and treated her poorly, why had she remained? Her decision to stay and work in Ximénez's hacienda is worth interrogating. After all, Apalachee was her land. She knew the trails, towns, and language.[79] She could have left or fled, but instead she stayed, demanded payment, and attempted to work within the Spanish colonial system. Her decision resonated with other Apalachee women. Although movement and mobility has often been posited as a source of Native agency and power, women like Chuguta Francisca expose the deeply gendered nature of that argument.[80] If she fled, would her family be punished? Who would "be afflicted with similar injuries and annoyance"?

The actions of Marcos Delgado, another Spanish official who resided near Our Lady of La Candelaria, showed that Chuguta Francisca's fears were well justified. Delgado "has in his power a family of three women, two [of them] young and one elderly, whom he carried off by force without authorization of the cacique or of the leading men; that although they have sent for them, he has not allowed them to leave."[81] These captured women involuntarily labored on his ranch, and in spite of the growing protests from the town, Delgado had little desire to let any of them go, including the woman who was too old to perform hard labor. He had kidnapped two generations of one family and, in doing so, turned Apalachee efforts to remain with kin and preserve matrilineal lines into a tool of slavery.[82] None of the three enslaved women ran away or followed the Apalachee delegations "sent for them."[83] Delgado made these Apalachee women choose between freedom and family. And that was not really a choice for any of them. Apalachee chiefs knew as much and said as much.

The petition saying "las muejeres están sufriendo" (the women are suffering) was more than a rhetorical trope in this matrilineal society. The Apalachee chiefs wanted the Native men to return to their town not so they could fix the "suffering" as if it were nothing more than a thatched roof that needed mending. Spanish colonialism was hurting Apalachee. For years, Apalachee leadership had benefited from their partnership, trade, and alliance with Spanish Florida. Apalachee had grown and become prosperous, even as its neighbors and rivals lost their footing. But at the eve of the eighteenth century, the balance was beginning to tip, and Apalachee women frantically rang the alarm bell.

Native women became the voice against Spanish colonial policies and the loudest supporters of Apalachee communities. Native women appear in almost every page of the 1695 *visitation*. They are in the concerns the caciques raise, and they are in the solutions they offer. In the caciques' demands and expectations for Apalachee, Native women emerge not as suffering victims but as powerful figures, or rather as figures with power in the Native political world.[84]

Ychu Francisca and Afac Gabriela were the only two Native women who spoke to the visitador Captain Florencia directly during his survey of Apalachee and Timucua. Of the twenty-nine separate pleas he recorded, only Ychu Francisca and Afac Gabriela made their own petitions. Both women were from the town of San Juan de Azpalaga.[85] Their chief, unlike the others in Apalachee, had openly critiqued the powerful Spanish Florencia family, which controlled much of Apalachee and, in the process, forced Captain Florencia to hear and record accusations against his own family. Interestingly, only in the one town council where the chief spoke decisively against Spanish authority did Native women voice their own requests. Perhaps this was merely a coincidence, but the chief's own defiant stance against the Spaniards might have eased any anxiety the leadership felt about letting Native women participate in political discourse.

Ychu Francisca and Afac Gabriela wanted their husbands back. Their audience with Captain Florencia was brief. They "requested that his Excellency deign to interpose his authority so that their husbands, Hijnac Andrés and Ocolasli Juan, who are in the presidio, may come to lead a marital life with them; that they find themselves with much work and need."[86] That was it; that was all they said (or all that the visitador recorded). The petition from Ychu Francisca and Afac Gabriela lacked the sentimentality or loneliness embedded in the male caciques' parlaying of Apalachee women's requests. Ychu Francisca and Afac Gabriela probably felt no need to make elaborate arguments about why they, and not the Spanish Crown or their town chiefs, should get to decide their husbands' movements.[87]

In Apalachee's matrilineal society, women had long determined where men lived and even worked. The visitador had seen firsthand this display of power. Antonio Entonado, chief of San Francisco de Oconi, had approached him on behalf of Pansaca Luis, who wanted to return from Ivitachuco to Oconi. It was a simple request that should not have involved the visitador at all. Pansaca Luis wanted to go home and his chief wanted him back. The only impediment was Pansaca Luis's wife. She was from Ivitachuco and expected her husband to live with her and work where she saw fit.

> The principal cacique of the said village stated . . . that one of his vassals named Pansaca Luis finds himself at the present married in the place of Hivitachuco and desirous of coming to this village [Oconi]; that in consideration of their needing the said Luis . . . and that, notwithstanding his being married, he begs his excellency that he grant him permission.[88]

Pansaca Luis needed a special permit to defy his wife.[89] A century of Spanish colonial presence and fifty years of mission activity in Apalachee had done little to alter matrilineality or matrifocal practices. Their endurance surprised no one, and even the visitador readily recognized their power: he "grant[ed] him [Pansaca Luis] the permission under the condition that it should be with the consent of his wife and not forced on her."[90] Pansaca Luis was back where he started, for even the visitador agreed he still needed his wife's consent to move about.

Native women thus had a critical role in shaping Native governance and autonomy as well as limiting colonial rule. Apalachees—like Chacatos, Guales, and Timucuas—repeatedly, loudly, and clearly said that Native women were necessary to the safety and resilience of their communities. Matrilineal practices, as well as the accompanying gender norms, expectations, and behaviors, could and did remain in place through the eighteenth century. They endured Spanish colonization, missionization, and interference into Native life. They outlasted Indian slavery and attacks. Centering women's bodies and voices requires, then, a different way of thinking about the violence and impact of colonialism. In the 1670 junta, in the 1675 unrest in Chacato, and in the 1695 petitions, Native women did more than describe the world around them; they disrupted colonial narratives of declension and loss by pointing to their power, and they demanded to be recognized, taken into account, and no longer made to suffer.[91]

CHAPTER THREE

The Wars Women Were Already Fighting

María Jacoba had been fighting for years. Hers was a long, quiet fight for the right to live as she saw fit. She wanted to choose what she did, where she lived, and with whom she interacted, and until 1678, she had expertly dictated the terms of that engagement. As a thirty-five-year-old Timucua woman from the Potano region, María Jacoba lived in a world notably different than the one her mother or grandmother had known. Consider her name. She self-identified as María Jacoba and was known and called by that Spanish name.[1] She was a practicing Catholic, spoke some Spanish, and wore clothing that adapted to Spanish norms. María Jacoba was unmistakably and firmly part of a colonial world. And yet, she was not. She was from a town Florida officials claimed no longer existed (but it clearly still did), and served a cacica who had, according to Spanish intelligence, relinquished power (but she clearly had not). María Jacoba's presence was enough to counter Spanish assumptions about a place and people they thought they knew; she was a living, breathing embodiment of the precarity of Spanish colonial control in Florida.[2]

María Jacoba lived "in her style" for the better part of a decade.[3] She forged a space for herself at the edges of an empire that could not control what she did, where she traveled, or who belonged in her world. She had married her husband in church but did not share a home with him and visited him only when she wanted to. Moreover, she knew she had to attend confession at least once a year to remain in the good graces of San Agustín religious officials, and that is exactly what she did. She came into town on a yearly basis to fulfill this minimum requirement but otherwise continued living the way she wanted to. Spanish sources do not let us see María Jacoba thriving, however. Instead, they show us only her moments of loss. She enters the archive right when the spaces she had so carefully carved for herself begin to fall apart.

In 1678, María Jacoba was brought to San Agustín in chains. She had been apprehended after coming into a nearby Timucua town alongside a known murderer, Calesa. María Jacoba argued that she should be rewarded, not imprisoned. She had done what Spanish authorities had failed to do: she had captured a dangerous man. María Jacoba explained how she had persuaded Calesa that she was on his side, urged him to walk into the nearby town of San Francisco, and then turned on him. But her actions and her rendition of events raised more eyebrows than support. Spanish officials immediately distrusted her. They had little appreciation for a Native woman who seemed more capable and better informed than they were. Governor Pablo Hita y Salazar cared less about how she had ended up in the company of a known criminal—or how she had managed to convince him to surrender, as she insisted—than he did about how she had managed to move in and out of San Agustín in the first place. He launched an investigation into her movements, rather than into Calesa's crimes.[4]

Testimony after testimony confirmed María Jacoba's story and autonomy, but that did little to ameliorate the distrust that Florida officials felt. Governor Hita Salazar decried her choices and declared her freedom excessive. After all, María Jacoba's movements had not taken place in some distant Indian village; she was traveling to and from the main Spanish town in Florida. Florida officials feared that María Jacoba's actions would inspire others to behave as she did. She was even accused of encouraging slaves to flee their masters. The Potano woman who had always lived in accordance with Spanish law, had gone routinely to confession, and had tried to bring a criminal to justice was now charged with inciting unrest.

The testimonies in María Jacoba's trial spoke of Alonsso, an Indian slave who had abandoned his master and followed her out of San Agustín. María Jacoba had insisted that "she dissuaded him many times from going away with her because he was in the service of his employer, but he followed her and came out on the trail to meet her." She had "urged him to return home," and her defense attorney claimed that "it was his [Alonsso's] persistence that won out over the pressing arguments which she made to him as a woman."[5] But if the defense contended that María Jacoba was a lowly woman overpowered by Alonsso's will, the prosecution portrayed her as a temptress, capable of seducing Alonsso or any man away from his proper place. The actual relationship between María Jacoba and Alonsso is hard to ascertain, and this ambiguity points to the complicated spectrum of freedoms that existed within this colonial context.

Due to her repeated abscondence, Spanish authorities labeled María Jacoba "una fugitiva," "una cimarrona por los montes," a fugitive, a cimarron who fled beyond the control of Florida officials.[6] The word *cimarrón* tended to refer to someone or something wild or undomesticated, and in Spanish America, the term was most commonly used to describe runaway slaves of African descent. In Florida, there are only a handful of instances where the word *cimarrón* was used to describe Native people who fled Spanish control, and it is "believed to be the origin of the name Seminole . . . [especially since] Muskhogean languages lack 'r,' [and therefore] Natives pronounced the name as cimallon."[7] María Jacoba was a *cimarrona* because she willingly abandoned her "settled" Christian life. Authorities deemed her decisions dangerous, and though her struggle for self-determination paled in comparison to Calesa's murders, she paid dearly for her actions. Sentenced to one hundred lashes, she faced the full wrath of a colonial apparatus that did not and could not accommodate her choices or freedom.[8]

The word *cimarrón* also racialized María Jacoba. It tied her transgressive movements and associations with those of the Black community, whose mobility and labor were far more restricted than her own.[9] And while Spanish officials never identified María Jacoba as a *parda*, *mulatta*, *morena*, *negra*, or anything but an Indian, they understood her actions in the context of a sharpening racial slavery regime that was steadily reshaping who could be enslaved and how to do so.[10] The Spanish need to control María Jacoba's whereabouts, body, and life was intimately connected to their ability to do the same for free and enslaved people of African descent living in San Agustín.[11] As Native women like María Jacoba pushed to make their lives in Spanish Florida more palatable, livable, or simply safe enough, they found their struggles enmeshed with those of Black women.

Black and Native women fought hard and repeatedly to protect their bodies, livelihoods, and freedoms. Their stories, though distinct, share many commonalities. Some dealt with the personal, communal, or even physical vulnerabilities endured in colonial settings. Others exposed the fraught and incomplete archival practices that failed to record their names or even acknowledge their humanity. But these women were not—or rather could not be rendered—invisible or silent. Tugging and pulling at snippets that mention them in the sources not only unravels some of these women's life stories, but also reveals the centrality of Black and Native women to colonial articulations of power and control, as well as to the gendered, racialized, and very real limits of both.

In 1687, as the summer air began to blow a little colder, two enslaved women and a group of ten others, including a small, nursing child, made the dangerous choice to flee Carolina, head south, and seek freedom, or at least safety, in Florida. The Spanish archive does not list any names of the enslaved, and English sources only record the names of the male fugitives: Mingo, Dicque, Jesse, Conano, Gran Domingo, Jacque, Robi, and Cambo. The women were described only by their skin color and sex. They were Black and women. One had a nursing child that was mentioned only once. Florida governor Diego Quiroga y Losada left the infant out of later retellings, even though the child offered the clearest bit of evidence for how these men and women understood their actions and each other. The infant, whose unpredictable cry could put the whole enterprise in danger, showed that these runaways were likely a family unit, if not by blood or marriage, then by circumstance and need.[12]

The small group of enslaved men and women had "fled from San Jorge [Charles Town] to be with the Spaniards and be Catholic," or so the Spanish deposition claimed.[13] But the Black men and women who escaped by boat in the cover of night were not merely running to Spanish Florida; they were escaping from English slavery. Almost nothing is known about who they were or what they did in Carolina. The large plantation economy associated with the American South, which forced millions of men and women to work sunup to sundown in fields producing staple crops, was still in its incipient stages at the eve of the eighteenth century. Nevertheless, the importation of enslaved people was already big business. By 1700, half of the population in Charles Town was enslaved. English chattel slavery was a racial, heritable, and deeply exploitive institution that was expanding rapidly.[14]

Spanish Florida offered these fugitives an alternative, not a guarantee. The Catholic Church and the *Siete Partidas*—a legal code compiled in the thirteenth century that sought to codify legal and customary traditions, including the treatment of women and slaves—gave enslaved persons in Florida certain rights and opportunities foreclosed to them by English law. Perhaps most importantly, enslaved people had access to *coartación*, the process by which they could buy their own freedom, which meant that Spanish law, as historian Jane Landers explains, "considered slavery a mutable legal condition, neither racially defined nor permanent."[15] In other words, though children born to an enslaved woman in Spanish America also inherited her status, they had other avenues for negotiating, redefining, and even ending their enslavement that were simply not available under the English legal code.

Both slavery and the fight for freedom were an integral part of Spanish Florida, not in an abstract or esoteric way but embodied in the lives and struggles of people of African descent.[16] Most commonly called *negros* and *morenos* in the sources, Spanish officials also used the terms *pardo* and sometimes *mulattos* to refer to people with mixed African and European ancestry, and the word *chino* to describe a person of Native and African descent.[17] These terms meant a great deal to those being described and those doing the describing, but they were also highly malleable. Someone who was *moreno* in one document could become *pardo* or mestizo in the next.

The fugitives from Carolina were identified as "negros and negras," and while they had left an emerging slave society built on the backs of enslaved African peoples, they found that the exploitation of Black labor was also a constant in San Agustín. From the very earliest Spanish incursions in the region, African and African-descended people played an active role in this colonial space. They served in the militia, worked on the construction of the Castillo de San Marcos (as the San Agustín fort was called), labored as overseers in the growing cattle ranches, and ran several businesses in town, including *pulperías* (grocery stores).

The status of Black people within this emergent Spanish society often proved tenuous, however. In 1608, Governor Pedro de Ybarra sent a report to the crown about the dangers San Agustín faced due to its shrinking Spanish population and its growing Black commmunity.

> There are no other people or citizens than the soldiers and one hundred blacks who on the day that the opportunity presents itself to fight, I have no assurances from them, because they are more likely to want their freedom . . . than to remain as slaves to their masters[.] And for that reason it has been two years since I issued an order that no person was to bring me a black person from elsewhere.[18]

Ybarra worried about the safety of a city protected by a Black population. He doubted that the enslaved would fight to protect their enslavers. If given the chance, the governor predicted that Africans and people of African descent would always "want their freedom."

The church and the army proved the two strongest pillars of the Black community in San Agustín. The Catholic Church recognized and recorded the marriages, baptisms, and burials of hundreds of Africans and their descendants. This powerful religious body also welcomed Black participation in *cofradías* (confraternity) like *Nuestra Señora de la Leche*, which served as a religious fraternity, provided funds for funerals, and held festivals hosted by its members.[19] Black men could also serve in the army. In 1683, Governor Juan Márquez Cabrera authorized the creation of a free pardo and mulatto militia. The surviving roster includes the names of six officers and forty-two men.[20] Jane Landers notes that while almost nothing is known about these men, where they came from, and how they had gotten to Florida, their service in the army "was also an effort to define their status as members of the religious and civil community, and as vassals of a King from whom they might expect protection or patronage in exchange for armed service."[21] During the 1680s, as pirate raids off the coast of Florida intensified, this Black militia repeatedly proved to be one of San Agustín's best lines of defense, disproving Governor Ybarra's earlier fears.[22]

Spanish sources from this period contain scattered mentions of Black men bravely acting as spies, interpreters, and soldiers, including some who rose in the military ranks, but Black women are conspicuously missing. Their empirical absence in the Spanish archive is not the same as actual absence. Black women lived, toiled, made lives for themselves, and defied Spanish authority. In her study on Black women in New Orleans, Jessica Marie Johnson has shown how French "officials especially failed to acknowledge or represent black women, enslaved or freed, in their census documentation."[23] The same could be said of San Agustín, and the two unnamed, fugitive women who arrived in 1687 prove a telling example. No longer English slaves but not quite free, these two women found themselves bound to domestic labor in the house of the Spanish governor, while the men in their group were sent to work on the Castillo de San Marcos, the main military structure in town.

In San Agustín, Black women, both enslaved and free, often worked in the homes of Spanish elites, serving as laundresses or cooks and performing tasks that the Spanish population relied on to survive but rarely bothered to quantify or record.[24] The two runaway women who arrived in 1687 might have disappeared entirely from the archive had the governor not been forced to make sense of them and their labor. Jennifer Morgan reminds us that "when gender, parenthood, or other familial relations make their way into the records, they need to be understood as a particular type of irruption."[25] The women who had fled from English slavery were an irruption, a force that had rushed into the governor's home and demanded freedom. Quiroga y Losada refused; he kept them in bondage, with no desire to acknowledge their experiences or lives. His most articulated expression was one of annoyance: he complained that no one would pay enough for their labor and now he was burdened by them.

The sudden visibility of these fugitive women came at his expense. He was "required to keep them [in his home] to avoid scandal through *recogimiento*," a loaded term that usually referred to the cloistering of women to protect their honor, virginity, and any element of their sexuality.[26] Quiroga y Losada's stated efforts to protect or rather to control the sexual lives of these non-Spanish women offers a complicated contrast with English society. Unlike Carolina, Florida was not steadily moving toward the racialized chattel slavery of Africans and their descendants. But like English officials, Spanish officials sought to regulate Black women's lives and freedoms. Thus, the governor argued that the only way to shield the two Black women from the physical and sexual violence that surely awaited them was to keep them enslaved in his home. These women had escaped English Carolina and arrived in Spanish Florida, but the freedom they had worked for and wanted still remained out of reach.

Governor Quiroga y Losada explained how an earlier attempt to sell these women had gone terribly wrong. During the auction, a soldier had lewdly commented that he would gladly buy them "for the day," as if they were prostitutes, and another had mocked them and offered a meager two pesos for each woman. The governor, embarrassed by the men's taunting, had quickly ended the sale and then downplayed the soldiers' actions as nothing more than a bad joke. Quiroga y Losada claimed that the men had shouted obscenities at the women "for the sole purpose of being scandalous."[27]

These were clearly threats, not jokes. The governor patently understood that; he had quickly removed the women from the auction block and asked for permission to purchase them himself. As the Spanish soldiers were openly stating their intentions to rape and physically abuse these Black women, Quiroga y Losada worried about himself. How was he going to feed and clothe these women? Would he be reimbursed for his troubles? How would his inability to sell these women affect his reputation and finances? In his letters, he made it seem as if these two Black women would certainly lead to his ruin.[28] But these women had bigger concerns than Quiroga y Losada's bruised ego or shrinking purse. They had to find a way to defend their own well-being and safety.

These two women left no testimonies or reports, but their bodies, first in bondage, then in flight, and finally somewhere in between in San Agustín, were their archives. They spoke of resilience and daring, but also of commodification and violence. Marisa Fuentes argues that examining "the workings of power on the bodies and historical afterlives of the enslaved . . . produce[s] new knowledge about their lives from the records left by the regime of power."[29] With their movements and bodies, these fugitive Black women pushed against the silences of the Spanish archive. They showed how gender shaped not only their experiences in slavery but also their access to freedom, a difference that becomes especially poignant when considering their struggles alongside those of the men who had absconded with them from Carolina. Their male companions had been "put to work in the making of the Castillo, which has already saved the treasury a great amount," and whereas the Black men were deemed valuable and useful, the Black women were considered both burdensome and exploitable.[30] Quiroga y Losada whined repeatedly that these women cost more than they produced and, if they were ever hired out, he would be responsible for the sexual violence that undoubtably awaited them. He even reprimanded them for spending their time "caring for two children," never acknowledging the reproductive labor of these women or the fact that these two children would likely remain in his possession. The degradation of Black women and their labor went hand in hand with the violent sexualization of their bodies.

The unnamed Black women were still in the governor's house when English officials arrived in San Agustín and demanded their return. The two women were not included in the list of runaway names presented to Governor Quiroga y Losada, but their absence did not imply that the Carolinians had somehow forgotten about them or that they were safe in San Agustín. Florida officials at first refused the slave owners, pleased with their new ability to undermine English advances. But the Carolinians proved relentless, asking, demanding, and then threatening violence if their property was not returned in a timely manner. When Spanish officials finally responded, they did so with ambivalence, unsure of what to do with these Black individuals who had chosen where and how they wanted to live their lives. The mere act of refusing to hand over to the English any of the fugitive slaves proved critical, however. Over time, this refusal became policy, and in 1693, Florida officials issued a *cédula* (edict) promising freedom to any enslaved person who arrived in San Agustín and vowed to serve both the Catholic Church and the Spanish Crown.[31]

Florida's small, free Black community began to grow in the late seventeenth century. Its members served as soldiers, shop owners, day laborers, overseers, cattle ranchers, interpreters, laundresses, maids, and any other occupation available to them. Enslaved and free people of African descent were both everywhere in San Agustín and almost nowhere in the records. Their presence and actions seem folded into the everydayness of colonial life in Florida.

Marriage and baptism records from San Agustín offer some of the only surviving bits of evidence for what was a booming and complex Black community.[32] These records show that people living in Spanish Florida, like those living in other parts of Latin America, engaged in endogamous marriage practices. Susan Richbourg Parker and Diana Reigelsperger have done extensive work on baptism and marriage records from San Agustín and have shown that Black women not only followed this pattern but did so at higher rates than Black men.[33] In other words, Black women tend to appear in marriage records only alongside free or enslaved Black men, both as their partners and as the witnesses to unions, as the marriage between García, a slave of Captain Lorenzo Joseph, and María, a slave of Captain Francisco Canisarez, on July 8, 1674, clearly shows. The church sanctified the "deposition and relation," and since there was willingness on both sides and no impediments, the marriage ceremony went on as planned. García and María had three *testigos* (witnesses) to verify their union, all of them male and all part of the emerging Black community in San Agustín. There was Simón, a free moreno who was employed as a bricklayer; Lorenzo, a slave in the service of Captain San Francisco de Lara; and Francisco, who was enslaved by María Ruíz, a member of the Spanish elite in Florida. García and María had found diverse and established members of the Black community to support their union.[34]

Black women depended on these relationships to negotiate their lives in San Agustín. Their *parentela* (a collective formed of kin, including relatives by marriage) and *compadrazgo* (godparents) represented their networks of support and allies. Although some Spanish officials and members of Florida's elite signed on as witnesses to these marriage records, most of the people in these Black women's networks were also of African descent.

Black men had slightly larger social networks. Whether free or enslaved, Black men could marry Native and mestiza women. The marriage of Juan, a "mulatto slave" of Captain Lorenzo Joseph de León to Isabel, "India Católica Yamase [sic] daughter of Pedro, gentile," on February 17, 1675; or the union between Bernardo Pediosa, a slave of Captain Don Lorenzo de Horryutiner, to Francisca, "Indian of Tolomato, widow of Ascensio," on June 30, 1675; or even the marriage of Phelipe de Santiago Candia, a pardo slave of Adjutant Joseph Rodrigues, to Micaela María, a Native of Pueblo de Nicolás who now lived in Nombre de Dios outside the city walls, on April 15, 1692, showed the intimate connections Black men could and did forge outside of slavery and San Agustín.[35] Black women were not afforded those same possibilities; they had to establish kinship and marriage ties with Black men in order to ensure some level of protection for themselves and their children.[36]

Of course, Black women had other relationships that were never recognized by the church, as evidenced in the baptism records.[37] There were about thirty infants baptized between 1687 and 1702 who were regarded as illegitimate, either listed as *naturales* (born out of wedlock) or with no known father. Enslaved Black women bore many of these children, and though it is impossible to know if these children were conceived from a relationship that was consensual, strategic, coercive, or shifting unpredictably along that range, these baptisms hint at the different relationships Black women entered into and to which they were subjected.

The church allowed the baptism of children born out of wedlock but still required *padrinos* (godparents) to perform the rite. Enslaved and free Black women in San Agustín worked hard to secure well-regarded and -connected padrinos for their children, even though they often faced an uphill battle trying to find padrinos for illegitimate children. On April 1, 1687, Theresa managed to baptize her daughter María, who had been born a week earlier and had "no recognized father." The priest warned Juan Anbrada, the selected godfather, of this young baby's parentage, "le adverti el parentesco." But Theresa had chosen well, and this padrino readily agreed to have María as his *ahijada* (goddaughter).[38] Following long-established patterns for other parts of Spanish America, in San Agustín enslaved women and "free women of color used compadrazgo [godparentage] to create powerful bonds of obligation between themselves and other free black and mulatta women."[39] Often enslaved women with illegitimate children listed only a *madrina* (female godparent) for their child, and that madrina was most often also Black and enslaved.[40] In other words, Black women relied on one another.

On occasion, Black women also served as madrinas for Spanish and Criollo children. Their documentation in non-Black or enslaved baptismal records shows how Black women created their community. Compadrazgo allowed them to extend kinship ties that were otherwise unavailable to them. They inserted themselves in the very foundational and intimate relationships that built Spanish colonial society. Why were these women committing to support the spiritual well-being of the children of slave owners, children who could grow up to own slaves and support the continued enslavement of their own godmothers? Perhaps the answer lies in the choice. Black women, enslaved or free, were never required to serve as madrinas; but in their choice, they could potentially provide for themselves and their families vital connections and access points to Spanish society.[41]

These records outline a growing Black population free or freed from bondage in San Agustín. By the 1730s, there were more than 1,500 people of African descent in Florida, and within thirty years that number doubled. In 1738, Governor Manuel de Montiano allowed the establishment of Santa Gracia Real de Santa Teresa de Mose, or Fort Mose, a free and autonomous Black town just beyond the border of San Agustín. The town was operational for only a short while, but it allowed Black men and women to own property, grow food, elect a governing body, and live away from prying Spanish eyes.[42] As people of African descent negotiated their place within (and outside of) Spanish colonial society, they also had to contend with the Native populations in the area. Black-Native relations in Florida were poorly documented, but it is clear that within city walls, people of African and Indigenous descent labored and struggled alongside each other. Sometimes they found comradeship in their shared, precarious arrangements, but often these relationships proved fraught, strained by the racial policies and violence of the Spanish colonial regime.[43]

In 1651, Don Manuel, the *holata* (chief) of the Timucua town of Asile, wrote a letter in Timucua complaining about rampant Spanish abuses. Don Manuel criticized a blatant land grab by some of the highest-ranking Spanish officials in Florida. He also wrote about the promises of goods never delivered, the damage done to Native crops by roaming cattle left unsupervised, and, more pressingly, the dwindling number of men left in his town due to exploitative Spanish labor policies. In his powerful and beautifully crafted epistle, Don Manuel displays immense care in how he presented and explained his complaints against Florida officials.[44]

The holata was careful not to insult Spanish sensitivities and showed respect to all the Spanish officials he mentioned. He used deferential language and honorific markings. But all that formality seemed to disappear when Don Manuel discussed Francisco Galindo, the *mayoral* (overseer) of the Aisle hacienda, who was known for his violent reprimands of Timucua laborers. The overseer is the only person in the entire letter not given an honorific marking: "Franco Galindo nanacu anonayoholata ma ano hebasinano apesola nimelabohihabe niohonihabe anomasiqiti niohonabela" ("Francisco Galindo speaking for the chief of the white people, said that I would be mercifully given the hoes, he said, they would be given to me"). Don Manuel employs and repeats the honorific participle *-ano* to show deference to the *ano*nayoholata ("chief of the white people"), as the holata called the governor of Florida; Galindo gets no such linguistic recognition.[45] In the Spanish translation of the letter, it is not immediately clear that the Native author was disrespecting the overseer in any way. But in its original Timucua form, there is something insulting about the way Don Manuel describes the overseer.

Francisco Galindo was a mulatto. He was the only person of African descent mentioned in the holata's letter and the only person who did not receive an honorific marking. This linguistic absence is hard to interpret properly. Did it mean that Don Manuel saw Galindo as belonging to a lower status than other Spanish and Criollo men? Did the holata simply dislike the mayoral? Was this lack of honorific marking due to the overseer's race, station, or a combination of those factors? Race was not the primary way that Native people talked about difference in the seventeenth century, but Don Manuel captured, at least linguistically, what he regarded as a clear distinction. He saw Galindo differently. The Black overseer was definitely part of the colonial power structures that were hurting the town of Asile—his town—but Don Manuel did not afford Galindo the same respect that he gave to the white men named in his complaint. In Asile, Don Manuel set the tone for these Native-Black relationships; in San Agustín, the situation and subsequent arrangements proved much messier.

In the 1660s and 1670s, Native men from Timucua, Guale, Apalachee, Yamasee, and the surrounding towns poured into San Agustín to assist with the building of the Castillo de San Marcos.[46] Some traveled willingly, and others went because they had to fulfill their town's labor draft required by the repartimiento. During their employment, these day laborers tended to live outside the garrison. Although laws prohibited Spanish households from enslaving or employing these individuals, there is evidence of both.[47] The increasingly diverse Indigenous population in San Agustín was not only male; Native women often accompanied their husbands in order to keep their families together or to seek employment within Spanish households in their own right.[48] As Criollo, Spanish, and Native workers moved into town to build the fort, small but significant waves of runaway slaves from English Carolina also began to reach San Agustín. African labor, both free and enslaved, had long been an integral feature of Florida life. But these new arrivals helped further politicize the labor and presence of Africans in San Agustín.[49]

Juan Méndez was one of these new arrivals. The archive reveals almost nothing about why he left (or, more likely, was forced to leave) Havana, Cuba. The journey to San Agustín was not his first, reluctant Atlantic voyage. In his brief confession, he explained that "he was from Cavo Verde" but was now "a slave to Don Pablo de Hita [y Salazar]," former governor of Florida, "and he was employed as *un hombre de campo* [to labor in the fields] and to do as his master commanded[;] . . . and he thinks he is older than twenty-five years old."[50] Méndez had been in the colony only a short while and knew little of the land or people surrounding the city, but after a violent altercation with his owner, he made the bold decision to flee San Agustín. Perhaps he had tried this tactic before. His relocation from Cuba to Florida may have been a punishment for previous attempts to escape slavery. In Spanish America, just like in many other slave-owning societies, relocation and sale were common punishments for enslaved people who repeatedly tried to escape.[51]

Méndez had not traveled far out of town when he encountered Silvestre, an Apalachee Indian who worked for or perhaps was enslaved by Isidrio Rodríguez, a Spanish soldier in the presidio. Silvestre was gathering wood in a *sabana* (field) when the runaway slave approached him and asked for directions to a nearby town. Though Silvestre initially conversed willingly, something about Juan Méndez's questions and manners made him uneasy. Within minutes, Silvestre correctly identified Méndez as a fugitive slave and tried to apprehend him. The sources are vague about what happened next, but a struggle ensued, leaving Silvestre mortally wounded and Méndez once again on the run.

Silvestre's death triggered an investigation that sheds light on the tense yet extremely close relationships between Black and Native peoples in San Agustín. In his confession, Méndez explained that his misfortunes had started well before he killed Silvestre: "Two days prior, when his mistress had sent him to get meat and when he returned home . . . he was missing some firewood and she threw a keychain [*llavero*] at him and it hit him in the face and it wounded him [*lo descalabró*] and for that reason he had not returned home."[52] Méndez thought his mistress had crossed a line, but Spanish officials disagreed. They did not regard this woman's violent actions as particularly noteworthy. She was merely doing what slave owners did, disciplining those under their command. By running away, Méndez was not simply challenging his mistress; he was also pushing against an existing power structure. But San Agustín's racialized social hierarchy held firm, buttressed by Spanish slave owners like this mistress but also by Native people, like Silvestre, who saw more benefit in apprehending Méndez than in aiding him.[53]

After wounding Silvestre, Méndez rushed back to San Agustín, but he knew that he could not return to his mistress's house. He needed to find safety elsewhere. His ability to hide in plain sight on the city streets of San Agustín reveals the ease and frequency with which Black people moved in and out of this small urban space.[54] Méndez did not rouse suspicion because there was nothing unusual about a Black man moving freely about the city. Perhaps he was on an errand for his mistress. Or maybe he was helping with the Castillo. If anyone had seen him coming back into town, they could have assumed that Méndez had been collecting wood or hired out to do some work in the sabana.

Nighttime presented a new challenge, however, and Méndez chose to seek refuge in what would seem an unlikely place: a kitchen. The kitchen in question belonged to the family of the former governor Don Pedro Benedit Horruytiner.[55] Most kitchens in San Agustín were removed from the main household building since they were made of wood, had thatched roofs, and often caught fire. In other words, most kitchens were not spaces occupied by Spaniards or Criollos, especially not after dark. Méndez knew that when he knocked on the kitchen window. It took some time, but eventually someone undid the window latch and Méndez crawled inside. The fact that he entered the kitchen through the window and not the door suggests that the main door was locked from the outside. The men in the kitchen were likely enslaved and thus had their nighttime mobility restricted by those in the main house. Méndez had hoped to find both support and sympathy for his ordeal; he found instead something far more complex in that kitchen.[56]

Méndez saw at least four other men sleeping in the small kitchen area. The first two were Native. Lorenzo Iguale, a Guale Indian from San Phelipe de Tolomato, and Adrian, an Apalachee from San Luis de Talimali, were still awake and conversing by candlelight when Méndez entered—at least according to Lorenzo's testimony. Adrian claims that he had been sleeping and was awakened by Lorenzo's warning that someone had unexpectedly entered the kitchen.[57] The other two men were of African descent: Juan de la Cruz, a mulatto, "Mexican slave of the heirs of Benedit Horruytiner," and "el negro Marcos," a Black slave.[58]

These men all worked in the same household and slept in the same tiny space, but during Méndez's trial, they actively dismissed any intimacy that their shared conditions predicated. The two Native men, Lorenzo Iguale and Adrian, testified that they had immediately identified Méndez as the murderer of Silvestre. They had heard about the violent encounter that had left one Apalachee man dead earlier that day in the sabana. When Méndez came into the kitchen seeking refuge in the middle of the night, Lorenzo and Adrian had quickly put two and two together. But they did not share their concerns or deductions with Juan or Marcos, the two enslaved Black men also sleeping in the kitchen that night.[59]

Juan even walked Méndez to church the following morning, supposedly unaware that he was aiding and abetting a known murderer. During his deposition, Juan sought to distance himself not only from Méndez but also from the Apalachee men testifying in the trial. Juan insisted that he did not know Méndez or his criminal activities and, more importantly, he argued that he could never have learned about them in time to stop Méndez because he did not converse with Lorenzo Iguale or Adrian, who mainly talked to one another in Apalachee. Juan made it clear that there was no friendship among these men. No matter how closely connected the lives, labors, and experiences of Native and Black men were in San Agustín, there was a profound divide between them.[60]

Several years later, another criminal case showed the continued tensions between the Black and Native communities in San Agustín. In 1695, two Apalachee men ingeniously counterfeited Spanish coins and used them to buy goods from Black-owned and -operated businesses. Andrés de Escavedo and Ajalap Cosme were two Native men who had come into San Agustín to assist with the building of the Castillo.[61] Sources reveal little about them, but they knew a great deal about San Agustín. Their plan depended on their intimate knowledge of the city, its shops, its economic arrangements, and social norms. First, Andrés and Ajalap carefully dug through the city's trash pits looking for broken plates and tin pieces. Second, they studied coins and manipulated the scraps to make them look like currency. Finally, they handed the fake money to a third party who would go to purchase items from several stores, including from a bakery and "a tienda de pulpería [grocery store]."[62] Andrés and

Ajalap mostly used their newfound wealth to purchase food, revealing how unsatisfying the meals provided to Indian laborers were; this practice also demonstrated their cunning, since they were buying items that were consumable and thus hard to confiscate.

Andrés and Ajalap seem to have specifically targeted stores operated by people of African descent. Chrispian de Tapia, a captain in the militia, was identified as a "free *pardo*" who ran the *tienda de pulpería* (grocery store), while Isavel de los Ríos, owner of a bakery, was described as a "free *morena*."[63] The two Apalachee men never explained the logic behind their plan, but, for their crime to work, the fake currency needed to circulate. Perhaps they assumed that the Black business owners would fail to recognize the true nature of the coins or, if they did eventually discover the offense, they would simply try to pass the coins to their Black clientele rather than report the crime to Spanish authorities. That Andrés and Ajalap lived in San Agustín only a short time before they devised a plan that preyed on the vulnerability of the Black community shows how clearly defined and identifiable Florida's racial order was.

At first, Andrés and Ajalap's ploy worked flawlessly. The fake coins quickly moved from hand to hand, accepted without any qualms by the store owners.[64] It was a little boy, or perhaps the woman he served, who helped unravel the case. When "a little Indian boy came to the store, whom María de Reina, a resident of the city was sending to ask for a half real's worth of provisions," Captain Tapia gave him as change some of Andrés and Ajalap's counterfeit coins.[65] The little Indian boy who had purchased the goods, or possibly his mistress, correctly identified the change as fake and demanded compensation from the store owner. Captain Tapia quickly realized his mistake and sought to bring the culprit to court.

Isavel de los Ríos, the other targeted store owner, took a different approach. Lacking the status or resources of Captain Tapia, she attempted to rid herself of the bad currency by recirculating the counterfeit tender. Spanish officials were then not too sure how they should treat Isavel de los Ríos.[66] She had not planned the heist and had been a victim of Andrés and Ajalap's clever fakes, but then she had failed to report the criminal activity and had wittingly participated in the circulation of fake coins. She offered a lengthy defense for her actions. To counter the fragmented ways Black women often appear in the colonial archive, I have included de los Ríos's testimony in its entirety.

> This present month an Apalachee Indian came to her house at about seven in the evening to buy two reals worth of rosquetes and she gave them to him. And he paid for them in little pieces of tin or pewter, each one the size of real, that she accepted because they seemed to be of silver. And, having looked at them closely on the following day, she saw that they were not [real], although they again seemed to be reals. Nevertheless, after having sold rosquetes for the house of the sergeant major don Nicolas Ponse de León and for the house of the corporal Ysidro Rodrigues, she experimented whether she could pass the said two reals. And she was not able to because they returned them, saying they were of tin. And on the following night a little pequatillo who serves Patricio de Monson, came with a little piece of the aforesaid tin the size of a real to buy two reals' worth of sugar syrup. And recognizing that they were not of silver, she took them away from him and along with them a little jar that he was carrying to hold the syrup and a little blanket and gave him a beating and threw him out the door. And later the said Patricio de Monson sent to ask for the blanket and little jar, saying that they belonged to an Indian of his. And the one who is testifying went to his house and she learned from the little knave pecuatillo that an Apalachee Indian named Andres, who serves the said Patricio de Monson, had sent the aforesaid pecuata to seek the two reals' worth of syrup with the little pieces of tin and that he had remained behind out in the street to see what happened, according to what the said little rascal stated. From this she presumes that on the first occasion when they deceived her with the two reals it was the same Indian of Patricio de Monson who sent for the syrup. And that what she has testified to is the truth under the oath that she has taken. She did not sign because of not knowing how.[67]

De los Ríos made no excuses. She had accepted the fake currency and, after realizing her mistake too late, she decided to "experiment" and see if she could get away with the same crime Andrés and Ajalap had committed. De los Ríos was a Black woman business owner, however; she was readily identified by her shop and her skin color, and she could not move in the shadows like the two Apalachee men who had swindled her. Her visibility and vulnerability went hand in hand.

De los Ríos, unlike other women in San Agustín, worked and lived in the public domain.[68] As a free morena woman, she had to find work outside her home. There was no indication she was married or had any other form of financial backing. And while Spanish officials understood de los Ríos's status, frequented her shop, and depended on the labor of other free and enslaved Black women, they also deeply distrusted her. De los Ríos's Blackness denied her the protections a Spanish or Criolla woman had within Florida's patriarchal ordering of gender.[69] She knew, just like Andrés and Ajalap had known, that if she presented Spanish officials with the fake coins, they would likely dismiss her concern or, worse yet, accuse her of criminal activity. The Apalachee men had sought to exploit her liminal status, but de los Ríos was not the owner of a successful bakery simply by chance; she had perfected her own ways of navigating the racial and gender regime of San Agustín.

Her first plan was to recirculate the coins. In her testimony, de los Ríos was very careful in how she narrated her efforts. Before detailing anything to do with the coins, she described how she had spent her morning selling goods to two prominent Spanish households. De los Ríos provides the full names and titles of the highest-ranking men in each household—*Major Don* Nicolas Ponse de León and *Corporal* Ysidro Rodrigues—reminding Spanish authorities of the important families she served and the reputable business she ran. Then she diminished, almost to the point of comedy, her dealings with the coins. De los Ríos testified that she was merely curious and wanted to know "whether she could pass the said two *reales*." When the reales were immediately returned to her, she learned her lesson and no harm had resulted from this failed exchange, or so she insisted.[70]

Then another customer came into her shop with fake coins. De los Ríos, being the responsible shop owner she was, decided to track down the culprit. She beat the Native boy who had tried to buy food with the counterfeits and then followed him to his master's house to find out who was behind this crime.[71] It is interesting to note that de los Ríos refers to this young boy as a "*pecuatillo*," which is a combination of *pequata*, a Timucua word meaning young person or servant, and the Spanish ending *-illo/a*, which functions as a further diminutive. We know almost nothing about de los Ríos, but with this simple word choice that combined both Timucua and Spanish she revealed an everyday linguistic negotiation necessary to navigate San Agustín's multiethnic, multiracial, and multilingual society.[72]

De los Ríos's sleuthing helped identify and find Andrés and Ajalap. As soon as the men's involvement came to light, confirmed also by the other Black store owner, de los Ríos was no longer considered a person of interest. As far as the trial details, she suffered no reprimand for her (failed) criminal activity. The two Apalachee men were less fortunate. They turned on each other, trying to cast the other as the main instigator. In the end, they both faced criminal charges and hard labor sentences. Andrés and Ajalap were right in assuming members of the Black community would only turn to Spanish authorities as a last resort, but they had not foreseen that de los Ríos would take matters into her own hands. She had not been the easy target they had expected.

De los Ríos likely faced many daily challenges to her wellbeing; this trial merely documents one. It shows her connections, determination, and knowledge and how she mobilized each to protect herself and her shop. It also shows that Spanish officials recognized and acted upon her knowledge; as much as they mistrusted de los Ríos's movements and freedom, they also relied on them to apprehend Andrés and Ajalap. Her testimony centered the struggles of Black women, emphasizing not only their work and role in the community but also the enormous amount of intellectual labor they performed to define and defend their autonomy. De los Ríos knew a great deal about a great deal. She had to. Otherwise, this trial would have been about her, not Andrés and Ajalap. She had learned to read San Agustín's urban landscape; the trick was getting Spanish officials to listen.

It was a Native woman who first warned Florida officials of the coming imperial war. The earliest news Spaniards received of what would be the first formal confrontation of Queen Anne's War came from an unnamed Chacata woman. She had adroitly fled the claws of Indian slaving and found her way to San Luis (near present-day Tallahassee) in late October 1702.[73] This Chacata woman had come into the city with great haste, and although the sources do not explain how she secured an audience with San Luis officials or how she communicated the pressing nature of her information, it is clear that these men listened to her intently. She brought news they had long feared: an army comprising hundreds of Indians and Englishmen was amassing quickly. This large force was planning to attack San Agustín.[74]

The Chacata woman had come all the way from Achito. She explained that she was not originally from this town but had moved there over a year ago. It is unclear if her relocation had been voluntary. It is possible that she had moved there with other Chacatos in hopes of finding respite from the constant threat of slave raids, but it is also likely that she had been captured and taken away from a Chacato town as a slave. The brief Spanish explanation for her movements—"who about one year ago was taken from this province to the one in Apalachicola by a Christian Indian from Sabacola, who lives in that province"—leaves both possibilities open.[75] Regardless of her status, during her time in Achito the Chacata woman witnessed several council meetings between Apalachee and Apalachicola leaders. Perhaps she had been invited into the council—Native women, especially Beloved women with prominent stature and respect within their communities, often sat in council meetings and were welcomed to share their insights.[76] Or maybe she had been there to prepare meals as the men talked into the night. Either way, she used her time in the council house wisely, listening with care as talk of war quickly transformed into martial preparations.

In the final council meeting she attended, the discussion had turned to Apalachee men and the roles they would play in the coming attack against San Agustín. Apalachicolas wanted more than hospitality from their southern neighbors; they encouraged the Apalachees to join the fight. By the end of the night, two important decisions had been made. The first came from the council house:

Apalachees would join the Apalachicolas in their planned attack against San Agustín. The second resolution came from the Chacata woman herself: she needed to leave Achito immediately. The alliances and relationships that balanced her world were quickly shifting, and there was no doubt in her mind that war was coming.

Once she reached San Luis, the Chacata woman provided a lengthy testimony. It is unclear if she spoke Spanish, but she understood enough Apalachee, Apalachicola, or Hitchiti to know what had been discussed at the Achito council house. Her testimony began by describing English plans to "wage war against this province" but then immediately linked this coming violence with the ongoing slave trade. In her understanding, the two perils were deeply interconnected. The testimony of the "Christian Yndia Chacata" provided detailed military intelligence framed through the gendered violence of the slave trade, which she argued sought "to kill the men and take the women prisoners." This Native woman was not just giving Spanish officials the intel they wanted to hear; she was offering them a unique understanding of how the Indian slave trade had redrawn the region's geopolitics:

> Yesterday in the afternoon of the current month arrived at San Luis a Christian Yndia Chacata. . . . She said that being in the place of Achito where she lived . . . she saw them make a Junta of all the places of that province. And they determined to come wage war against this province. And come to the place of Bacuqua and Escambe to kill the men and take the women prisoner. . . . [A]nd this Indian woman explained that they would come to this place of San Luis, where they would make strongholds in order to lay claim over the whole province, and that at the same time they would go with many English vessels from San Jorge and fall on this presidio and take it, and once and for all end with all the Spaniards and the Christian Indians . . . and they [the English] would remain the sole masters of the land. Having convened this junta and council, they gathered in the said place of Achito four hundred Chisca men, Apalachicolas, including no other nation but ten Chichimecos and three Chichimeco women which they

> also say come with firearms as well as other women from Apalachicola.[77]

The Apalachicolas were getting ready to fight. Native men and, as the Yndia Chacata made clear, also Native women prepared to go to war. Native women in the Southeast saw war as their responsibility: they advocated for battle or advised against it, determined the fate of those captured, integrated captives into the community, and called for safety. Native women belonged in war, something the Yndia Chacata conveyed explicitly to Spanish officials: "In the said place of Achito, [there came] four hundred Chisca men, Apalachicolas, including no other nation but ten Chichimecos and *three Chichimeco women* which they also say come with firearms as well as *other women* from Apalachicola."[78] Apalachicola and Chichimeca women were accompanying Native men into battle. Native women were mobilizing against Spanish forces. Although the participation and involvement of Native women in military campaigns are poorly documented, the gendered martial moment described by the Yndia Chacata was far from unique.[79]

With her testimony, the Chacata woman also displayed her vast geopolitical and military knowledge. She had not merely eavesdropped on council meetings; she had understood the implications of a changing Apalachee-Apalachicola alliance, discerned the immediacy of this shift, acted on her geographical literacy, and communicated her findings in a comprehensible way to an audience that was not always receptive to Native women. San Luis officials asked her about the invading forces' numbers, armaments, munitions, movements, and long-term strategy. She answered all their queries with detailed responses. But she also spoke about what *she* regarded as important. As San Luis officers asked about the joint Apalachee-Apalachicola attack coming against San Agustín, the Chacata woman detailed instead a planned attack on the towns of Bacuqua and Escambe.[80] She dwelled on the violence consuming Indian country.

The Yndia Chacata repeatedly highlighted the real, present, and extremely close danger of Indian slavery. As she had walked from Achito to San Luis "she left following a path where she saw traces" of a slave party led by an English man, likely Anthony Dodsworth. This party was heavily armed "and according to the signs she learned that they were carrying many prisoners because they had left many stocks (*cepos*) that they make to apprehend them."[81] The cepos remained; the captives did not. The Chacato woman knew how to read this absence. She was more than a humble messenger: she overheard, translated, and retold the events at the Achito council house, contextualizing them within her own fears and expectations. She could make sense of "the signs" of a ravaged land, finding paths that were still open and safe for her. More poignantly, she comprehended Indian slavery and its social, environmental, and physical impact, in ways that almost no Spanish official could do at the time.[82] Like Isavel de los Ríos or María Jacoba, the Yndia Chacata had taught herself how to expertly navigate this complicated and increasingly violent landscape.

San Luis officials attentively listened to her report and quickly communicated her findings with their higher-ups in San Agustín. It is worth repeating, then, that the military reconnaissance conveyed from one Spanish official to another was based on the political consciousness of a Chacato woman and on her ability to understand, negotiate, and manipulate the contested world she inhabited. Moreover, Spanish officials trusted and relied on her report. Her words resonated beyond her as she detailed a world quickly coming undone and the threats of Indian slavery that Florida officials could no longer disregard.

Despite the significance of her warning, no one bothered to write down the name of the "Christian Yndia Chacata." Her knowledge and agency are quietly folded inside Spanish concerns, while she disappears from the archive as quickly as she entered it. But her experiences cannot be dismissed either: they had led her to being in Achito at the right time and place, and they allowed her to develop the right linguistic, geographical, cultural, and historical background to understand the geopolitical changes affecting her land.[83] As San Luis and San Agustín officials began preparing for war, the Yndia Chacata spoke about a past and present struggle waged on and through Native women. As she curtly reminded Spanish officials, the fact that violence had occurred out of their sight—away from San Agustín or San Luis—did not mean that it had not happened. The thousands of missing and murdered Native women told of a fight already underway.

PART II
Fighting Women

CHAPTER FOUR

Women Besieged and Besieging

The women were screaming, and Florida governor Zúñiga y Cerda feared losing control of the situation. He had tried to ignore them, but he found their cries distracting, annoying, and above all else loud. And they were getting louder. Governor Zúñiga y Cerda had done his best to protect the main Spanish town in Florida from the large English and Native army that had laid siege to San Agustín during the first week of November 1702. Over one thousand people had crowded uncomfortably into the small Castillo de San Marcos as English and Native forces surrounded the town. The invasion had quickly faltered and become a stalemate. The English failed to penetrate Spanish defenses, and Spanish counterattacks failed to drive the English away.

On Christmas Eve, Spanish sentinels spotted two English supply vessels. News that the invading army had received reinforcements swept through the Castillo. Hushed whispers of surrender grew to a steady murmur, and within a matter of hours the fort was wrapped in a chaotic commotion. Defeat now seemed inevitable. And the women began making a bad situation even worse, the governor complained. Their wails soon proved infectious, increasing anxiety and lowering morale. Spanish officials could not deal with both the new English advantage and the loud, growing, gendered unrest within their own fort. With every additional supply and weapon unloaded from the English vessels, Spanish chances for success seemed further away. With their loud cries, the women heralded the imminent Spanish downfall.[1]

Zúñiga y Cerda urged calm. He needed to organize a response. He hoped to send several scouting missions to figure out what supplies the invading English forces had received, and he began preparing to send more letters to nearby Spanish colonies requesting immediate aid. But as he tried to resume control, the women started shouting again, even louder than before. The governor soon learned that more ships had been spotted in the far distance. Were these vessels English or Spanish? If these were English ships, as the shouts within the Castillo despondently predicted, and the enemy received additional troops and supplies, Spanish hold on San Agustín would not last much longer. But if these vessels were Spanish, then they had arrived at the most opportune moment and could inflict serious damage on the English forces currently unloading and organizing their new supplies.

Zúñiga y Cerda remained unsure. Identifying vessels that did not clearly display colors was a trying task. And this fleet, which was, in fact, Spanish and coming from Cuba, had purposefully concealed its identity, fearing Spanish forces no longer controlled San Agustín.[2] The events that followed took place in quick succession. The women were shouting. Governor Zúñiga y Cerda struggled to ascertain the provenance of the vessels. Then the women made more noise. Soon other men joined the governor and the sentinels in their reconnaissance. The women's screams made communication among the officers increasingly difficult. Despite repeated efforts and the governor's growing frustration, no one could properly tell if these newly spotted vessels were English or Spanish, and the women continued crying out. Left with few options, Zúñiga y Cerda did something no other governor had ever done, or at least not in an official capacity. He issued an order demanding the women shut up.

Zúñiga y Cerda's complaints about the noise of "the women" homogenizes what were, in all likelihood, very different and competing demands.[3] He was mostly worried about Spanish and Criolla women. Even then, he was far more concerned with the distracting effects their voices had on his men than on what these women were actually saying. The records he produced reflect perfectly this tension, revealing a great deal about his fears and anxieties and much less about the women's. But Spanish and Criolla women were not the only ones making unwelcome noises.

The cries of Timucua, Guale, Chacato, and other Native women in the Castillo also spoke of the immediate dangers. But unlike most Spanish men and women in the fort, these Native women had faced these enemies before, many times.[4] Some had dealt with encroaching and violent slaving raids for over thirty years; they had moved their towns, fled attacks, and had loved ones captured and sold; others had only recently felt the full effects of the expanding Indian slave trade. Now inside the fort, Native women were face to face with a force they had been directly or indirectly fighting most of their lives. They had experience with the danger that surrounded them and knew that if the Castillo de San Marcos fell, they would be captured and sold.[5] Their yells, which annoyed and overwhelmed Zúñiga y Cerda, were likely filled with anger for how long they had endured these attacks, with fear for what was at stake, and with commitment to the fight, for it was their task in war to sing, pray, and shout to encourage the defense of their homelands.[6]

The women of African descent also raised their voices. Some knew well, intimately well, the English attackers beyond the Castillo's coquina walls. They had labored in their houses and fields, hungered in their homes, and suffered physical, emotional, and sexual abuse at their hands. Starting in the late 1680s, many enslaved Black women fled the abuses of English bondage and sought refuge in San Agustín.[7] In Spanish Florida, they worked hard to transform the conditional safety provided to them into a vibrant, autonomous Black community. Thus they fully grasped, perhaps better than any of their counterparts, what would happen to them if the fort fell. Their cries were of fear and anger but also of longing for the safety and freedom that they had traveled so far to secure, which now seemed at risk once again.

The governor found the women's voices—all the women's voices—disconcerting and inappropriate, and thus issued an order for "the most silence possible."[8] Though the documents give no sense as to how Zúñiga y Cerda's command was enforced, it seems to have been carried out because a sudden and brief daytime quiet enveloped the fort.[9] This momentary silence, punctuated only by the occasional rumbles of the livestock, contrasted sharply with the anxious noise and the unsteady but persistent bombardment San Agustín had endured for almost two months. In this quiet, Zúñiga y Cerda could finally "see and hear the movements and sail signs" of the two approaching ships. The much-awaited news was then confirmed: the vessels had come to aid San Agustín. With hope restored, the Castillo once again erupted in noise, but this raucous celebration had none of the melancholy or irrationality the governor had attributed to women.[10] It was the sound of the tide turning and a now possible Spanish victory.

Zúñiga y Cerda's unusual order, as well as the gendered noise it sought to contain and control, hints at the uneasy but important role of women during the 1702 siege.[11] Women and noncombatants made up the vast majority of those trapped inside the Castillo de San Marcos, so it should not be surprising that their cries, complaints, demands, and endurance are recorded in Spanish sources.[12] But it is surprising—in part because common misconceptions about eighteenth-century warfare as an exclusively male venture (which it was not) make women seem out of place in the siege; in part because when women are finally allowed to make an appearance in narratives of war, they tend to be presented as the victims, not the agents of change; and in part because women told other stories that unsettled what colonial officials said about the war, the siege, and themselves.[13]

The attack against the Spanish Castillo is often described as the first battle of Queen Anne's War, the moment when violence raging in Europe crossed the Atlantic and spilled directly onto colonial rivalries. This imperial conflict over the succession to the Spanish throne redrew European alliances and saw the transition of power from Hapsburg to Bourbon dynastic rule. Historians most often frame the war, which lasted a little over a decade and ended with the 1713 Treaty of Utrecht, as part of a larger conflict led by the expansion of France under Louis XIV. English and Dutch rulers, in particular, saw their continental and overseas enterprises jeopardized by Franco-Spanish unity.

In the Americas, Queen Anne's War had many fronts. The conflict touched the New England colonies, Canada's eastern coastline, and Newfoundland. Perhaps the most recognized moment of this long war came in February of 1704, when a joint Indian-French force raided the English town of Deerfield, Massachusetts. The attack resulted in the death of over fifty English colonists and the capture of over one hundred men, women, and children. But Queen Anne's War did not start or end with Deerfield.[14]

There were also fronts in the Caribbean, including confrontations in St. Kitts, Guadeloupe, Nassau, and Nevis. México experienced violence along its coastline, including assaults on Tancochapa, Lerma (near Campeche), and the Chiltepec Bar. There were key naval skirmishes off the coast of Panamá and Cartagena. In South America, forces from Buenos Aires launched an invasion of Colonial do Sacramento (present-day Uruguay).[15] Queen Anne's War was truly a global conflict. It was also part of a cycle of violence that seemed to shuffle and then repeat itself throughout the long eighteenth century—preceded by King William's War (1689–1697) and followed by other, equally long, multi-imperial conflicts, such as the Guerra del Asiento (1739–1748) and the French and Indian War (1754–1763).

In 1702, however, as a large Native-English force stood at the gates of San Agustín, no one knew what was to come or that the conflict would soon spread beyond the walls of the Castillo. The following years saw bloody battles in Apalachee, Timucua, San Luis, Pensacola, and Mobile.[16] These violent conflicts reshaped the geopolitical landscape of the Southeast, and while they were certainly part of this imperial, global conflict, they also unfolded in deeply local and colonial ways. After all, those invading San Agustín in 1702 were not there simply because Queen Anne told them to be. The war had brought additional supplies, men, and political incentive to long-established animosities.

In the 1670s and 1680s, Carolina officials and slave traders sponsored raids into Guale (present-day Georgia). These attacks both devastated the populations living in the region and encouraged the powerful Yamasee Indians to move away from Spanish lands and form a closer partnership with the English. In 1686, Spanish forces retaliated for these earlier attacks and destroyed

Port Royal, a Scottish colony south of Charles Town. In October 1702, one month before the San Agustín siege, over eight hundred Apalachee, Timucua, and Chacato Indians, supported by fewer than thirty Spanish infantrymen, marched against four hundred English-armed Apalachicola Indians. The massive confrontation near the Flint River proved a decisive victory for the English-allied Indians and led to the capture and enslavement of over half the Spanish-supported army.[17] By the time row upon row of soldiers disembarked near San Agustín in late 1702, open, violent, and large confrontations between English and Spanish forces were nothing new in the region.

James Moore, governor of Carolina, had confidently stated that the San Agustín fort would fall easily and that the loot would be bountiful. In particular, Moore stressed to his Native allies the great number of slaves, both Native and African, that could be apprehended during the attack. For English settlers, San Agustín was more than the symbolic seat of Spanish power in the region; it was a roadblock to their expansion. English trade and slaving networks had grown exponentially in the last decades of the seventeenth century, destroying Spanish missions in Guale and Timucua, as well as Apalachee and Chacato towns. Queen Anne's War did much to sanction this ongoing violence.[18]

Residents of San Agustín watched in horror as a force of over one thousand men reached their town. The Spanish decision to protect San Agustín, much like the English decision to attack it, deeply intertwined imperial and local pressures. Since the 1670 founding of Charles Town, the uncertain boundaries and acrimonious interactions between Florida and Carolina had made for tense geopolitics. The majority of the people who lived in the Spanish city had been born there.[19] Florida was their home. Their familial ties, economic connections, and material/property wealth rested in and with the colony. They defended the Castillo for Spain as well as for themselves.

The people of San Agustín had just begun preparing for an invasion, gathering their belongings and boarding up their homes, when English and Native forces descended on Guale. The attack had come much sooner than anticipated, and these Guale towns, the last Spanish holdings before San Agustín, had fallen far more

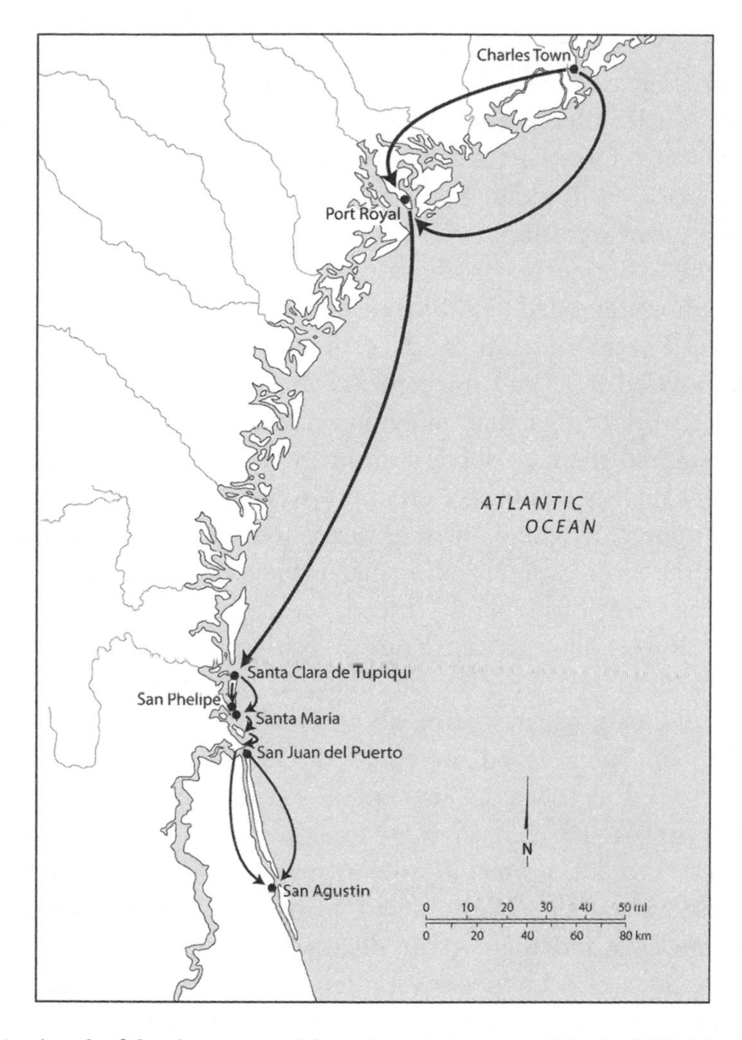

6. *Attack of Guale towns and San Agustín in 1702 (Map by Bill Nelson)*

quickly than predicted.[20] Neither Spanish soldiers nor missions had offered much protection, and the vast devastation caused by the attack became evident in the region's new soundscape. The first and perhaps most disturbing sound was of silence. As the enemy burned and attacked towns, Spanish officials waited for Guale women and children to come pouring into San Agustín seeking safety and protection—but they never came.[21]

Spanish expectations turned first to disappointment and then to fear, as the news of a coming English attack seemed only amplified by Guale absence and silence. On November 4, 1702, Governor Moore's forces attacked the three remaining Guale towns: Santa Clara de Tupiqui, San Phelipe, and Santa Maria.[22] These mission towns were about one hundred miles north of San Agustín, along the Atlantic coast.[23] Those Guale who were not immediately captured or killed fled. Some went south, toward the village of San Juan del Puerto and into areas claimed by the Spaniards. Many more traveled west and north, following established kinship and trade networks rather than obeying Spanish instructions that basically required them to serve as human shields for San Agustín.[24] The first reports from the front lines were vague mentions of the enemy approaching and "having heard some gunfire." Indians appear in the most generalized terms: as nameless, Christian victims fleeing a ferocious enemy intent on capturing and enslaving them.[25] But as soon as the English-Native forces made landfall, Captain Francisco Fuentes de Galarza, the Spanish officer in charge of Guale, began writing about Guale women.

Captain Fuentes had served in the Guale province for many years. Since the 1680s, he had made repeated calls to fortify the mission towns and increase their defenses, a demand he had long tied to the need to protect Native women. Without a fort or Spanish military support, Fuentes had feared that the Guales would leave the area and that "great disgraces would happen to some women," by which he meant rape, enslavement, and a return to a pre-missionized state.[26] Fuentes deployed a common wartime rhetorical strategy of citing violence against women to demonize the enemy. His concerns about safety were more about showcasing the brutality of English violence than about properly representing Guale women. The captain wanted to emphasize Guale women's vulnerability as well as the need for the Spanish to defend them. But in the process, he exposed something far bigger and more fundamental: without women, Guale would be no more.[27]

Spanish reports had previously noted how the specifically gendered violence of Indian slavery was affecting the region. During the 1702 attack, however, a connection emerged between the shrinking numbers of Native women and the loss of Spanish control. At a quick glance, the mentions of Native women are easy to miss. "Las mujeres" appear in lists, next to "church ornaments, altars, women, and children . . . destroyed by the enemy."[28] But Guale women made their presence felt and heard. With English-Native forces advancing, they took action. They rushed Fuentes and began yelling. The captain narrated this incident with disdain, complaining how, in the midst of a disorienting attack, he found himself accompanied "by no Spaniards or Indians" but surrounded by "los clamores de las mujeres" (the clamors of the women).[29] In English, *clamor* refers to a loud, confused sound; in Spanish, the word can also mean supplicant pleas. Were these women shouting at the captain or requesting his help? For Fuentes, the semantics mattered little. In his report, he sought to communicate both his calm leadership and the irrationality and helplessness of women in war. In their cries, the women sought something altogether different. They wanted to communicate both their responsibilities in wartime and the inadequacy and failings of the current Spanish military response. These Native women rooted their demands to be heard within a longer Indigenous tradition.

In the Southeast, Native women had a role in warfare. They counseled for or against battle, decided how captives would be treated, and called for protection. In 1708, Thomas Nairne, an English trader, described a martial performance by Chickasaw women: "The Chickasaws usually carry ten or Twelve Young women with them to the Wars, whose business is to sing a fine Tune, during any action. If their own men succeed, they praise them highly and degrade the Enemy, but if they give Back, the singers alter their praises into reproaches."[30] The Guale women were not just clamoring in fear; they were likely admonishing Captain Fuentes and demanding action. The literal and loud voices of these women speak of their agency—audible not only at the time but still echoing in the archive now. The voices of Guale women were neither silent nor silenced. They made clear that their fate and that of Guale were one and the same. Their clamores spoke of an imminent war, one that Native women had been fighting for decades and that the Spaniards could no longer tune out.[31]

Governor Zúñiga y Cerda wanted to stop the invading army before it crossed the Salamototo (now the St. Johns) River. He ordered Captain Joseph de Horruytiner to reinforce Captain Fuentes, hoping that a show of Spanish force, though likely not enough to defeat Moore's army, could slow the march toward San Agustín or, at the very least, convince their Native allies that going after the Spanish presidio would prove more effort than it was worth. Captain Horruytiner marched north with a small contingent while Captain Fuentes fled south with some refugees, his family, and a couple of Franciscans. But the two men never met. The details of Fuentes's actual deeds are hazy, but Captain Horruytiner heard secondhand reports of Fuentes's bravery: he had risked his life to protect women and children, he had defended the Franciscans, and he had managed to save many ornaments from the churches. In the end, it mattered little, because English forces apprehended Captain Fuentes and those under his care, taking them all to Charles Town.[32]

Fuentes's wife was also captured during the attack. Though Spanish and English documents refer to her only as "Captain Fuentes's wife," María Francisca Guerrero, born and raised in San Agustín, can be identified from her marriage record.[33] She had lived in Guale a long time and watched in disbelief as entire communities she had known for years fled their homelands taking only what they could carry. María Francisca, like most of the women who experienced this attack, is described only in the broadest strokes as frightened and defenseless. Her association with a high-ranking military officer, however, offers a rudimentary outline of her life. She was not young; she had been married since 1686 and had several children, including an older daughter who, according to local gossip, was having an affair with the governor of San Agustín. She must have become a mother at a very young age, because she was visibly pregnant at the time of the attack.[34]

The captivity and eventual childbirth of Captain Fuentes's wife in Charles Town reveal a different process of warfare. Hers is not a linear military narrative: attack, fight, and victory or loss. María Francisca's wartime story is one of silences and uncertainties, punctuated by small moments of profound noise. Before the English took her prisoner, her life in Guale had outlined the expanse and possibilities for Spaniards in La Florida. As Susanah Shaw Romney has shown for the Dutch colonies in New Netherlands, "creating households along contested frontiers" was essential to establishing European control. This was also true in colonial Florida, where Spanish rule "demanded the presence of women and families."[35] María Francisca, with her body, children, and household, had validated and strengthened the Spanish and Catholic enterprises in Guale. Her capture exposed the weakness of both.

María Francisca's pregnant body immediately set her apart from the other Spanish prisoners, a difference noted and rearticulated by English reports.[36] Though Carolina's officials made little reference to the Native captives taken to Charles Town, they specifically detailed "a Spanish woman, the wife of Capt. Fuentes, being bigg with Child, is in Great Want of necessary relief." The English vowed to "provide such things for the immediate relief of the said woman as are necessary."[37] María Francisca would be taken care of because she was "bigg with child" and "in great need" but also because she was a Spanish Criolla, and one married to a prominent man at that. Her gender was not an isolatable or merely additive category; it manifested itself in conjunction with her other socially legible identities: class, race, and religion.[38]

Missing, once again, were the Guale women. They had been there, next to María Francisca; they had urged her husband, Captain Fuentes, to take charge; they had undergone the same reluctant march to Charles Town; and they had endured physical and sexual violence. But their English and Native captors never contemplated, not even for a moment, selling María Francisca into slavery. Unlike the Native women, the Criolla was a prisoner, not a slave. Moreover, María Francisca's pregnancy was not seen as a potential source of revenue for her captors. On the contrary, it had spurred the English government to spend money and pass an order providing care "for all the Spanish prisoners now in this province."[39] No such accommodations were made for the captured Native women. Their bodies were not just caught up in the fighting; they were their own battleground.

Guale women's wartime travails differed from those of María Francisca. This difference, perhaps unsurprising, nonetheless matters greatly. It reveals, first and foremost, that "there was no unitary or univocal position of women in relation to war."[40] María Francisca and the Guale women might have stood together, but not on equal footing. Their asymmetrical relationships to both power and subjugation showed gender as a process that, on the ground, had tangible and radically unequal manifestations. For the captured Native women, as for María Francisca, gender proved a compound experience, one that was mediated and transformed by other social categories and understandings.[41] Hence, María Francisca appears in the archive, while the Guale women do not.

On November 6, less than one day after the attack on Guale, Governor Zúñiga y Cerda issued a proclamation ordering everyone inside the fort. Spanish officials and couriers read the order all over town. For most Spanish and Criolla women in San Agustín, the governor's words were the first sounds of war they heard. They were a stern warning as well as instructions, telling everyone to gather all the necessary provisions, supplies, and animals under their care. Women had been on Governor Zúñiga y Cerda's mind as he issued this order. He argued that, although they would not help with the fort's defenses, women needed to relocate inside the Castillo immediately.[42] They could not be left alone in the town as the men prepared for war.

The governor feared that if only the men went into the fort, they would be distracted and worried, more concerned about protecting their families than defending the presidio. "For the preservation of the families, they [women and children] have left their homes for now" and have come into the fort, where soldiers "would think their own families safe."[43] Eilish Rooney, who has explored the use of gendered rhetoric in contemporary warfare, argues that women often enter "war discourse as an exploitable rhetoric of vulnerability that required masculine protection."[44] Zúñiga y Cerda thought of women in a way Rooney would readily recognize. He viewed them as defenseless and in need of "masculine protection" and then used both that vulnerability and need to legitimate his military decisions.[45]

The governor then commanded that anyone who resided beyond the city limits had to move into town. Every man fourteen years of age or older who did not already have a military appointment had to report for service.[46] The governor also vowed he would fine those who did not carry provisions into the presidio as well as those who brought too many unnecessary items. His order teetered between plea and punishment, hinting at the complications of getting a noncombatant population ready for battle. Zúñiga y Cerda made it clear that anyone who wandered beyond the town limits and fell captive to enemy forces would receive no reprieve. He would not risk his soldiers to rescue anyone who had defied his instructions.[47] "For the maintenance of your families," Zúñiga y Cerda's evacuation order explained, "you must leave, for now, your houses."[48] Prioritizing Spanish families over Spanish properties, the governor revealed not only a core tenet of his wartime strategy but also the prominent roles families played in the maintenance of colonial rule.[49]

The evacuation into the fort proceeded with haste, and within a couple of days 1,500 people who had long lived in close proximity to one another—San Agustín was only several square miles—now began to share an even more intimate and public living space inside the Castillo de San Marcos. The fort was soon overcrowded. Only a select few—the governor, the treasurer, and a handful of other officers—enjoyed the comfort of a private chamber. Most of the soldiers were forced to share one large room. Everyone else crowded into the fort's open plaza. The shared space quickly became dirty, malodorous, and noisy. That many people, dwelling together, in a small, open-air space, occupied also by some of their animals, made for unpleasant living conditions. The limited access to water also meant that the washing of clothes, linens, and bodies, already a limited activity in wintertime, became almost nonexistent.[50] In San Agustín, women were the ones responsible for cleaning clothes, a particularly onerous chore that required hauling heavy loads and buckets of water and spending hours hunched over scrubbing. Elite Spanish women often employed Native and Black women to do the laundry for their households.[51] But during the siege of 1702, few women (if any) brought their washboards into the Castillo.

The governor wrote sparingly about these mundane topics. Although his daily reports, council meetings, and seemingly endless letters requesting reinforcements focused primarily on the fighting, provisions and food supplies also proved a recurrent topic. Zúñiga y Cerda had at first complimented the people of San

Agustín for heeding his orders and bringing sufficient food into the fort, but he quickly realized that his initial praise had been premature. The governor found some relief from the Castillo's resources and the fact that five of its twenty rooms were already devoted to food storage.[52] The water supplies also seemed stable; there were no recorded complaints of water shortage during the siege, a fact that suggests the three functioning wells provided enough water for those within the Castillo walls. Moreover, right as English forces surrounded San Agustín, the Spanish had managed to drive over 150 head of cattle into the moat without losing any of the herd to enemy forces or fire. This quick maneuver ensured a steady access to meat for those within the presidio.[53]

There is no description of what people ate during the siege. Colonists throughout Spanish America preferred to keep an Iberian diet whenever possible; in Florida, the unreliability of the *situado* (subsidy from the Spanish Crown) that brought the necessary food staples, such as flour and wine, forced colonists to consume more local resources, including the "indigenous trinity: maize, squash, and beans."[54] But Spanish colonists in San Agustín did not fully or willingly adopt Native culinary practices. Fish bones speak to that difference. Though both Native and Spanish households show evidence of fish consumption, Native homes from the pre-Hispanic period contain the bones of smaller fish such as silver perch, which could be caught with baskets or nets in shallower water, like estuaries. Spanish homes had evidence of much bigger fish, like red or black drum caught in deeper waters. In other words, everyone in Florida ate fish but not the same type or in the same ways.[55]

Concerns about foodways in Spanish Florida usually revolved around issues of sufficiency, however, rather than type or variety, and the siege did much to compound the existing problem of food scarcity.[56] During the siege, Spanish officers and soldiers received their rations from the fort, but noncombatants had to make do with what they had brought into the Castillo. María and Gertrudis Diaz Mejía recalled how women and children, especially those without active-duty male relatives, were left to scavenge for the remains.[57] While Spanish, Criolla, and Black women were not allowed to leave the presidio, Native women and men left the safety of the Castillo to fish and gather additional resources to supplement their caloric intake. It is not clear whether these individuals left of their own volition or were instructed to go out and find additional food for their mistresses and masters also inside the fort. Any movement in and out of the Castillo was a dangerous enterprise, one that became increasingly so as the English forces moved closer and food supplies dwindled.

By mid-December the invading army "had carried a trench to within a pistol shot of the moat, which was the last they threw up to the north, to prevent the Spanish Indians from securing the sea food which was *their* sustenance."[58] The mention of "*their* sustenance" suggests that Native people had to provide their own meals and would not always receive rations from the storage house. Food became an increasingly contentious issue as the siege stretched on for days and then weeks; food, though a shared need, was clearly not distributed in equitable ways. The siege reinforced, rather than redressed, existing inequalities within San Agustín.[59]

Unsurprisingly, then, Spanish officials took aim at the Black community within the fort. Enrique Primo de Rivera, one of the governor's trusted commanders, explained that while he understood the need for every able-bodied man to carry a gun and serve in the defense of the fort, he thought that "neither Indians, blacks, nor mulattos were to be trusted."[60] This position, which Primo de Rivera had developed during the siege, was out of step with the entrenched Spanish practices and policies in Florida. San Agustín had a long-standing Black regiment and routinely employed Black men in the militia. Moreover, Spanish officials had sponsored, encouraged, and even armed Indian-led attacks, including some in which Primo de Rivera had participated.[61] Despite these experiences—or maybe because of them—he feared the loss of control that could come from arming all the different men living within the Castillo's shared, small, and enclosed space. European and Criollo soldiers were in the minority, and their small numbers would have been acutely pronounced during the siege. These tensions surrounding food and safety show that as much as the siege was a conflict between those inside and those outside the Castillo, this violence did not create unity among the different people seeking refuge in San Agustín.

The dark complicated matters further. The fort's commanders, despite having received several orders to improve conditions, had never adequately lit the Castillo. There were numerous complaints that it was too hard to see within the presidio; one observer noted, "the main guard of that plaza in the Castillo lacks light. This is a great inconvenience for all those who keep watch and carry weapons at night."[62] Spanish officers like Primo de Rivera worried about being able to distinguish *who* was carrying a gun at night. The darkness also forced people even closer to one another since there were few fires that lit the Castillo at night. The fort's highly flammable materials meant that fires had to be closely monitored and kept small.[63] Moreover, the siege took place during the months of November and December, when it became dark in the early evening and remained so until past six in the morning, meaning that for most people, darkness and limited field of vision were not just problematic obstacles: they marked the rhythms of life during the siege.

Shelter also proved challenging. Though Florida is generally hot and humid, during the winter months, temperatures could drop to the forties and the periodic precipitation made the outdoor conditions miserable. Governor Zúñiga y Cerda had tried to create temporary shelter. He ordered all the shingles "that were brought to make the roof of the church" stripped and delivered to the Castillo. He explained that the church's "planking [*tablazón*] will help make lodging and housing in which women and children could find refuge and comfort since it is not possible that they fit in the existing quarters." Zúñiga y Cerda insisted that these provisional rustic housing structures "would keep them from the cold and rain . . . which are particularly rigorous in these parts during these months."[64] Capitan Don Juan Saturnino de Abaurrea, a soldier who had served for many years in Guale, complained that the governor's efforts were insufficient. In addition to sharing a room "with eighteen other musketeers," he had suffered from exposure since he "was unable to find anything with which to erect any kind of shelter."[65] The captain's complaint fell on deaf ears. This was war; he was supposed to tolerate certain hardships.

So were the women. At least two babies were born in the Castillo in early November: "Francisco, son of Marta María, a Guale wage worker (*naboría*) married to a slave, and María, daughter of a soldier from Spain and his San Agustín wife." Another baby was baptized "in necessity," a phrase that hints at her impending death and, perhaps, at the inadequate shelter and food available in the Castillo. Susan Richbourg Parker, examining extant baptismal and marriage record from San Agustín, argues that the siege had long-term effects on daily life. "The impact of inadequate shelter and food showed itself in the drastically lower birth rate for 1703. That year infant baptisms fell to one-third of the number of pre-siege christenings."[66] Wartime had lasting and visible effects on San Agustín's female population, so much so that in the aftermath of the siege, Spanish officials even reissued a sixteenth-century decree encouraging Spanish women to immigrate to Florida.[67]

Before the siege, women had little reason to venture into the fort.[68] Their lives were centered on their familial duties, though it is abundantly clear that women's spatial movements in San Agustín extended far beyond the home.[69] Spanish women went to mass and confession; they walked around the city visiting shops, chatting with their neighbors, and attending fiestas. Other women, especially lower-class and non-Spanish women, had even greater mobility. They ran shops, tended fields, and even traveled between towns. They knew how to negotiate spaces defined by male power and privilege. Still, the Castillo de San Marcos had remained mostly off limits.

In 1702, everything changed. The once almost exclusively masculine space of the fort now included women. And rather than a contradiction, women's presence became a sort of rallying cry. In his correspondence, Zúñiga y Cerda depicted the fort as the last beacon of Spanish family life in the region. It was as if the English invasion had radically transformed the purpose of the Castillo de San Marcos. The once critical military outpost designed to protect Spanish imperial interests in the region suddenly became a place that kept women safe. This transformation rested on clearly patriarchal ideas that diminished and infantilized women's war experience.[70] Even so, Zúñiga y Cerda's inclusion of women in his military calculus evinced that, while he considered men the central actors in this conflict, he knew men did not make military decisions, prepare for battle, or wage war in a vacuum: women, children, and other civilians were always present. As much as Zúñiga y Cerda hoped otherwise, women were more than rhetorical devices—they were real—and their needs, demands, and voices often disrupted the governor's plans.[71]

Zúñiga y Cerda surveyed the fort's soldiers, ammunition, and supplies, and what he found only deepened his sense of dread.[72] There were only 323 men on his rosters: 137 infantry soldiers; two Indian translators; sentinels and infantry units scattered in Guale (which had just fallen), Timucua, and Apalachee; and twenty-three soldiers injured or incapacitated. In all, a mere 250 professional soldiers protected San Agustín at the time of the invasion. The governor tried to increase his odds by arming every able-bodied man, releasing prisoners from jail in exchange for military service, and ordering the commanding lieutenants of Timucua and Apalachee to return to San Agustín with as many troops as they could rally. But he knew those reinforcements would not suffice. "This number [of soldiers] is not enough to try to go after . . . the enemy," he said.[73] The governor came to realize that the vast number of people who now resided in the Castillo were not—and would never become—combatants.

The governor knew, as did most Spanish officials, that if the invading forces penetrated the fort's defenses, San Agustín would fall immediately. Unbeknownst to the Spaniards, however, Moore's large army lacked weaponry strong enough to breach the Castillo's coquina walls. Rather than heavy, low-trajectory cannons with solid shots that could pierce the fort's walls, the English had high-trajectory cannons that could project shells inside the fort, but these shots, no heavier than twelve pounds, did little damage to the San Agustín presidio.

Almost as soon as English forces reached the Spanish Castillo, Moore sent Colonel Daniel to Jamaica to secure heavier cannons and exploding bombs.[74] Meanwhile, Zúñiga y Cerda wrote frantic letters asking for additional men, ammunition, supplies, and basically anything anyone was willing to send. Both governors connected their fates to that of their empires. Moore sent requests back to Charles Town and Jamaica, showing how the attack on Florida was bound to the larger English Caribbean. The Spanish governor sent word to Havana, but the majority of his messages traveled within mainland Florida to Timucua, Apalachee, Pensacola, and Mobile. Moore and Zúñiga y Cerda understood that whoever received reinforcements first would be victorious.[75]

The siege began November 10. English forces launched their attack by land, since the bar had proven too narrow and shallow to invade by sea. Moore and his men moved through the abandoned town, looting and setting fire to Spanish houses. They even plundered Nombre de Dios, the only urban mission in the colony. "At this time the enemy arranged to raise the siege by setting fire to the city," the Florida governor lamented, and "in a short while some [houses] were burned and the fire spread to others."[76] The Carolina governor seemed pleased by the havoc he had wreaked, and the noisy rampage of his men taking and burning the town seemed to communicate clearly (and loudly) his intention to destroy San Agustín. Moore set up camp in the Franciscan monastery, one of the largest structures in town, and then ordered his officers to take over the handful of two-story buildings that remained. These tall structures proved strategic strongholds that allowed English soldiers an unobstructed shot of the fort.[77] Spanish homes had become dangerous liabilities in enemy hands.

From the Castillo, it seemed as if endless waves of English and Native enemies poured into town. By midday, the shock of the invasion had turned to anger, and Spanish forces began firing at will at their enemy. As Moore's men returned fire, the sound of bullets announced that San Agustín was at war. Most people within the fort did not have the enemy within their line of sight, but they could hear the bullets, cannon shots, and yelling. In other words, for the women inside the Castillo, the war began as an auditory experience. The aural quality of war was not one of constant shelling, at least not yet. After an intense offensive maneuver, "the enemy ceased cannonading," the Florida governor recalled, "and I as well did not continue with the previous frequency; since the gun-carriages were already weakening and some of our cannon fell . . . I continued firing infrequently since I could not know how long the siege might last or if the enemy might receive reinforcements."[78] The first day of the siege was punctuated by moments of loud intensity followed by silences that were neither calming nor ever particularly long.

7. *Jaune Quick-to-See Smith,* Shock and Awe *(2011). Smith's layered work, rooted in Native myths and stories, depicts a violent and (almost) loud landscape that centers the suffering of a woman and her child. (Courtesy of the artist and Garth Greenan Gallery, New York)*

The irregular but intense cannon fire had changed the soundscape of San Agustín. And while war has a tendency to do just that, the sonic violence of the 1702 siege was, both in its impact and effects, particularly gendered.[79] The tactile nature of sound meant that those inside the presidio could hear and feel the enemy they could not see. Women felt the reverberations of the English cannon shots; they bore witness to the loading of Spanish cannons, smelled the exploded powder, and saw the bursts of light as the shots fired. Women were also allowed to respond to this belliphonic onslaught with their own sounds: they could scream, cry, and pray for relief. The women's distress reflected an affective landscaping of sound that resounded literally and figuratively throughout the presidio.[80]

Then came the boom. A loud explosion suddenly overpowered the uneven pattern of gunfire that had reverberated throughout the first day of the siege. The deafening sound came from within the Castillo: the largest cannon, improperly loaded, had exploded and killed three people, including Juan de Galdona, one of the most knowledgeable gunners within the fort. Zúñiga y Cerda's description of this incident evinces the profound sensorial disruption of the explosion. He began his daily report by detailing English troop movements, but after eight lengthy sentences about forces landing and unloading supplies, he brusquely, without any transition or warning, wrote: "Reventó un cañón" (a cannon exploded).[81] Even though he was writing hours after the events had transpired, he made no effort to contextualize the disorienting and loud explosion. It was as if his ears were still ringing.

The sound unsettled a fort already tense from the day's long bombardment. Panicked and confused shouting soon followed. Everyone within the Castillo started looking and pointing at the blast zone. The governor reached the wrecked cannon in time to watch one of the soldiers succumb to his injuries. This quick response reveals the governor's close attention to the noises within the presidio but also shows how truly small this structure was. As he assessed the situation, Zúñiga y Cerda became aware that he had an audience. It was not just the soldiers watching the tragic scene. Women and children might not have had a direct view of the enemy, but they could see the Spanish soldiers struggling in a very public and loud way.[82]

The lines between public and private became blurred in the uncomfortable intimacy of 1,500 people sharing a common, albeit open-air, space.[83] Within the confines of the besieged Castillo, women were far more visible to Spanish military and political decision makers than in their daily, prewar lives. As a category in wartime, "women and children" are usually understood as victims, sufferers, and seekers of masculine protection, not as actors in their own right. But during the siege, women were agents that could and did affect military policy. Maybe all they could do was listen—but even the seemingly passive act of listening required them to process and evaluate information that they would never have had access to in peacetime.[84]

Zúñiga y Cerda and his officers did not particularly enjoy having their military acumen, so closely tied to their manhood, out on display. They complained constantly about the "muchedumbre de las mujeres" (throngs of women) that impeded their work. When a *junta de guerra* (war council) decided that a Spanish vessel should try to break the English blockade and send word to Cuba, the Florida officers made painstaking efforts to hide both the meeting and its plans.[85] As the junta attempted to implement a military initiative taking into account, even fearing, women's aural registers of war, the women's cries open different ways to understand how war was experienced, embodied, and lived. Women's sounds, particularly their lamentations, unnerved an already turbulent soundscape.

Within a week, the siege had become deadlocked. English and Native troops could not breach the Castillo's defenses and Spanish forces could not drive the invading armies back. Every attack was foiled, every counterattack deflected. Moore soon decided to change his strategy. In addition to bombarding the fort, he would surround it, prevent anyone from entering or leaving, and starve out those who remained inside. It was a good plan; however, the perimeter he established was not. Time and time again Spanish officials managed to send messengers, spies, and scouts past enemy lines.[86]

On November 10, Zúñiga y Cerda sent letters to Lieutenant Governor Solana of Apalachee and Lieutenant Governor Diego de Jaén of Timucua. He also corresponded with the governors of Pensacola and Cuba. On November 16, Francisco Romo de Urisa, an infantryman traveling from Apalachee to San Agustín, captured a spy: Jalaph Baltasar, a Native man from Apalachee working for the English.[87] This level of mobility shows how porous the English perimeter was and how those inside San Agustín remained connected to the outside world during the siege, but it also offers a glimpse of an Indigenous world that continued to operate even as war raged on.[88]

On December 14, that very world would force the presidio's doors open. A month into the standstill, a man approached the entrance of the fort, claiming he was a Yamasee who had escaped the English and now wanted to return to Spanish care. Everything about Juan Lorenzo, from his English gun to his Spanish baptismal name, aroused suspicion. He would probably have been denied entrance into the Castillo had it not been for his travel companions: a woman he identified as his wife, who was nursing a baby, and another young girl. Juan Lorenzo offered no additional explanations for these Native women by his side, but they seemed to be there to communicate his peaceful overtures. Their presence mattered enough for Spanish officials to make note of it but not enough to rouse suspicion or prompt more questions.

The nameless woman referred to only as Juan Lorenzo's wife is as easy to miss as she is to dismiss. She appears only in a passing mention, and the rest of the account turns to Juan Lorenzo and his surreptitious activities during the siege. But her presence forced open the much larger context in which the siege was unfolding. She was a reminder that this siege was as much a Native conflict as a European one. Of the thousands of men attacking the Castillo, far more of them cared about women like this one than the one who sat on the English throne. Colonel James Moore had promised his Indian allies that there would be many Indian captives ready for the taking once they breached the Castillo's walls.[89]

Slavers were after women just like Juan Lorenzo's wife, which was exactly why Juan Lorenzo had brought her "with an infant at her breast" to San Agustín. Without uttering even a single word, she conveyed both the precarity of life under constant English slaving raids and her desperate need for protection.[90] Performing a vulnerability and victimhood that the Spanish had come to expect from Native women, Juan Lorenzo's wife transformed Juan Lorenzo into someone Spanish officials needed to care for, even pity. Juan Lorenzo posed no threat; he was just a man trying to protect his wife and child from the English, a responsibility those inside the Castillo understood well.

Juan Lorenzo explained that he came bearing good news. He had spotted Apalachee reinforcements on their way to help those confined inside San Agustín, and had overheard English troops debating when and how to retreat.[91] There are no specific details on what Lorenzo said or did, but it is clear that Spanish officials were intrigued enough to let him enter the fort while they discussed this latest and surprising bit of intelligence. Juan Lorenzo's news about aid from Apalachee was nothing more than a ruse, however, intended to distract Spanish officials. As the officers debated, Juan Lorenzo rallied the Indians within the fort and tried to convince them to blow up the powder room. The Yamasee man was a double agent who aimed to destroy the Castillo from the inside.

Juan Lorenzo's plot faced immediate opposition. The Indians he thought would be friendly and eager to join his cause had little interest in exploding their last line of defense. They alerted the governor straightaway, and Juan Lorenzo was promptly apprehended, thrown in jail, interrogated, and likely tortured.[92]

Juan Lorenzo had lived and worked near San Agustín for a long time. Like many Yamasees, he had decided to leave Florida in the 1690s, fed up with Spanish policies that not only failed to protect him or his family from encroaching Indian slaving raids but also seemed needlessly punitive. But unlike most Yamasees, Juan Lorenzo left archival evidence of the moment he made his decision to leave.[93] It happened in early 1695, when Pedro de la Lastra, *doctrinero* (parish priest) of Santa Clara de Tupiqui and San Felipe, ordered Juan Lorenzo to travel to San Agustín and collect some items that had arrived with the situado. Juan Lorenzo was not too keen on leaving his family and argued that married men should not, or perhaps could not, travel without their wives' permission.[94] The friar insisted, and, feeling pressured, the young Yamasee agreed to comply with the Franciscan's request and left his family for what he assumed would be an easy errand.

When he reached San Agustín, however, the items the friar had demanded were not yet available. Juan Lorenzo waited for several days but then grew weary and returned home. Friar Lastra and Captain Diego de Jaén, lieutenant governor of Guale, were furious with the empty-handed Juan Lorenzo and threatened to "punish him in the morning and . . . make him go to San Agustín at his own expense to seek the said" goods.[95] Juan Lorenzo thought this threat excessive, as he had done all that the Spanish officials had asked and his failure to retrieve the goods was not due to any fault of his own. Already tired of Spanish abuses, he made the decision to leave that night. By the following day, before any punishment could be carried out, Juan Lorenzo, along with his wife, child, and three others, fled the Guale missions. Following a path taken by many

Yamasees before him, Juan Lorenzo led others away from Spanish towns, relocating closer to English towns and trade.[96]

During the 1702 siege, Juan Lorenzo returned to San Agustín to fight against Spanish officials once again. The almost immediate failure of his plan eclipses the deep historical and personal experiences that informed his strategy. Juan Lorenzo had once guided people away from Spanish towns and thought he could replicate his success, but the Native people within the Castillo had little in common with this Yamasee instigator. They had hungered, cooked, cleaned, soldiered, and lived next to Spanish officials and noncombatants for over forty days (or even more, depending on where they had resided before the siege started), and whether they liked these officers and civilians or not, they had long decided that their best chance of survival came from withstanding the English invasion, not from destroying the presidio.

Taking Juan Lorenzo's actions seriously, then, requires a reexamination of all components of his plan, including the women by his side. The one referred to as his wife might have been the same woman who left Guale with him ten years earlier, but there is no mention of her Spanish name or baptism. It is just as probable that she shared no matrimonial bonds with him and was actually his captive, thrown into this political intrigue against her will.[97] The latter option seems quite plausible because, when given the chance, she spoke readily against Juan Lorenzo. Juan Lorenzo's supposed wife and the young girl, maybe another captive related to her by kin or blood, confirmed that this Yamasee man was working for the English and planned to blow up the Castillo.

These supposedly Yamasee women were never formally interrogated. Their words were paraphrased and summarized, rather than taken down verbatim or under oath. The testimony explains that, after realizing Juan Lorenzo "was a spy and it was further confirmed, and being so the girl verbally declared it so."[98] "La muchacha bocalmente [sic] lo declaró" literally means that the Native girl confirmed, with her voice, the allegations against Juan Lorenzo. Lynn Stephen and Shannon Speed urge us to pay attention to Native women's voices: "Women's resistance to interrelated violences is often expressed in ways that may be outside of how we are accustomed to seeing . . . or conceptualizing resistance. To tell a story, speak up, request asylum, or ask to be heard can be seen as a revolutionary act when women do it in a context where they are supposed to be silent and are punished for asserting their presence and voice."[99] As much as the young girl's words sealed Juan Lorenzo's fate, they also emphasized her place in this story. Spanish officials, as well as Juan Lorenzo, might have treated these Native women as props, intended to support, even serve as physical proof, of men's claims. But these women who had entered the Castillo during the siege were agents in their own right. They had intimate knowledge of Juan Lorenzo's military plans and were instrumental in his apprehension. They were at the front lines of war.

Their invisibility is further reinforced in the documentary record. After their declarations and Juan Lorenzo's imprisonment, these Native women (and baby) disappear from the Spanish archive just as abruptly as they entered it. They were deemed irrelevant to what happened next, and yet they were deeply significant to understanding Juan Lorenzo and the larger violence and pressures of the Indian slave trade. These women were connected to the larger Indigenous world beyond San Agustín, but Spanish sources tell us almost nothing about them. Their quick appearance and equally quick disappearance and their simultaneous irrelevance and deep significance were dual and dichotomous processes that are not unique to these women but are instead recurring tropes in the testimonies of Black and Indigenous women in colonial documents throughout the Americas, particularly in times of war or unrest.[100] But for Juan Lorenzo, these women, as well as the gendered assumptions and expectations that underlaid their presence, had a very real impact. They were the reason for his admittance into the fort and, ultimately, the source of his plan's failure. Their significance thus cannot be solely measured by colonial records and practices intent on silencing them.

The excitement from Juan Lorenzo's failed uprising had barely quieted when Moore's forces launched a new assault. By December 19, the Spanish soldiers discovered that the English had dug three new rows of trenches, limiting access to the grasslands near the fort where the Spanish cattle grazed. Even more terrifying, these trenches had some gabions made of mud and rock that offered protection from artillery fire.[101] The well-orchestrated offensive attack did not have the intended consequences, however. Spanish officers managed to fire at the advancing forces and push them back to their starting position. Moore failed to breach the Castillo, and those inside failed to inflict any significant infrastructural or physical damage on the invading army. The stalemate continued.

As the month of December wore on, both sides became increasingly exhausted. Supplies were running low on the English front; morale was depleted along with food stores within the Spanish Castillo; and, to make matters worse, the end was nowhere in sight. Then on Christmas Eve the balance shifted. Inside San Agustín, arrangements were underway to celebrate one of the holiest nights of the year when two ships peaked over the horizon. Panic erupted. Rumors spread that not only were these enemy vessels but they came armed with the dreaded *bombas de fuego*. Zúñiga y Cerda complained that "certain people" were "spilling their voices" (*demarrar voces)* and proclaiming "that the said brig and sloop had come with the bombs that [the English] went to get from Jamaica." These reports "were so widespread that the bad effects of those voices were already felt[;] in particular they made the women disconsolate."[102]

Unlike standard grenades, which were round shells filled with gunpowder that, depending on the size, could be lit and thrown by hand or propelled by small mortars and howitzers, bombas de fuego were about ten to thirteen inches in diameter, they were fired from a cannon, and they could burn up or explode the intended target. This piercing weapon could accomplish what the English had failed to do thus far: blast a hole in the presidio's defenses and loudly announce the beginning of the end for the besieged Castillo. Then came confirmation. The ships were indeed displaying English colors, and Spanish officials, who had long desired the siege to be over, now feared the worst kind of ending. San Agustín officers and civilians had endured a long siege, a naval blockade, and repeated attacks. They had repelled all assaults on the Castillo, but now, as the new vessels reached land and began unloading goods, their previous efforts seemed in vain.

Narrating loss is never easy, and Governor Zúñiga y Cerda had to do it in real time. As he tried to describe a defeat that seemed all but certain, he turned to the women once again and the burden they had placed on his leadership, on Spanish ability to withstand the siege, and on the presumed Spanish loss. The governor explained how, when the provenance of these two ships "had been uncovered by the Castillo . . . the spirits of the soldiers and the rest of the people, especially the women, [we]re without consolation, having seen the enemy and their [new] food stocks and their reinforcements."[103]

Rather than preparing for an imminent attack or launching a preemptive strike, Zúñiga y Cerda tried to console these women. It was less a choice than a necessity, because before he could make a plan or call a junta de guerra, he needed to deal with the noise and unrest caused by the anxiety-ridden women inside the presidio.[104] Zúñiga y Cerda openly feared that these female cries would make his soldiers "lose their better judgment."[105] The governor insisted that "the trouble that these dismaying voices produced" could not be ignored.[106] He found himself fighting two enemies: the one outside the Castillo's walls, who had just received new supplies and a renewed sense of energy, and the one inside, which was also growing in number and, if unrestrained, would consume the whole presidio.

Sound was gendered. Spanish officials described how the irrational and irritating noise produced by "la muchedumbre de las mujeres," had become increasingly dangerous during the siege. The women's desolate cries affected what men could hear, enact, or attempt. For Zúñiga y Cerda, focusing on the women within the Castillo was not just about shifting attention away from the English reinforcements or downplaying Spanish inability to withstand a new attack—although it certainly did those things. It was also about taking care of the people within the fort, especially the most vulnerable. Even if all that he and his soldiers could manage was consoling the distraught populace, then he could claim a small but significant victory: he had kept 1,500 people ordered and disciplined in the face of unbeatable odds. Zúñiga y Cerda did not personally express fear or anxiety in his writings. He let the women's loud cries do that for him. By communicating *their* worries, the governor could both narrate the desperate state of San Agustín and evoke his control over the situation.

The governor decided to counter the women's uncontrolled noise with his own, officially sanctioned sounds. On the night of Christmas Eve, "to prevent the growth of disconsolation," Zúñiga y Cerda ordered the playing of instruments. He commanded that "like some other nights in this place they play harps and vihuelas with lively tones and [carry out] other diversions and, through those means," the people in the presidio would forget, at least momentarily, the foreboding threat the enemy posed and think more rationally about their options.[107] The "lively tones" were intended to calm the "ramblings of the women" and silence any talk of the bombas de fuego.[108]

The governor had limited success in countering women's wailing with music or authorized sounds because Spanish sentinels spotted two new ships on the horizon. Women within the Castillo, already anxious by the Christmas Eve arrival of English reinforcements, now seemed incapable of calm. It appeared that the ships had come to aid San Agustín, but the women's panicked clamors made communicating with these vessels impossible. Increasingly worried that the fleet was going to sail past San Agustín, the governor issued his order of complete silence. He wanted quiet in order to best determine a course of action; the women insisted on sound. Their lamentations shifted Zúñiga y Cerda's perception of who mattered in war. He not only had to hear the voices of all those involved in the siege, even those who never fired a gun; he also had to listen to them, to appease them. Women's sounds had a power not often acknowledged.

The arrival of General Esteban de Berroa from Havana officially ended the siege. Colonel Moore, who only two days prior thought he had the upper hand, now concluded that he could not overtake the resupplied presidio. The Carolina governor began a hasty evacuation and burned the few structures that were still standing in San Agustín. Even John Ash, a prominent colonial official in Carolina who wrote a scathing critique of Moore and the invasion of Florida, had to acknowledge that the governor "retreate[d] with such caution and dispatch, that he lost not one Man by the enemy."[109] As the English troops managed to depart undisturbed and unharmed, Zúñiga y Cerda's exasperation was unmistakable. Reinforcements had finally arrived and given Spanish forces a notable advantage, but the inability to communicate and coordinate with the Cuban fleet had left the governor stranded in the Castillo as the enemy continued to destroy the town.[110]

With precious time slipping away, Adjutant Sebastián López de Toledo managed to break through the English blockade in a rowboat, carrying orders from Zúñiga y Cerda to General Berroa entreating him to launch an attack.[111] He argued that the San Agustín forces now had a clear advantage. They had men, supplies, and firepower. Moreover, the once formidable enemy was now disillusioned; their numbers and strength had dwindled and they had resorted to destroying their own equipment in order to abandon the region faster.[112] But Berroa had other plans, and the only fighting that ensued was the hostility between the two Spanish commanding officers.

Berroa and Zúñiga y Cerda seemed to have disliked one another immediately. The general complained that his efforts to communicate with San Agustín had been ignored. He had orders to support the Spanish presidio and expel the English forces, but he had no desire to endanger his troops by attacking an army already on the run.[113] Zúñiga y Cerda accused the general of delay and obstinacy. "If General Berroa had done his duty he should have pursued the enemy as I ordered," insisted the governor, especially "since there was no lack of guides, and the bar of San Juan [where the enemy was regrouping] is not more than 12 leagues distant." The governor drew a sharp contrast between the "brave and loyal" men who had kept San Agustín safe and Berroa's troops, who were "boys and . . . so useless that even after many years they would not be of any service."[114]

The ways in which armed conflicts find resolution provide insight into the different experiences of war. For Zúñiga y Cerda, who had prioritized safety over open confrontations throughout the siege, Berroa's arrival presented a vital opportunity to showcase his military prowess. This was no time for caution. Any bravery or manliness he had assigned to staying in place during the siege now evaporated. It was as if the panic and desolate cries of the Castillo's women had become inaudible, overwhelmed by a sudden and louder call to battle.[115] Zúñiga y Cerda argued for a profound change within San Agustín. Even though the fort still offered a safe haven for women and children, the Castillo and the governor had now reclaimed their masculine military purpose. Both were ready to fight.

In a savvy political move, Zúñiga y Cerda sought to shift the blame for any perceived military ineptitude or deficiency onto Berroa. It was Berroa who had thwarted his efforts to engage the English. It was Berroa who "had given the enemy space . . . and they burned more parts of town."[116] It was Berroa who had let the English forces slip away. Zúñiga y Cerda's more aggressive military rhetoric and orders showed a governor already looking ahead and strategizing on how to communicate, contextualize, and justify his actions during the siege before the Spanish Crown. "I do not doubt Sir, that some persons, disaffected and offended by the present hostilities, the damage inflicted by the enemy, with such great destruction and uncertainty, would lodge some charges against me for their losses," explained the governor to the king. But Zúñiga y Cerda hoped to be absolved of any wrongdoing since he had done everything possible to protect San Agustín and remove the enemy.[117]

The Florida governor's final efforts involved calling a junta de guerra. Flustered by Berroa's lack of action, Zúñiga y Cerda made a vocal and lengthy plea for an assault on Moore's retreating forces.[118] But like Berroa, the junta de guerra also resisted the governor's bellicose plans. The officials and soldiers deemed the proposed attack against Moore's army needlessly dangerous and likely to fail. The junta argued that the people within the presidio were weak, exhausted, and in no condition to march against the English. With San Agustín still burning, ash and smoke filled the air as people filtered out of the Castillo. The enemy most of them had heard but never seen was finally gone. Unfortunately, so was their town.[119]

CHAPTER FIVE

Narrating War and Loss

SAN AGUSTÍN WAS IN RUINS. The impressive coquina presidio had weathered the siege, but the surrounding town was ravaged. Two sisters, Doña Francisca and Doña Juana Ponce de León, recalled their desolation "after the siege of the enemy, in which the great fire devoured the house where we dwelled with all our goods [and] furniture." Their loss ultimately proved material as well as personal: their father and sole provider, Nicolás Ponce de León, died in the chaotic years immediately following the English attack. The sisters remembered how the enemy had uprooted the entire city, "destruyendola de raizes," and engineered long-term damage by targeting "a hacienda of livestock, which had helped us maintain the city."[1] The San Agustín fort had managed to repel the invading English army, but now the city was in a precarious state. As the Ponce de León sisters recalled, people in San Agustín were starving, disease-ridden, and, to make matters worse, still required to fight powerful Native and English forces, who had suffered a setback but whose resolve to destroy Spanish holdings in Florida had only grown.[2]

In January 1703, English and Native forces had hastily retreated from San Agustín after the arrival of Spanish reinforcements from Cuba, but most of the people huddled in the Castillo de San Marcos feared they would soon return. Though the English siege had failed, the region felt more violent and unsafe for the Spanish colonists. Doña Francisca and Doña Juana Ponce de León explained how "the heathen Indians aided by the English population of San Jorge have done and continue to cause much death and atrocities in the ports and surround this city with extreme inhumanity and in a manner that deprives us completely of the support of our food supplies." The Ponce de León sisters recounted how the English siege of 1702 deeply affected their daily lives, limiting access to even the "most basic provisions."[3] The woefully understaffed and undersupplied San Agustín seemed no match for a determined and relentless English enemy. The concerns raised by Doña Francisca and Doña Juana echoed the larger community's distress about the state of the Spanish enterprise in Florida.

Doña Francisca and Doña Juana Ponce de León, like so many women in San Agustín, were left destitute by the 1702 siege and the subsequent waves of attacks. Committed to recovering from their financial and property loss, they petitioned the Florida governor for monetary support. Their appeal was an intimate and immediate request for aid. It was also part of a long-established and widely practiced tradition of petitioning performed by women throughout the Spanish empire. Oscillating between first- and third-person narration—exclaiming "please help *us*" but referring to their destroyed property as "the furniture that accommodated *them*"—the Ponce de León sisters balanced the specifics that afflicted them with the larger context of war.[4]

Their petition was one of many. There were more than fifty other individual and group petitions (and probably many more) issued in San Agustín from 1701 to 1713, with certain individuals filing multiple claims to explain a change to their original filing, expedite their case, or merely express frustration about the long delays. These petitions for aid came overwhelmingly from Criolla women, or women of Spanish descent born and raised in Florida. There are so many petitions that the stories and voices of these women prove easy to find—it was as if women in La Florida went from being implicitly everywhere to explicitly somewhere. The sudden ease with which they take over the Spanish archive after the siege of 1702 is worth exploring and points to women's important roles in defining and narrating war.

The presence of these women, while refreshing, was also poignantly unequal. Only certain women were allowed to request support. Only certain women were allowed to record their experiences. Only certain women's suffering was worthy of attention.[5] The copious sources from women of Spanish descent in the colonial archive reveal two often unconnected processes. The first is about women and war. These petitions generate a discourse about war that centers women's experiences and knowledge, exposing the many taxing burdens women carried during and after bellicose conflicts in the early eighteenth century. Yet these understudied stories prove as fascinating as they are selective. Spanish and Criolla petitions, with all their intimacy and loudness, underscore the silence of Native and Black voices. The second process found in these sources is thus about exclusion and racialization. It shows how the efforts by women of Spanish descent to safeguard their bodies, families, and inheritances not only played out through existing colonial dynamics but also emphasized the power imbalances of those relationships.[6]

In the aftermath of the 1702 siege, Spanish officials in Florida developed careful ways to narrate loss during wartime, relying on the interconnections of race, class, and gender to do much of the heavy lifting. The suffering of Spanish women allowed for a more expansive definition of war and its impact, but it also began to craft a sanctioned narrative about whose stories count and whose lives matter.

The 1702 attack proved so utterly devastating that most of what historians know about San Agustín's houses, living arrangements, and neighborhoods comes from after the siege. The few and relatively scattered earlier accounts describe a humble, poorly populated, unremarkable city. In 1675, Bishop Calderón conducted a survey of San Agustín, which praised its "spiritual welfare" over its physical condition:

> The city is built lengthwise from north to south. It is almost cut off by an arm of the sea, which surrounds it and buffets it, leaving it half submerged from hurricanes as it lies at sea level. Its climate is somewhat unhealthful, being very cold in winter, with freezes, and excessively hot in

> summer[;] both . . . extremes are felt the more as there is no protection nor defence [sic] in the houses, they being of wood with board walls.[7]

Jonathan Dickinson, a Quaker castaway rescued by Florida Indians and brought to San Agustín in 1696, left a brief description of the Spanish town. Though thankful to have been delivered to a European hub by his Native captors, Dickinson seemed rather unimpressed with the decrepit wooden houses of San Agustín, noting that many of these buildings were empty. Six years later, on the eve of the siege, San Agustín could boast several more structures than Dickinson had spotted, but the city remained small and its buildings unimposing. Governor Zúñiga y Cerda himself had requested masonry walls to reinforce his home, but at the time the English forces under Moore marched into the city, the governor's residence was only half-built.[8]

The siege further exacerbated San Agustín's housing woes. The destroyed and damaged property claims filed after the siege provide insight into the precarity of daily life, but they also show the importance of female-owned real estate in the city. Of the roughly 150 different petitions, eighteen specifically mention property owned by women. Women owned at least 12 percent of the damaged property, and it is noteworthy that more than 76 percent of the listed women owners had properties valued at one hundred reales or more, which was almost double the average home price listed. Moreover, many of the female owners had several properties under their name. On average, it seems that women in San Agustín owned more numerous and more expensive properties than their male counterparts before the siege.[9]

Ana Ruíz provides anecdotal evidence that corroborates those numbers. In 1696, she petitioned the crown to receive payment for housing the newly appointed governor as he got situated in the colony. She explained how Governor Juan Márquez Cabrera "had stayed at one of her residences"—note the plural here—and she commented that this was also "where his predecessors had stayed in the past." Ruíz had not lodged this governor or any of the previous ones simply out of the kindness of her heart. She expected payment for the use of her property. Márquez Cabrera had evaded her request several times and Ana Ruíz had been forced to file at least two separate petitions before receiving any restitution. Her endeavors showed that even well-paid and influential men like the governor struggled to find housing in San Agustín without the support of women.[10]

Women had owned property in Florida since the colony's earliest years. But the decision to refortify the Castillo de San Marcos in the early 1670s changed the stakes of land ownership. The first coquina stones arrived in 1672, but it took over twenty-three years to complete the fort.[11] This long-term building project increased the number and diversified the provenance of male workers and soldiers in San Agustín. Small but noticeable waves of Spanish, Cuban, and Mexican soldiers arrived to build, work, and staff the fortification. Their presence shifted more than the town's demography.[12] First, these new arrivals threatened the labor opportunities for Criollo soldiers, some of whom lost their military posts as the additional laborers and soldiers took their place. Second, these new soldiers could improve the marriage prospects and social mobility of Criolla women—though it is worth noting that the period from 1683 to 1702 saw a rise in births but a decrease in church-sanctioned marriages. Since most Spanish or Criollo men who arrived in San Agustín had no previous holdings in the colony, a woman's access to land proved a coveted commodity that helped incentivize new unions.

Houses, rather than coin or imported goods, were a common form of dowry for women in Florida.[13] Both Gertrudis de Morales and her daughter, Gerónima Rodríguez, used their homes as dowries to marry soldiers who had recently arrived in the colony. Gertrudis even managed to retain her property through all three of her marriages. Spanish law allowed a woman to keep her dowry after her husband's death, which in San Agustín meant that women like Gertrudis and her children always had a safe place to live even if they lacked the protection of a male head of household.[14] Access to property allowed Spanish and Criolla women social stability or even mobility through marriage, but it also provided a safety net for the women who outlived their partners or were forced to endure lengthy separations.

Determining how many women owned houses during the presiege period is difficult, as men assumed control of property during a marriage. Treasurer Juan Menéndez Marquez is a case in point.

After the siege, he reported the loss of his home, but this property was actually part of his wife's dowry. Doña Antonia Basilia de León had brought the home with her when she entered the marriage.[15] Menéndez Marquez had likely also contributed some of his assets to the dowry; called *arras*, this financial support was under the husband's purview during the marriage but had to be returned in full to the woman if the marriage ended (by either death or separation). The arras, along with the dowry, allowed women some financial stability and independence, not simply for themselves but also for the dependents under their care.

Though it might surprise us that women owned property in colonial Florida, this practice was quite common in Spanish America. Unlike English legal tradition, Spanish law, based on the *Siete Partidas* (1265) and *Leyes de Toro* (1505), offered several protections for women. It allowed married women to acquire property, write legal documents (such as wills and petitions), and litigate in their own names. Moreover, women's property (*parafernales*) appeared as distinct from that accumulated during their marriage (*gananciales*).[16] Widowed women retained control of their *bienes parafernales*, their dowry and arras, as well as half of the *bienes gananciales* they had accumulated during their partnership. All these legal protections were at play in Florida, which helps explain why, when the smoke cleared from the English attack, Spanish and Criolla women were banging down the governor's door demanding that their losses be recognized and their wealth restored.

Native and African-descent women did not follow suit. They did not file petitions after the siege even though they had, at least in theory, access to the existing legal and governmental outlets in the colony.[17] Moreover, Native and African-descent women had played a vital role in maintaining Spanish and Criollo households in Florida; the destruction of these spaces also affected them.[18] Where did these women live and work as San Agustín rebuilt itself? Why were they not offered the same relief as Spanish and Criolla women? It is possible that Governor Zúñiga y Cerda simply made a choice. With limited resources at his disposal, he chose to privilege the requests of Spanish and Criolla women, reasoning that if these homes were once again running, Native and Black women would be able to find employment and thus have no need for additional assistance from the crown. It is also possible that the women petitioners lied or, more specifically, that they carefully selected which relationships and familial ties to detail in their requests. The fact that they only mentioned their Spanish and Criollo relatives does not mean that they only had Spanish and Criollo relatives; it simply means that emphasizing these connections afforded them a better chance of securing monetary relief.[19]

Governor Zúñiga y Cerda, like most of San Agustín's dwellers, spent the days after the siege trying to understand the extent of the damage. Overwhelmed by requests for aid, food, restitution, and, above all else, permission to leave Florida, Zúñiga y Cerda offered a sympathetic ear; served as a key witness for many depositions; filed a comprehensive report chronicling more than 150 individual properties destroyed and 47,000 pesos in damage; and vehemently demanded the crown take action to protect Florida's loyal subjects who had valiantly withstood a devastating English attack. But Zúñiga y Cerda refused to let most people leave the tattered city. He feared that the war was far from over and believed that Spanish and Criollo families needed to remain in San Agustín if Spain had any hope for retaining its holdings in the region.[20]

The governor was right. Over the next four years, English and English-supported Native attacks threatened the very existence of Spanish Florida. The raids of 1704 utterly devastated the missions in Apalachee and forced the evacuation of San Luis. Closer to San Agustín, the few enduring Timucua missions and towns faced new waves of violence. In 1705, one of the few remaining Timucua towns suffered its own lengthy and violent siege. A poorly organized French and Spanish campaign against Charles Town failed miserably in 1706 and further weakened Spanish holdings in the region. In 1707, the English laid siege to Pensacola (twice).[21] Spanish forces were losing the war all over Florida.

With their missions attacked, their allies enslaved, and their lands burned over and over again, San Agustín officials had to engage in some careful diplomatic gymnastics with the Spanish Crown as they recounted loss and demanded aid without admitting fault. Women played a central role in that political exercise, but the rhetoric was decidedly different than it had been during the siege. During the English invasion, women had been an unwelcome but unavoidable presence in the juntas de guerra and other military discussions held in the crowded Castillo; they had become the loud mouthpieces for the general anxiety and fear that consumed the fort; and, because they had forced San Agustín men into a defensive posture, they were blamed for any Spanish military shortcomings. But this gendered discourse had begun to shift as soon as the siege lifted, with the arrival of reinforcements from Havana. If the movements, actions, and even the mere physical presence of women during the military conflict had helped Spanish officials explain the dangers of their colonial world coming undone, the same movements, actions, and presence of women after the 1702 siege meant something different.

As the war moved away from Spanish homes and returned to Indian country, women—particularly Spanish and Criolla women—signaled the possibilities of a colonial world being put back together, however haphazardly. Women held the key to remaking the city; they were central to Spanish recovery in Florida.[22]

The years of violence and destruction that followed the 1702 siege created a war with many fronts. Spanish and Criolla women did not partake in the fighting, but the violence wore on them. Famished, struggling to support their families, and reeling from material and personal losses that felt never-ending, these women at the edge of the Spanish empire, much like those at its core, turned to legal and governmental avenues for aid. Most women's decision to file a petition began in the same way: with death, or more specifically, with the death of the male relative who had been responsible for supporting them.

Reports about the casualties during the 1702 siege vary, but estimates are low. Enemy fire killed far fewer than did illness, prolonged exposure, and limited access to basic necessities, such as clean water and food.[23] There were a handful of soldiers on both sides who died and others who were captured, but the biggest human toll likely came from the attacked towns in Guale, as many of the Native inhabitants were enslaved and taken to Charles Town.[24] The deaths that frame the women's petitions, then, were most often not the direct result of a military confrontation. The men these women had lost had certainty fought in the war but had not necessarily died in battle or in the 1702 siege. Most had died in the months or even years after the English invasion. San Agustín women could only appear before the governor after their main provider, be that their father, husband, father-in-law, or uncle, had passed away—though many petitions bitterly alluded to long years of distress and loss the women had already endured.

It was the Spanish and Criolla women petitioners' job to link the life, service, and death of their male relatives to the ongoing war and thus to the ongoing need for support. Through the pleas of Spanish and Criolla women, the siege becomes a much longer affair, one with consequences and implications that reverberate for decades. The chronological, emotional, and familial parameters of the conflict expand in the women's petitions. In other words, while these documents certainly attested to Florida women's legal agency and power, they also created a different framework for the ongoing war, one based on experience rather than in the military events. The women were living through a war, and they had much to say about it.

The Spanish Crown had an infrastructure and colonial apparatus designed to safeguard women who had been left without male support, though it also patronized and restricted them in the process.[25] These petitions were mostly dictated, and they were accompanied by a letter of support from the governor. Even so, at least 40 percent contain the signature of the woman petitioner, implying not that they had written the documents themselves but that they had been in the room when their request was transcribed or, at the very least, that someone had read it to them.[26] Some of the Spanish and Criolla women petitioners identified themselves as Doñas (an honorific title that alluded to their prominent place in society); others listed their important male relatives; and all vowed to be "hijas légitimas," legitimate daughters. None identified as mestiza or Indian, and none claimed to be parda, mulatta, or Black.[27]

The supposed homogeneity of the petitioners not only contrasted with the diverse population that actually made up San Agustín but also revealed the highly racialized nature of these documents, which affirmed and naturalized the Spanish/Criollo experience while erasing all others. As Marisa Fuentes argues in the context of Barbados, women of European descent "accumulated racialized and gendered power" by creating these petitions that Black and Native women could not (or were not allowed to) make.[28] Spanish and Criolla women were seen as women and thus allowed to suffer and demand protection. Black and Native women were gendered differently: excluded from the institutional mechanism that offered financial restitution and recorded the loss of their homes and businesses, they were denied the promises of a safe future in San Agustín.[29] Intended to recognize and even uplift women's voices, these petitions showcase the racialized ways gender was understood, enacted, and enforced in colonial Florida.

The petitions women filed for aid and money after the siege of San Agustín followed a simple pattern. The women first humbled themselves before the governor and crown and then they detailed the reasons for their request: usually a combination of their own debilitating circumstances and the impressive deeds and services performed by the male family member who, until his untimely death, had cared for them, at least financially.[30] After providing evidence for their claims, or sometimes merely insisting on their validity, the women explained their specific needs and particular situations, listing any children they cared for and physical ailments they suffered. Finally, they concluded by demanding the standard rate of four reales per day for the remainder of their lives in San Agustín.

This daily sum would still be theirs even if they remarried. Furthermore, if these Spanish and Criolla women petitioners made a special request at the time they filed the claim, the monetary support they received could be transferred to their daughters and even granddaughters. With this guaranteed income, women hoped to receive some additional source of revenue to feed and support their children, especially their female offspring who had little chance of securing independent employment. The four reales could help beyond the much-needed immediate relief, serving as a dowry or investment in the future of young Spanish and Criolla women left without male protection. The income could help these women secure a favorable marriage match for themselves or their offspring, ensuring along the way the stability and prolongation of Spanish society in Florida.[31]

Women had made petitions in Florida long before the 1702 siege, but Queen Anne's War rapidly expanded the use of this long-established practice. A claim dated May 15, 1701, by Catalina

Hernández de la Cruz, widow of Ensign Alonso Solana, provides an example of a petition filed before the war whose approach and content mirror those made after the siege. Hernández de la Cruz began with a plea: "At the mercy of her Majesty, I beg . . . for my husband who served in the offices of public scribe and government and military engineering." Her petition then explained how her husband's loyal service had ended abruptly "when lightning struck him." Without her husband, Hernández de la Cruz avowed, her family suffered greatly, "leaving me very poor, with six children, three of them girls." Moreover, she was unable to work, since "I am also missing an arm and my house is broken into many pieces due to the impact the lightning had." All her hardships, including caring for three girls with no prospect of employment, could be mitigated by "asking her Majesty for alms of four reales per day."[32]

Hernández de la Cruz's request demonstrates her savvy legal and political know-how.[33] Hernández de la Cruz wanted to rebuild the life literally "broken into many pieces" by the sudden death of her husband, and the crown readily complied. The positive result of her petition was typical; although a response often took longer than the petitioners wanted, delayed by the slow Atlantic communication from and to San Agustín, Spanish and Criolla women in Florida routinely received monetary support from the crown.[34]

The destruction of the siege of 1702 prompted a flurry of petitions very much like the one made by Hernández de la Cruz. The most important difference was, quite predictably, mentions of the war itself. In addition to their standard reports about suffering in "extreme poverty," the petitioners also began to include details about the siege, the violence that had persisted, and the difficulties of living during what would turn out to be a decade-long conflict. Spanish and Criolla women inserted in the prescribed petitions information about their life before and after the fighting, and they produced along the way a previously unexplored, gendered, and oral history of San Agustín during Queen Anne's War.[35]

On October 12, 1706, María Mendoza, widow of the ensign Diego de Argüelles, asked for support, detailing the "thirty years her husband had served in the line of duty . . . and especially the services and time her husband did during the siege, rushing to the defense of the strong house and going to fight the said enemies in all the opportunities given to him."[36] Although other women were far more precise about their husbands' length of service—Antonia de Argüelles reported how her husband had served "twenty four years, nine months, and three continuous days," and Juana Cordera Meriaz recalled how hers "had served forty nine years, six months, and five days"—María Mendoza pointed to her husband's eager and devoted military activity during the siege.[37] Mendoza asserted that her husband had wanted to fight. By emphasizing his willingness "in all the opportunities given to him" and his specific deeds during the war, rather than just pointing to his military career generally, Mendoza's petition differed in a small but important way from similar requests made before Queen Anne's War.[38]

Prowess in battle, like "rushing to the strong house" and "fighting the enemy," now seemed to matter more than the length of the service. Spanish and Criolla women petitioners understood that their husbands' most recent military deeds took precedence: if they included an example of their spouse's bravery, they made sure the incident related to the ongoing war, especially the siege of San Agustín or the defense of a Spanish outpost.

María de Pedroza's husband had not served long but had done so heroically, a point she made repeatedly in her petition, and one that was reiterated in the accompanying witness report by the governor. Governor Zúñiga y Cerda amplified Pedroza's praise for Ensign Francisco de Pedroza, noting how "during the siege he served in the defense of the strong house with his arms during the day and the night I always saw him very alert."[39] According to the governor, Francisco had not stolen any weapons from the strong house and had been alert in the line of duty. Although refraining from theft and staying awake on the job seem fairly basic and hardly remarkable deeds, the point was that the ensign had behaved honorably at every turn. Wartime could bring out the worst in people, but it had shown the very best in her husband, or so Pedroza insisted.

The petitions of San Agustín women were like answers to an unspoken question—"What did *you* do during the war?"—in which "*you*" was understood as being explicitly male and military. Unsurprisingly, the descriptions of the men's activities and services were the central part of the women's petitions. Antonia Grosso's petition makes it seem as if her father had singlehandedly won the war.

Sebastián Grosso "had gone to Havana to give warning of the siege of this Real Garrison, exposing himself to the dangers posed by the enemy and the sea . . . having gone during a time of many storms . . . and returning with the armada from which he gave chase to the enemy."[40] Sebastián had traveled past the English blockade, secured aid from Cuba, chased the enemy away, and brought peace to San Agustín. Grosso claims her father was fearless.

In her petition, Gertrudis de Uriza follows a similar approach when discussing her son. "My son is there held prisoner in the town of San Jorge [Charles Town] for over seven years," Uriza explained. "He has been a prisoner since the time of the siege, having been serving an important post about eight leagues from this plaza." Uriza makes clear that her son did not desert his post or surrender quickly. He rode out to meet the enemy and "was wounded by a bullet." He had faced "this extreme danger" without hesitation and with courage.[41]

The heroic actions of these men were the core of the petitions, but the women could not or did not excise themselves completely from the story. Uriza mainly discussed her son but contextualized his military service in the "extreme poverty" she now faced and the many brushes with death she had endured: her husband had died during the siege and her daughter shortly thereafter. Linking their deaths and her son's captivity with the "doubling of her work and her difficult time," she focused on her son but showed how the war had affected her more broadly.[42] Antonia Grosso took this connection a step further. In her petition, she drew particular attention to the dangers of the 1702 siege, remarking on the sizeable enemy army, the blockade off the coast, and the dangers outside the city gates. At a quick glance these descriptions seem only to emphasize her father's courage in the face of such adversity. But, as her petition makes clear, her father had been in Cuba, getting relief for the presidio. He had not endured the siege; she had. These details reveal some of what *she* saw, feared, and heard while he was away.[43]

In other words, while Spanish and Criolla women petitioners featured the deeds and accomplishments of their deceased male relatives, they still managed to say a great deal about their own trials during the war. María and Gertrudis Diaz Mejía, two sisters who filed their petition together, portrayed a world upended by conflict, both imperial and personal.[44] Early in the war, they had lost their father to the enemy, but it was the more recent death of their mother that had left them unprotected and utterly alone. The brief petition of the Diaz Mejía sisters is slightly unusual, as it gives almost no facts about the family or the father's service records and instead devotes most of its text to the sisters' experiences during the siege. María and Gertrudis described how the enemy "had completely destroyed and annihilated" San Agustín. "We could not go outside of the place [the Castillo] without risking certain death," they stated, and just like that, they left one of the only first-person accounts of the siege and its aftermath.[45]

María and Gertrudis spoke at length about food and the lack thereof. They were hungry and had been so for quite some time, and there was nothing to eat in the city or its surrounding areas. The Diaz Mejía sisters did not accept this hunger as a normal outcome or expected state in wartime. They blamed their suffering on the brutality of an enemy that not only attacked the presidio but also targeted and burned San Agustín's fields and basic sources of sustenance. "It is heartbreaking," María and Gertrudis concluded, "to see all the *creaturas* [young children] crying from hunger and [to] lack any resources to give them."[46] The sisters asked the crown to have compassion for their community's shared plight. The Diaz Mejía sisters had suffered, and they had seen others suffer as well. Their own vulnerability compounded their inability to aid others and fulfill any maternal expectations. The crown owed them. María and Gertrudis deserved recompense for their fear, hunger, and strife, as well as for their powerlessness to help others, especially children.

The Diaz Mejía sisters requested only two reales, instead of the standard four, but they asked for additional flour allocations. Their expected payment was perhaps lower because it rested on their own articulated needs and experiences, rather than on their father's service. Though the sisters made no mention of an earlier effort to secure funds, the family had, in fact, made an earlier attempt. On April 20, 1708, eight months before the sisters appeared before the governor, their mother, Doña Gertrudis de Argüelles, had stood in the same place and asked "for the remuneration of the sixty eight years of service one month, and twenty days which her father had served and the fifty years, nine months, and five days that the said Captain Diego Diaz Mejía [her husband] had served."[47] Though she briefly mentioned her daughters, María and Gertrudis, Doña Gertrudis devoted most of her petition to her lost wealth: "The enemy had ruined her houses and heads of cattle and now she had no way of providing for her family suffering under extreme poverty."[48]

Houses. Heads of cattle. Doña Gertrudis spoke in the plural, revealing the sizeable wealth that had once been under her control. She had owned multiple properties and had a profitable source of income. Her future and that of her daughters had seemed secure until the war. She still had María and Gertrudis, but what good were daughters who could not provide for themselves and needed dowries to marry? Doña Gertrudis concluded her petition by asking for "four reales . . . for the rest of her lifetime," never demanding, as so many others did, an extension to carry over this claim to her daughters in the event of her death. Despite her omission, whether unintentional or a concerted effort to continue controlling the family purse, Doña Gertrudis's petition strongly resembled the one subsequently filed by her daughters. The almost identical details and phrasing of the two claims hint at a barely visible female communication network.[49]

Surely Doña Gertrudis and her daughters talked about the war, about their suffering, and about how they could improve their situation. In these conversations an important learning took place, both about their family's personal history and about their privileged and legal access to aid. Though women's communication networks are more often assumed than seen, Doña Gertrudis and her daughters, Gertrudis and María, used similar language to describe the English attacks and, more interestingly, all three focused on their own suffering. The inclusion of details about their personal loss, hunger, and fear is rather unusual, as almost none of the other women's petitions include these topics. The similarity of these petitions reveals a shared family history of the war that was deeply personal, but also public.[50] Whatever remained of their private world, these women emphasized their communal experiences; their voices were testaments of the war's destruction and, more importantly, guides for San Agustín's recovery.

Believing women does not have a robust history. The women who filed petitions from San Agustín tried to prove their authenticity by including additional letters of support. Doña María de Argüelles y Canizares, for example, not only declared in her petition that "her poor state [was] due to her lack of vision" but also included proof from a third party: "I have certified this with a surgeon."[51] Argüelles y Canizares knew all too well that women could play up their physical limitations to ask for additional aid or expedite their requests. To prove that her eyesight was indeed a real problem, not a rhetorical strategy, she offered two accompanying documents: the governor's letter certifying her claims and a surgeon's note attesting to her injuries.[52] Most women, however, only included a letter from the governor to corroborate their claims. Filed alongside, but usually placed ahead of any woman's request, the governor's statement was both an introduction to the woman's plight and a testament of its veracity.[53]

The extant accompanying letters from Governor Zúñiga y Cerda do little more than duplicate the Spanish and Criolla women's original petitions, validate their stories, and enthusiastically support their assertions. After all, Zúñiga y Cerda wanted and needed the crown to provide money to San Agustín.[54] Yet there was one important difference between these similarly purposed documents: Spanish and Criolla women petitioners wrote at length about their daughters. It was not as if they ignored their sons, but there was an understanding that boys, even very small ones, would eventually find some form of employment and relieve their mothers' financial burden. Both the governor and the women mentioned the children left in their mother's care, often remarking on their age, especially if they were too young to work, and on their number, in order to emphasize how many mouths needed to be fed. But Spanish and Criolla women petitioners, unlike the governor, explicitly mentioned their female relatives. Sometimes the petitions only list the names of the other women in their lives; other times they recount in some detail the experiences and struggles of their kinswomen.

In her petition, Doña María de Argüelles y Canizares discussed her daughter in detail. She asked that the money for the forty-six years of combined service for her deceased husband, Juan de Monzón y Uriza, her father-in-law, Ensign Agustín de Monzón, and her father, Capitan Alonso de Argüelles, continue after her death to support her young daughter Sebastiana de Monzón.[55] If Argüelles y Canizares had any sons, she never mentioned them. At the time of her petition, Doña María Argüelles y Canizares was ill and close to death; she knew that even if the crown agreed to pay her four reales, it would take months or perhaps years for the money to reach her purse. Without sentimentality and never bemoaning her mortality, Argüelles y Canizares simply sought to prevent her husband's and family's lifetime of work from vanishing into the bureaucracies of empire. She was also thinking about her daughter. Born in a time of strife and uncertainty, Sebastiana's health had always been poor. During the fighting, she and her mother were left to their own devices, and now they were alone in a war-torn city.[56]

Helena de Aldeco, widow of the ensign Alonso Lanzarote, asked for money for her granddaughter. Helena first disclosed "her extreme poverty" and explained how the English had burned her home during the siege and left her completely destitute. But Aldeco focused more on what remained than on her long-gone wealth and house. She devoted the bulk of her petition to Juana Theodora Pérez. Juana was the daughter of Aldeco's daughter, who had died during or shortly after the start of the conflict. Juana and Helena now only had each other.[57] Aldeco makes no mention of the Native or Black women who probably worked in her house and did her laundry and cooking; it was her Spanish blood relations that mattered most. Aldeco framed her request as a way of promoting and preserving the struggling colonial society in Florida.[58]

Similarly, Agustina Rodríguez de Mesa, widow of Captain Antonio Argüelles, requested that her four reales pass on to her granddaughter, María Regidor. Although most Spanish and Criolla women petitioners tended to emphasize the needs and prospects of their daughters, granddaughters and nieces were also important. Dionisia Gonzales de Villa García, daughter of Francisco Gonzales de Villa García, asked that after her death, her niece, Francisca Plazida, who was an orphan and poor, should receive her payments. In the same line, almost as in the same breath, Dionisia stated that her niece was legitimate and thus merited financial government assistance.[59] These petitions showed how Spanish and Criolla women's identities were constructed by and depended on their relationships with other women, not just based on their connections to the men their petitions were intent on praising.

These women's networks were deeply racialized, however. Spanish and Criolla women proudly prioritized extended, female, and familial connections that actively and repeatedly excluded Native and Black women. For all their insistence that their suffering needed to be heard, Spanish and Criolla women had no problem silencing other voices. These petitions often extended across generations, and as Spanish and Criolla daughters took up the causes of their mothers, nieces of their aunts, and granddaughters of their grandmothers, they affirmed and validated the status and rights of Spaniards and Criollos in San Agustín. Spanish and Criolla women petitioners thus created a legacy of wealth and power for their families that depended on restricting the same opportunities for Black and Native women.[60]

Some of these petitions took decades to resolve, as was the case for María, Manuela, and Lorenza de Aspiolea. In 1698 their mother, Antonia de Barbossa, had petitioned for a *plaza muerta* (payment for her deceased husband, Francisco de Aspiolea).[61] The men in the Aspiolea family had served the crown dutifully for decades, and Antonia demanded payment not merely for his services but also to counter the "extreme poverty and exposure to the dangers of the world" Barbossa now faced. She had also insisted that when she died, her husband's plaza muerta should "pass to her daughters."[62] The crown had agreed, and payments seemed to have been made—or at least were made until the siege. In 1705, María, Manuela, and Lorenza de Aspiolea issued a complaint stating that the plaza muerta had failed to transfer to them after the death of their mother.[63] Antonia de Barbossa had done everything right, María, Manuela, and Lorenza insisted. In the aftermath of war, the crown needed to honor their father's legacy and their mother's petition.

For María, Manuela, and Lorenza, their father's and mother's struggles were related. The Aspiolea sisters had not only seen their father serve and their mother request a plaza muerta; their entire livelihoods had depended on this system working properly. The legal and social structure of their world rewarded male military service and female suffering. For María, Manuela, and Lorenza, now orphaned and without familial protections, the consequences of violence that had begun long before the English laid siege to the city reverberated for decades. Though their father's lengthy service record spoke to a lifetime of work, the women's petition had connected his (and by default their) struggle to the subsequent years of violence. Their petition was a record of wartime that extended well beyond their father's death.[64]

Death was an active player in these petitions. Spanish and Criolla women petitioners often named every single person whom they had lost, beginning with the male relative the petition was based on but also including their children, siblings, and other family members. Gertrudis de Uriza poignantly recalled her daughter's death. After asking for the four reales in return for her husband's and son's valiant service, Uriza explained the limited terms of this clemency: "[the payment] will only be during my lifetime since my daughter has already passed away."[65] This brief reference, present only in her petition and not in the governor's certification, served two purposes. First, Uriza wanted to assure the crown that her request was minimal. She was old and certain to die soon, so the crown would be required to provide its monetary support for only a handful of years and, since she had no dependents, the payments would end with her death. Second, Uriza wanted to enumerate all that she had lost. She testified to her pain and her sacrifice. Her son and husband had died during the fighting, and whatever comfort her daughter might have provided was now also gone.

Women's lives and losses were just another part of war. Juana, Helena de Aldeco's daughter, had died in a cold makeshift bed, not on a battlefield. But for Aldeco, Juana's death was as much part of the war as her husband's service, and she included her daughter in her petition. The governor, however, did not incorporate Aldeco's deceased daughter or her still living granddaughter in his letter of support; these details probably seemed irrelevant to him in this context. Governor Zúñiga y Cerda saw how war touched and undid the lives of women—after all, he had served as the main corroborating witness for many of their petitions—but time and time again, he omitted personal information about the Spanish and Criolla women, privileging instead male military service.[66]

Women saw things differently and said as much in their petitions. On October 4, 1704, Doña María de la Rocha, frustrated by administrative delays, filed a final claim that inadvertently—or perhaps quite purposefully—omitted almost all mentions of her male relatives. Rocha's petition, which cited the many times she had filed similar claims (and even "had procured approval several times," though not a single real had been paid), does not mention her husband or any other male family member.[67] She chastised the Spanish Crown for forgetting her suffering and failing to fulfill its duty. By her last petition, Rocha seemed to suggest that it was not her husband's service or death in the line of duty but her own endurance and that of her children that more clearly embodied the long-term effects of war. Rocha's petition and those of Argüelles y Canizares, Uriza, and Adelco did not try to equate the sacrifices of their husbands, sons, or other male relatives with their own or their daughters' experiences. But they did demand acknowledgment of women's presence in wartime and their significance in Spanish colonial communities. Their petitions argued that women's experiences were not less valid or real.[68]

Most San Agustín women alluded in vague terms to the suffering and limited futures that awaited their daughters if the crown failed to support them. Gertrudis de Uriza took this reproach a step further.[69] She explicitly linked government aid for her husband's service with her daughters' ability to marry. In her petition, Uriza demanded the expected four reales "so that they [her daughters] have a secure income and so then they can get married."[70] The crown and governor agreed to support Gertrudis and the other women because the men in their lives had died, not because they hoped to invest in the future marriage arrangements of these women. Honoring military service and marriage were not equivalent projects for Spanish officials. For Gertrudis, however, her husband's sacrifice and her daughters' future went hand in hand. Women petitioners argued that Spanish presence in Florida depended both on men's military might and on women's ability to produce and reproduce Spanish families and norms in the area.

Ana María de Argüelles agreed. She had endured the violence, disorientation, and unsanitary conditions of war for years. Like most petitioners, she narrated her suffering and demanded support for her everyday needs, such as food and shelter. But she also looked ahead. Argüelles took the time to list all her daughters in her petition: "all who are minors, the eldest is nine years of age and is called María Gertrudis, [then there is] María Teresa, Francisca, and Josepha."[71] In identifying each one of her daughters, in saying their names and having someone write them down, Argüelles did more than list her dependents. She reminded the governor that without a dowry, the war-weathered women in her family would be less likely to marry, to birth children within the Catholic tradition, or to promote Spanish society in Florida.[72] The future of Spanish Florida depended on women.

Men were not encouraged to file claims. Soldiers who had a plaza muerta and survived the war would continue receiving a military salary or pension, especially as they got older. Those without an established plaza would be able to find employment in San Agustín now as laborers rebuilding the town. A petition from a former soldier for additional money and aid seemed, at best, unmanly. Unlike a defenseless woman, a man had a harder time asking the crown for aid, but desperate times forced desperate men to try desperate tactics. A handful of soldiers and enlisted men without permanent military appointments appealed to the crown for aid.[73] Male- and female-authored petitions from Florida were very similar. First, male petitioners depicted the services they had performed and the bravery they had displayed, and then they explained their particular ailments and circumstances that had motivated the request for additional monetary support. Second, like Spanish and Criolla women petitioners, men stressed the needs and vulnerability of their daughters.

Diego Caro, master of ships, for example, asked the crown for aid for the protection and well-being of his two adult daughters. Caro, who also had five other young children, drew particular attention to the financial burden of having unmarried daughters, especially ones who were unlikely to fulfill this sacrament because they lacked a dowry to help secure a respectable match.[74] In his petition, Caro narrated his military service, explaining that he had served the crown for "twenty four years, nine months, and twelve days as a soldier, sailor, and master of ships."[75] Moreover, during his lengthy and illustrious career, he had displayed "special zeal" during the 1702 siege, offering his maritime knowledge to carry news of the attack to Havana. He was a brave, committed, and experienced soldier. In short, he was someone who deserved special recognition and maybe even additional support.

Diego never mentioned his wife, and she was a telling silence in his petition. Had she died during the war? Had he been a widower for a long time? It was her absence that made it so difficult for him to care for his "five children who are all minors and his two adult daughters." In their petitions, women argued that neither they nor their families could function without a man; in his petition, Diego wanted to have it both ways. He showed himself as a man, a capable and committed soldier, and a loyal subject; he also showed himself unable to support his family without government aid. In the end, his claim, like those of most male petitioners, was not approved, even though it was very similar to the ones made by Doña María de Argüelles y Canizares or Helena de Aldeco. The crown refused Diego Caro, leaving his daughters with a father but without a dowry or a stable future.[76]

Governor Zúñiga y Cerda produced a long report identifying all the individuals who had lost property during the siege. There were 149 entries, each listing a name and the amount of that person's monetary loss. Most were men, but the governor included eighteen women. One, and only one, was listed as not being of Spanish descent. "Victoria la Yndia" claimed she had suffered 100 pesos' worth of damage, and she demanded restitution.[77] The document says nothing more about her. The lack of information about who her people were, her age, her relationships, or any of her experiences nonetheless makes one thing clear: she owned a sizeable extent of property that was considered part of San Agustín. Her singularity on the list speaks not to the small number of Native women in the city but to the obstacles they faced within the colonial world. Many Native women lived, worked, prayed, sold goods, and spent much of their lives in or near San Agustín. But their access to property was clearly limited, though not prohibited.[78]

Victoria la Yndia illustrates that belonging to and participating in Spanish society were not the same as receiving its protections and privileges. The petitions by Spanish and Criolla women make no reference to the Native women who labored in their homes, whether willingly or by force. In their beautiful and painful genealogies of female suffering and endurance during the war, Spanish and Criolla women omit any mention of Indigenous women, as if their struggles were not valid or real. Their absence, especially compared to the plethora of Spanish voices, creates a powerful narrative of loss and even disappearance. The Floridiana petitioners in San Agustín were not the first nor would they be the last to erase Black and Native women from Florida's history.[79]

Their silence repeated a larger story of Native population loss and declension that had gained traction with Florida officials during the second half of the seventeenth-century and would be further solidified with the attacks against Apalachee in 1704. But Native people remained. Their lives, labor, and military acumen continued to be central to the everyday operations of San Agustín. An expense report filed by Governor Zúñiga y Cerda right after the siege included a specific account of the costs owed to the Native and enslaved soldiers that served in Florida.[80] These men needed to be paid for their service. They had fought and helped repel English forces, even if they did not get to decide what that victory looked like.

Enslaved and free people of African descent, much like Native actors, were absent from the post-siege petitions. It was clear that they had fiercely defended the Castillo and endured much loss as a result. It was also clear that despite their lack of petitions, they remained in the city during the war. In 1703, only three weeks after the English withdrawal, Joseph Carabina, "negro slave of Capt. Juan de Ayala," married "Barbara de León a mulatta slave of the Adjutant Juan Ponce[;] . . . her godmother was Josepha Maria mulatta slave of the Major Sergeant Don Enrique de Ribera."[81] This relationship had withstood the siege, or perhaps it had blossomed during the conflict, as Joseph Carabina and Barbara de León had enjoyed more access and time together. While this union reveals a great deal about the strength and adaptability of the Black community in San Agustín, it says little about everyday life during the war. The struggles of Black individuals and families had no place in the official narrative of loss, bravery, and empire that Spanish and Criolla women petitioners helped create.

Confronting historical silence is never easy, especially when other voices clutter the archive. The women's petitions, much like their clamors and shouts during the siege, proved powerful. They recorded the ongoing war in different ways, articulating the familial and individual suffering that was muffled in official reports and creating gendered genealogies of struggle. The petitions also reaffirmed the racialized and gendered power of Spanish and Criolla women through their ability to silence or altogether disregard the existence of Native and Black women. It was as if they were not quite women and thus did not require the same protection or aid as Spanish and Criolla women.[82] Their absence is a reminder of the incompleteness of the colonial archive, but also, and perhaps more importantly, of the careful, racialized, and gendered ways the colonial documents were generated and preserved.

As English and Native attacks continued to threaten Spanish holdings in Florida, the ability to protect Spanish and Criolla women became both more important and more difficult to achieve. The safety of these women and the stability of the colony seemed bound together. They rose together; they crumbled together. And as the violence intensified, women's voices came to narrate not only the impact of the ongoing conflict but how it would be remembered.

CHAPTER SIX

The War That Never Ends

Doña Juana Caterina (sometimes Cathalina) de Florencia lived a full life in Florida until Queen Anne's War displaced her and most of her relatives.[1] Born into one of the wealthiest families in the colony, she enjoyed a life of privilege. She married young and she married well.[2] Her family ran cattle ranching and trade operations, with overland and maritime networks (both legal and illegal) that allowed the family to develop a small fiefdom in Apalachee. The power of the Florencias rested on their economic and political connections, as well as on almost daily negotiations with the Apalachee leadership and people.[3] But the war changed everything.

After the failed siege of San Agustín in 1702, English and Native forces opened a new theater of operations to the west (near present-day Tallahassee), targeting the populous yet poorly defended towns, missions, and ranches in Apalachee. Two waves of attacks, the first in early winter and the second in late spring of 1704, utterly decimated Apalachee. English-armed and -sponsored attacks led to the capture and enslavement of thousands of people, the destruction of most Apalachee towns, and the end of Spanish hold over San Luis. Once a booming mission town with growing connections to Caribbean entrepôts, San Luis became little more than a haven for those displaced by slaving and war.[4] Spanish officials, including many members of Doña Juana's family, deemed the situation in the region untenable. As Queen Anne's War escalated, they chose to abandon and burn down San Luis themselves rather than see it fall into enemy hands.[5]

With that decision, Doña Juana lost everything. Her house was gone, her prized possessions scattered. One by one, the well-connected and rich men in her life were consumed by the war and its violence. In a matter of months, her once robust familial network and wealth had shrunk significantly.[6] Like many Spanish and Criolla women, Doña Juana filed a petition documenting her struggles, but her 1709 petition is almost fifty times longer than any other similar request filed during Queen Anne's War in Florida. Most of its pages are filled with the testimonies of Spanish officials, soldiers, and other "disinterested persons worthy of belief."[7] The story they told and retold focused on the impressive deeds and sacrifices of the Florencia family, blending race and class interests to bolster Doña Juana's gendered claims for aid and support.[8]

Every time Doña Juana enters the Spanish archive, she wins. From her baptism to her marriage record, and from her children's births and marriages to her petition, Doña Juana's archival footprint reveals the inner workings of someone who masterfully navigated the war-torn world she both inhabited and helped shape. Doña Juana's narrative has a clear beginning, middle, and end that build to a critical crisis from which she emerges victorious, all the while providing riveting details and unprecedented access to the lives of women in Florida. In both its legibility and arc, Doña Juana's story proves incredibly seductive. It is, after all, the account of a strong and important Spanish woman withstanding all odds to protect her family and good name; but it is also an account Doña Juana carefully crafted about herself.

Native people told their own stories about Doña Juana.[9] Apalachees described her entitlement and cruelty. They discussed her involvement in enslaving and abusing Native women. They blamed her for wanton violence. They spoke through and against the silences in her narrative, centering Apalachee resilience and adaptability within a story that otherwise seemed to be about Spanish accomplishments. But Apalachee voices do more than disrupt Doña Juana's seamless narrative; they point to starkly different understandings of and experiences in Queen Anne's War. For them, the war had begun long ago and would continue long after Doña Juana left Florida. The war included people and disputes that Doña Juana, or most Spanish officials for that matter, knew little about or outright dismissed.

Apalachees specifically mentioned Doña Juana. For them Doña Juana was like a needle threader, allowing them to put long and often tangled pieces of thread through the eye of the needle. And as much as Doña Juana spun tales of her time in Apalachee for her own advantage, Apalachees used Doña Juana for their benefit and to tell their own stories. Taken together, the narratives by and about this elite Criolla woman bring to light the competing ways Spanish and Native records discuss and remember Queen Anne's War. Doña Juana's physical and archival presence shows the fault lines pulling this region apart as well as the gendered and increasingly racial ways that colonial officials and Native leaders were trying to weave it back together.

Doña Juana de Florencia had quite the legacy to live up to. Even before she was born, her family had been busy making its mark on Florida. Her birth actually came at a moment of tremendous economic and political growth for the Florencia family.[10] In the late 1650s, the Florencias had moved to the Apalachee region and begun developing an expansive and profitable ranching empire. Members of the family had served actively in the military and commanded several expeditions, and some had consistently occupied political office, ranging from visitador of Apalachee towns to lieutenant governor of San Luis, the highest-ranking Spanish position in the area.[11]

By the start of the eighteenth century, close to forty members of the family resided or made a living in Apalachee. The taxes the Florencias paid in a two-year period (1698 to 1699) hint at their remarkable wealth. The crown took a 10 percent tax on any increase in their herds and, complying with the law, Jacinto (Juana's husband), Francisco and Diego (her brothers), Diego Jiménez (her brother-in-law), and Francisca (her mother) counted their animal stocks and paid the tithe. The cattle reported by the Florencia family members amounted to the largest herd in Spanish Florida, and that number did not reflect the unreported ranching activity rampant in the colony. According to their taxes, the Florencia family had close to five hundred head of cattle, and it is safe to assume that they owned almost double that number.[12] They also controlled almost all the different elements related to their massive enterprise. They decided which fields their cattle freely pastured—or, in other words, which appropriated Apalachee lands would feed Spanish livestock instead of Native families. The Florencias were also known for exploiting their Native labor force, compelling them, through intimidation and force, to work long hours away from home for little pay.[13]

Juana was born on December 11, 1662, just as the Florencia family's wealth began to skyrocket. Her baptismal record contains little more than her name, date of birth, and the names of her parents and her padrino (godfather). Six sentences in all, the record looks like most others. The previous entry in San Agustín's baptism ledger is for a girl named Cathalina, who was born just a week earlier. Cathalina's entry is only a sentence longer, and it contains an important distinction: she was baptized "por necesidad" (by necessity), which implies that Cathalina was ill and not likely to survive. In contrast, Juana was a healthy baby, a fortune she enjoyed for most of her life.[14]

Compared to what is known about other girls baptized in Florida around the same time, there is a remarkable amount of information about Juana's family and lineage. Her mother was Francisca Urisa, whose parents were Diego Mejía and María de las Nieves y Urisa. Juana's father was Pedro de Florencia, whose parents were Claudio de Florencia and Francisca Leyba de Artega. The parents of Doña Juana's paternal grandmother were Gaspar Fernández Perete and Francisca Leyba.[15] Juana knew a great deal about these connections, which linked the affluent Urisa, Menéndez, Mejía, and Florencia families together.

The history of the Florencia family, especially its long Spanish heritage and deep involvement in Apalachee, was well known. Doña Juana grew up in a town where everyone recognized her and told stories about her family, especially the feats of her grandfather, Claudio de Florencia, who was murdered during the so-called Apalachee Revolt of 1647.[16] Juana's wealth and power rested on a violent past, one that was never quite past since the Florencia family made a point to tell and retell the story of Apalachee—*their story* of Apalachee.

Claudio de Florencia, Juana's paternal grandfather, had served as the first lieutenant governor of Apalachee from 1645 to 1647. Though initially invited into the region, the Spaniards found that the Apalachee were increasingly displeased with the expansion of cattle ranching operations (spearheaded by the Florencia family), the demanding missionizing activities of Franciscan friars, the increasing labor demands coming from San Agustín, and the meddling in intra-Apalachee politics.[17] When Claudio received an invitation to the town of Bacuqua, he took it as a sign of good things to come. He was wrong. The Apalachees turned on the Spanish delegation, killing Claudio, his wife, daughters, and grandchildren, as well as several Franciscan friars. Doña Juana's father was spared since he was not present during the attack.

The Florencia family murders at Bacuqua were called the Apalachee Revolt of 1647, and the violent ends of some of the leading members of this prominent family quickly became part of Florida lore. Nicolás Mendes, a soldier who served in Apalachee, remembered that one of the first stories he heard when he arrived at his Florida post was about the Florencia family. He had come to Apalachee in 1675, twenty-eight years after Claudio and his family were killed, yet the Apalachee Revolt remained a topic of conversation.[18] For Mendes, this story had taught him about the dangers lurking in Apalachee, but it also served as a guide to who was who in Florida society. Through the gruesome story of Bacuqua, Mendes learned a great deal about the Florencias, whose "persons are highly appreciated," as well as "the political and military positions that their parents, grandparents, and great grandparents" had held.[19] The Florencia family was Florida royalty.

Alonso Naranjo, another soldier with no direct connection to the Florencia family, had also "heard as public knowledge in this city that the caciques of Vacuqua [sic] had invited the lieutenant and all of his family to a gathering and that they had killed them with blows from axes and with other cruel tortures. And in the midst of them [the tortures], they [the Florencias] were preaching the evangelical doctrine to the Indians."[20] Naranjo, like Mendes, had been introduced to the history and political reality of Florida through the Florencias' devastating experiences in the so-called Apalachee Revolt. It was "public and well-known" that the Florencias were a "highly regarded," "devoted" family, whose members had laid down their lives to serve the church and crown. They were local Florida heroes.[21]

Apalachees obviously told their own stories of the events at Bacuqua. Juan Francisco, a soldier in the region, recalled "how he heard the old Indians from the province tell of this many times."[22] While he did not reveal any of the specific details shared with him, the lessons of the 1647 attack were manifold for the Apalachees. First, it confirmed what they already knew: Apalachees had a lot of say in how they dealt with Spanish colonos. Apalachees were both numerically and militarily superior. Second, the murder of Claudio and his family, much like his initial welcome into the region, had failed to garner universal support. Apalachees were divided; not every Apalachee town had agreed that the violence at Bacuqua was the right course of action.[23] And finally, the attack had shown that Apalachee and Spanish worlds were increasingly intertwined. Apalachees could expel Florida officials from their towns, but they could not simply ignore Spanish advances. After 1650, Spanish presence, both welcomed and contested, became increasingly common in Apalachee lands.

Doña Juana was quite familiar with the history of Apalachee. This was her past, but it was also her future. In 1675, at the age of thirteen, she wed Jacinto Roque Pérez, a well-respected officer, who seemed poised for leadership in Apalachee.[24] Jacinto had been one of the first colonos to return to Apalachee after the events at Bacuqua had hastily driven Spanish officials, friars, and soldiers out of Apalachee lands. Jacinto had followed Pedro de Florencia, Juana's father, and other Florencia family members in their efforts to reclaim Apalachee for the Spanish Crown. Jacinto had made his way through army and governmental posts in San Luis, and though he had known and worked alongside the Florencia family intimately before his wedding to Juana, his marriage to a member of this influential family helped consolidate his status. He went on to serve as lieutenant governor of Apalachee for three terms and became one of the region's largest landowners.[25]

We know very little about Juana's relationship with her husband, except that she followed him to Apalachee and became pregnant very quickly following their marriage.[26] Juana would go on to have ten full-term pregnancies and perhaps others that ended in miscarriage.[27] These numbers were not atypical for upper-class Spanish families in the eighteenth century. Better nutrition, support during and after labor, and wet nurses helped radically improve survival rates among babies and mothers of wealthy Spanish families.[28] Doña Juana might have been afraid of establishing her home and raising her children near the site where Apalachees had murdered her grandfather and aunts, but fear alone was not enough to deter her from the profits that awaited her in San Luis. Her presence serves as a simple but important reminder that the Florencia family's power—built on cattle ranching, trade networks, government posts, military connections, and even the support of the church—was not purely male. It needed women.

It needed Juana. During her many years in San Luis, Doña Juana and her familial relations anchored the Spanish ventures in Apalachee. She understood well that it was her family, her households, and her role as a daughter, wife, and mother that affirmed as well as engrained Spanish power in the area.[29] As it had been for her grandfather Claudio de Florencia in the 1640s, the settling of Apalachee for Doña Juana was a family affair that gradually folded her, most of her siblings, and many of her relatives into a powerful political and economic network that connected the area from the 1660s to 1704. Then it all abruptly ended. In the winter of 1704, the violence of Queen Anne's War rapidly toppled the Florencias' regime in Apalachee.

Juana and Jacinto, her husband, were roused from their beds when Apalachee men and women poured into town on January 25, 1704. These Native refugees had stunned expressions and horrible news: the town of Ayubale was gone. The enemy had launched a brutal attack, capturing many Native women and children and burning what little remained.[30] The towns of Tolome, Capole, Candelaria de la Tama, and Ocatoses soon also suffered attacks.[31] As the war moved away from San Agustín and opened a new front in Apalachee, the influence of the Florencia family was put to the test, endangering also the lives of most who lived and worked in San Luis. Since Ayubale was close to San Luis, Captain Juan Ruíz de Mexía, the lieutenant governor and official in charge of the Spanish fort, decided to organize a swift response. Captain Mexía feared that if he did not stop the sizeable English-Native forces at Ayubale, the violence would spread like wildfire. He knew that San Luis was far smaller and less equipped than San Agustín; if the enemy laid siege to San Luis, it could not endure as long as San Agustín had in the winter of 1702. Unlike Governor Zúñiga y Cerda, who chose to wait out the danger inside the presidio, Captain Mexía chose to bring the fight to the enemy.

This military decision proved costly. Mexía left Doña Juana's husband in charge of San Luis and rode out "with about thirty Spanish soldiers and settlers, and four hundred Apalachee Indians." The Spanish-led forces "surrounded the enemy and killed six or seven of the English and about one hundred of the pagan Indians." But eventually, "for lack of munitions," the Spanish and Apalachee forces "were defeated," and Captain Mexía "was wounded by a ball which toppled him from his horse."[32] The battle at Ayubale proved a double blow for Spanish officials, who not only failed to turn back the invading army but also showed their weak military hand. As poorly supplied and ill-staffed as San Agustín had been, San Luis was clearly in worse shape.

No one was more pleased by the decrepit state of San Luis than James Moore. The former governor of Carolina had suffered both personal and political attacks after leading the disastrous 1702 siege. Eager to clear his name and exact vengeance, he had helped organize the attacks against Apalachee. To gain support for his cause, Moore made almost the exact same arguments he had articulated for sieging San Agustín: the fighting would be quick, the loot would be plenty, and there would be many slaves for the taking. This time, however, Colonel Moore's promises proved right. In Ayubale, the well-armed Apalachicola, Yamasee, and English soldiers overwhelmed the large Spanish-Apalachee army. They killed many Apalachees and some Spanish soldiers, and they even managed to take captive key Spanish officers. Moore had hoped to negotiate a handsome ransom for the return of these unscathed prisoners, but diplomacy with San Luis quickly went awry. Moore had released some men as a sign of good faith, but when San Luis officials refused to offer any form of payment, the colonel took the remaining prisoners to Charles Town.

Diego Jiménez, Juana's brother-in-law, suffered this fate. Jiménez had led the charge to expel the enemy from Ayubale with Captain Mexía. Though the injured commander had managed to make his way back to San Luis, Diego was not so lucky and spent four years imprisoned in Charles Town. Diego was married to María Magdalena, Doña Juana's youngest sister. Thirteen years and a world of experiences divided Juana and María Magdalena, but the two had grown close with time, shared a household, helped care for each other's children, and endured the start of the war together.[33] María Ana de Arguelles, wife of another of Doña Juana's brothers, Francisco, also lived with them. Ana had one son and three daughters, one of whom was born sometime in 1704, probably in Juana's house. In all, Doña Juana, María Magdalena, and Ana were running a household with nineteen children and very little male supervision.[34] Then Diego Jiménez was taken captive, Captain Mexía was injured in battle, and Jacinto was thrust into a leadership position just as San Luis's future seemed most uncertain.

Doña Juana's husband wasted little time gathering everyone and everything he could inside the garrison. The cattle, church furnishings, and of course the women and children were relocated inside the palisade for protection. In a parallel to the siege of San Agustín eighteen months earlier, Moore and a large Native army reached San Luis, a meager fort now housing over 1,400 people, most of whom were not soldiers. The English colonel had no intention of repeating his earlier mistakes. With less arrogance and pleased by the massively successful slave raids in the nearby Apalachee towns, Moore tried his hand at diplomacy.

The colonel magnanimously promised that he would spare San Luis. In truth, he had little desire to engage in another costly siege. In exchange for his peaceful overture, Moore merely asked that any Chacato Indians found in the fort be turned over to him and his army. This peculiar request hinted at the deeply local reasons and pressures that encouraged most Native people to fight in Queen Anne's War. It was unclear if Moore himself had any stake in his demand for the Chacatos in San Luis, but much of his Native army, especially a sizeable Tasquique unit, cared deeply about the fate of these Indians.[35]

As it happened, in 1699, a group of Chacatos, guided by none other than Francisco de Florencia, Juana's brother who had a troubled relationship with the law, had raided a Tasquique hunting party and stolen deerskins. The Tasquique Indians who had joined Moore's efforts sought justice, or at least financial restitution, for this assault that had taken place five years earlier. It was a dispute between Indian towns that underpinned the demands made at the gates of San Luis. It was Native tactical and military knowledge that directed the course of the attacks on Apalachee. And it was Indigenous-centered geopolitics that determined which towns the invading forces targeted and which they spared. Past and present inter-Indian relations did more than inform Moore's request to Jacinto; they shaped the course of Queen Anne's War in the region.[36]

Jacinto refused to surrender any Chacato Indians. "The said captain replied to him that he could not hand them over because of their being vassals of his Majesty and because they [Chacatos] had given obedience and because of having promised them security under the protection of royal arms." The captain gave an impassioned speech, declaring that the only "silver he had" to give Moore's army "was the lead in bullets."[37] Jacinto's decision was a strategic political move intended to both defy English advances and inspire support among the dwindling numbers of Native people in the Spanish town of San Luis. The Spanish forces needed to show they could protect those loyal to them. After some tense back-and-forth, Moore, much to the displeasure of the Tasquique Indians, decided to leave San Luis empty-handed and look for easier targets.[38]

Spanish officials understood that their grip on the region was slipping, yet the decision to evacuate San Luis still proved contentious.[39] Jacinto Roque Pérez, who had abruptly taken command of the town after the lieutenant governor had been injured in the battle of Ayubale, organized a war council. At first, San Luis officials seemed determined "that they should wait out the enemy," much like the San Agustín leadership had done during the 1702 siege. Then reports about the brutality of the nearby attacks against Apalachee towns began trickling into San Luis. Tales of burned homes, families torn apart, and injured bodies left on the road to die shocked and dismayed the San Luis population.[40]

Moore's forces seemed determined to enslave Apalachee people and destroy their homelands, or that was how Spanish and Apalachee voices represented these slavers. Apalachicolas, Creeks, and Yamasees comprised most of Moore's forces in 1704; they had their own motivations and reasoning for engaging in this conflict. Important work has shown how these different Native nations used their involvement in the slave trade to build their communities, expand their influence, and negotiate their connections in an increasingly volatile colonial world.[41] But at this time and from the Spanish archive, slave raiders emerge as little more than a ferocious other, intent only on violence.

Spanish officials quickly realized that their defenses would not hold. Even if they managed to keep English forces away from San Luis, they could not ensure the safety of Apalachee. Manuel Solana, a leading officer stationed in the fort, argued, "It is impossible to defend the blockhouse with fewer than fifty soldiers," and thus "those who here remain should be transported to that presidio [in Pensacola], and that all of the cattle be driven, for if not, all will be lost."[42] To save San Luis—its people, resources, and potential—Spanish officials needed to abandon it.[43]

The last days of San Luis are poorly documented, but the scattered sources left speak of chaos and panic. People frantically attempted to salvage what they could. They gathered any valuable goods and rounded up as many heads of cattle as they could find. The Franciscans turned their attention to the churches. They stripped the missions bare, itemizing and packing many precious ornaments, such as candlesticks and Eucharist dishes made of silver.[44] But anything that could not be carried or carry itself had to be destroyed. Jacinto feared that if enemy English forces took the fort after the Spanish settlers departed, they would have a ready-made stronghold in the region. Governor Zúñiga y Cerda, stationed in San Agustín, shared the Captain's concerns:

> The hostilities of the pagan Indians, led by the English have succeeded in depopulating the Province of Apalachee. . . . Consequently, should the enemy return, they could

> readily take it; and their finding it fortified and with artillery would be sufficient motive for them to occupy the province. In this light, it was decided in council, to destroy the blockhouse and withdraw [from San Luis].[45]

As acting lieutenant governor, Jacinto first ordered "to demolish the defensive feature, consisting of a stockade in the convent." He then wanted "the trench filled" and the "taking down of the corral and reducing it all to firewood." Finally, "He ordered that all the houses of the Spaniards should be burned and that they should begin with his own."[46] From the safety of the blockhouse, Doña Juana could see her home, the sizeable Apalachee council house, and the convent burning. Her husband had set San Luis on fire.

Jacinto, like most Spanish officials, never depicted the events of San Luis as a failure.[47] Instead, he insisted that the costly burning and abandonment of the town was a savvy military maneuver that, in spite of its explicit association with loss and defeat, worked to ensure the safety of Spanish society in Florida.[48] A 1708 report echoed Jacinto's claims, arguing that although the province of Apalachee might have been left "defenseless and helpless without Indians and with enemies who had burned towns and the garrison . . . the plaza of San Agustín in Florida was safe and secure."[49] San Luis had sacrificed itself to protect both its people and the whole of Spanish Florida. The linguistic acrobatics Spanish officials in Florida, México, Cuba, and Spain performed to avoid mentioning the loss of San Luis were as creative as they were gendered. No officer or soldier was responsible for "the accidents of war"; on the contrary, these men were courageous, even selfless, making decisions against their financial, familial, and even historical interest.[50]

Juana saw Jacinto for the last time during the hurried evacuation of the city. She was to head west, with all the female relatives and children living in her home. This included her ten offspring; María Magdalena, her sister, whose husband had been captured and taken to Charles Town, and their five children; as well as Ana Argüelles, her sister-in-law, and her small children. Meanwhile, Jacinto was to journey east. Along with Francisco de Florencia, Juana's brother and Ana's husband, he organized and accompanied a military escort with all the valuables and weapons removed from

San Luis. According to Doña Juana's petition, Jacinto put duty above family, "neglecting to accompany Juana and his children in order to fulfill his position to defend the presidio."[51] He accomplished this trying task and reached San Agustín with all the precious cargo and without incident. But the journey in the heat of summer took a heavy toll on his and Francisco's health. Within days of reaching the Castillo de San Marcos, both men were dead.

Doña Juana learned about her husband's passing after reaching Pensacola.[52] The trek for Spanish and Apalachee families journeying west from San Luis had also proven very difficult. Raiders repeatedly attacked the slow-moving caravan composed of six hundred (some sources say eight hundred) people. These assaults did more than terrify the displaced population; they also drove "all of them [cattle] away, as well as all the horses of the Spaniards."[53] With few if any animals left in their care, Spanish and Apalachee refugees had to walk, side by side, not quite equals but bound together by circumstance and war. Spanish officials lamented how "even the women" like Doña Juana de Florencia were stripped of all their comforts and exposed to the elements during the evacuation.[54]

Doña Juana suddenly found herself without her husband, home, or any source of income from which to support her family. To add insult to serious injury, a little "vaulito" (chest) of jewels she had managed to salvage before her home burned was stolen as she fled from San Luis. The once wealthy and powerful Juana did not even recognize herself. Her status and widely recognized persona, rather than affording her protection, had left her more exposed. Robbers had targeted her, betting that the Florencia matriarch was carrying items of wealth and taking advantage of the fact that she lacked the male network that had supported her in San Luis.[55] By the time Doña Juana reached Pensacola, she was penniless and destitute.

Soon she was also alone. Her sister and housemate for many years, María Magdalena, had marched west with her, but then she took her five children to Cuba, where she awaited the release of her husband, Diego Jiménez, from his imprisonment in South Carolina.[56] It is not clear why Doña Juana chose to travel to México instead of to Cuba with her sister, or if she had any choice in the matter. It is also unclear what kind of life she managed to build for herself and her family in Vera Cruz. But we do know that after her long and difficult travels ended, she petitioned the crown for support. Like most women petitioners, Doña Juana requested aid because of her family's long service and the valiant wartime achievements of her recently deceased husband. Unlike the appeals of most women, however, her petition contained eight expert witness reports and the support of twenty-six prominent men in San Agustín, including the governor.[57] The petition was eventually approved, and though it took many years Doña Juana was awarded over 1,000 pesos from the crown. Although it is unclear whether she received one lump sum or recurrent payments like the other women petitioners, her award was almost 250 times greater than what anyone else from San Agustín had managed to secure.[58] The large sum was owed in part to the many children left in her care, her enormous loss, and, undoubtedly, the sway of her illustrious family history.

With her 1709 petition, Doña Juana engaged in an exercise in memory and myth making. The petition had to remind the crown of all that the Florencia family had accomplished in Florida. It also had to convey all that they had lost, and it had to make Doña Juana an exemplar of both merit and suffering. The petition began with a letter of support by the governor, Francisco de Córcoles y Martínez, and ended with Doña Juana's own testimony, a two-page account that is almost identical, both in tone and content, to the other petitions made by women in San Agustín.

Claudio de Florencia, Juana's brother and a leading Franciscan in Florida, remained in San Agustín after the evacuation of San Luis and took it upon himself to summon the leading eight witnesses. He wrote the fifteen questions these men had to answer and ensured that all the proper documentation accompanied his sister's request.[59] Claudio's methodical approach created a long, thorough, and repetitive petition that told the same story over and over again, amplifying Juana's struggles and needs with its multiple, echoing versions. According to the petition, Doña Juana was the anchor of San Luis society. She used her wealth and influence to help others. Nicolás Mendes, a soldier in San Luis during the war, argued that Doña Juana was a kind and giving mother to them all:

> [She was] curing the entire province from her house, the religious as well as the soldiers and Indians and with such great love and open arms *that if all of them had been her children*, she would not have been able to do more for them, nor with more promptitude and charity.[60]

Mendes explained that Doña Juana's caring nature had preceded the war, but when Moore's forces began attacking Apalachee towns, she and "her children went to the very beds of the sick with medicines, meals, preserves, wine, firewater, and whatever else as a gift."[61] Doña Juana saw it as her duty not only to feed the hungry but also to clothe them. She and her daughters "deprived themselves of the clothing they wore to serve the poor Spanish women, both widows and married ones . . . so that they would not leave off going to hear Mass" because they were improperly dressed.[62] Doña Juana was nothing short of a saint. She provided food, medicine, and clothing, and she ensured that everyone went to mass. Moreover, she performed this bountiful charity to make her husband proud: "her husband took great pleasure in it."[63]

Interestingly, but perhaps unsurprisingly, it was the witnesses who were not related to Juana and who thus had less intimate contact with her that provided the most laudatory descriptions of her actions.[64] Unlike Mendes's rosy view of Doña Juana, Joaquín de Florencia hardly mentions her, focusing instead on her family's long history of service for the Spanish Crown. Joaquín thought Doña Juana's main achievements had nothing to do with feeding the poor or helping the sick. Instead, what mattered was that she (like Joaquín) had been born into the Florencia family, she had married a notable man, and she now needed support because she was a widow with ten children in her care. Doña Juana was little more than the sum of her family relationships—a gendered specter who mothered and supported others and deserved aid to ensure the continuation of her celebrated family lineage.[65]

All the questions Claudio de Florencia composed for Doña Juana's petition were leading, intended to reflect positively on the Florencia family. The sixth query is particularly revealing: after providing a brief history lesson on the so-called Apalachee Revolt that vilified Native people and extolled Spanish courage, Doña Juana's brother asked the witnesses "whether they know it was considered public knowledge and well-known that they [the Florencias] were considered to have died martyrs."[66] Better said, the testigos were given the opportunity to elaborate on the Florencias' greatness, not to question these events or their impact. And that is exactly how the testigos' accounts read. Doña Juana's petition is like a hagiography of the Florencia family.

The final questions in Doña Juana's petition discussed the fighting and eventual evacuation of San Luis. Though this document was mostly concerned with recording the triumphs of the Florencia clan, it had to explain why a member of one of the wealthiest families in Florida now needed monetary support. Gender served as the main framework for descriptions of Doña Juana's loss. Her suffering as a mother and widow took center stage. Ruiz Mexía described her as "a poor widow without any wealth . . . who went to Panzacola [sic] from Apalachee and he has heard it said that there in Vera Cruz she is very, very poor, with ten children."[67] Juan Francisco described her wretched state "because of having lost all of it [her property] in Apalachee."[68] The financial and emotional toll Juana carried allowed the men who testified in her petition to describe the immense and costly defeat the Spanish had endured in Florida without ever addressing their own incapacity to protect her or the others in Apalachee.[69] Her wartime loss and thus her request for money seemed to have nothing to do with the policies San Luis officials adopted or the course of actions they had taken. They talked about *her* loss, not theirs.

Narrating their own struggles during and after the war proved far trickier for these Spanish officers and soldiers.[70] It was not easy to admit that they had lost San Luis, that they were no match for the advancing English-Native army, or that their shortcomings had pushed Doña Juana, along with the rest of the Spanish and Indigenous population of the city, to leave and burn their homes. Moreover, the one time they had faced the enemy in open battle outside the raided city of Ayubale, the Spanish militia and their Native allies had fared very poorly. In relating some components of this disastrous sequence of events, the men testifying in Doña Juana's petition rewrote the history of the final days of Spanish rule in Apalachee.

They did not claim that the Spanish forces had somehow won, but they did insist that they had faced formidable odds that made their withdrawal both necessary and correct. Juan Francisco, who had participated in the clash at Ayubale, explained that "during the battle that took place, the enemy Indians fled and all the rest hid themselves, with only eighty Englishmen staying in the battle. And with the Spaniards not amounting even to forty, victory was almost ours." As "enemy Indians" fled or hid, the eighty English and the forty Spaniards engaged in a fierce battle that the San Luis forces would have won, had not the better-supplied English army shot and "wounded the lieutenant." The honorable Spanish soldiers had then rallied to protect their fallen commander and withdrawn to safer ground.[71] Juan Ruíz Mexía also alluded to the bravery of the small Spanish forces that "fell upon him [Moore] with war and battle against him and his troops," calling special attention to how "all the enemy Indians had surrendered terrified" and the Spanish were left "fighting only the English."[72] Juan Francisco told a fantastical tale of how, deep in Indian country but apparently without much Native involvement, Spanish and English forces waged a pivotal battle of Queen Anne's War.

Native people were not completely excised from Spanish narratives of war, however. Apalachees, Yamasees, and Apalachicolas can be seen fleeing, cowering, and abandoning their posts.[73] In Spanish sources, Native people seem to appear only in their disappearance. The testimonies in Doña Juana's petition point to Spanish superiority over the invading Indian forces, who all seem to run away or surrender at the sight of the Spanish army, and to English inability to control their own Native allies, who refuse to follow orders and who go where they please. These same testimonies, however, remain relatively silent on the many Apalachees who had fought alongside the Spanish militia from San Luis, both at the initial confrontation in Ayubale and throughout the war. Rather than as fighters, Apalachees were portrayed much like Doña Juana, as passive victims losing their homes, relatives, and wealth.[74] This gendered belittling of Native people allowed Spanish officers and soldiers to sidestep their military loss in battle and argue that they had, in fact, succeeded in protecting the defenseless women, children, and Indians of San Luis. Native people were thus included in

Doña Juana's petition as a way to bolster the bravery of colonial officials, downplay Native military prowess, and vindicate the collapse of Spanish Apalachee.

Apalachee men and women contested Doña Juana's curated story of Spanish courage, wealth, and influence. Although their voices were often not as loud as Doña Juana's and their stories were not as easy to understand or corroborate, their words and actions forged a different kind of record, one that quickly moves past Doña Juana and speaks instead of Apalachee strength, connection, loss, and resilience. Taken together, the three extant Apalachee accounts that mention Doña Juana—a testimony from 1687, a letter from 1699, and a report from 1702—create a collective and corrective biography that challenges the elite Criolla woman's rendition of events and instead highlights the struggles and importance of Native women in Apalachee.[75]

In 1687 Matheo Chuba, acting chief of San Luis, and his *inija* (second in command), Bip Bentura, met Doña Juana in jail.[76] She had burst into their cell under the cover of night to set them free. The surprising ordeal had begun earlier that day, when Matheo Chuba and Bip Bentura had gone to San Luis to ask Antonio Matheos, the newly appointed lieutenant governor of Apalachee, for permission to travel to San Agustín. After listening to their request, Matheos deemed the Native leaders dangerous and imprisoned them.[77] Antonio Matheos had only recently arrived from Spain as part of a new effort to Hispanicize the leadership and military of La Florida.[78] He had little command over Apalachee, its people, or its needs. He also did little to endear himself to the leading families of San Luis. Doña Juana and her relatives took an immediate dislike to Matheos, considering him a threat to their authority and influence in Apalachee, and the Florencia family sought to undermine the lieutenant governor at every turn.[79]

Matheo Chuba and Bip Bentura cared little about this internal Spanish rivalry. But their desire to journey to San Agustín and meet directly with Governor Juan Márquez Cabrera got the attention of Doña Juana's husband. Jacinto began to encourage other Apalachee leaders to use Matheo Chuba and Bip Bentura's planned visit to San Agustín as an opportunity to present grievances against

Matheos. Jacinto had urged "the said Indians and other caciques that if they had anything to ask before the governor against the said adjutant and lieutenant that they should tell it to said Matheo Chuba and Bip Bentura."[80] A rather inexperienced and somewhat paranoid leader, Lieutenant Governor Matheos became convinced that "a wild scheme" was taking shape and accused the Apalachee chiefs of trying to undermine his policies.[81] He denied Matheo Chuba and Bip Bentura's travel request and threw them in jail to ensure that they would not defy his orders.

Matheo Chuba and Bip Bentura were powerful men with powerful connections.[82] Slaving raids, disease, and the repartimiento had forced Apalachee leadership to think carefully about where they located their towns and with whom they forged alliances.[83] Apalachee leaders had adapted well to their changing landscape, welcoming groups like the Chacatos into their lands and expanding their trade and communication networks. Demand for Apalachee-grown grain had increased in San Agustín, and Apalachee leaders like Matheo Chuba and Bip Bentura knew that as much as they needed an alliance with their Spanish neighbors, the Spanish needed them more. The corn Apalachees harvested fed Spanish bellies and the labor Apalachees provided helped build the Spanish presidio. The new lieutenant governor of San Luis had failed to understand what important allies the chief of San Luis and his inija were.

Juana and Jacinto made no such mistake. They defied Matheos's orders and freed Matheo Chuba and Bip Bentura from jail. "And that same day of imprisonment, at night, the Captain Jacinto Roque Pérez, and his wife, and his mother-in-law came asking about the said prisoners and to facilitate matters they freed them."[84] Matheo Chuba and Bip Bentura were awake and still visibly shaken by the events of the day when the three unlikely figures entered the cell.[85] There are no records of this clandestine meeting, although later Jacinto stated that their unforeseen imprisonment had left "the Indians agitated."[86] Without explicitly mentioning the events of the so-called Apalachee Revolt of 1647, Jacinto pointed to his family's firsthand experience with "agitated" Apalachees and their terrifying capacity to unravel Spanish efforts in the region. Doña Juana, was afraid that history would repeat itself. After all, she was standing near where her grandfather and aunts had been murdered and once again facing an escalating situation, Doña Juana offered a direct and physical link to a past Jacinto dearly hoped to avoid.

The imprisoned Apalachee chief spoke about the future, however, not the past. In his account of the events that led to his capture and release, Matheo Chuba devoted most of his time to talking about Apalachee women. Rather than discussing his unfair imprisonment, planned journey to San Agustín, or the internal struggle among rival Spanish factions in San Luis, the chief talked about the safety of his people and the growing limitations on his power. He began his testimony not with Doña Juana or her husband, but by correcting the claim that he had "ordered some women to the community fields." Matheo Chuba explained how he had stationed four young men to patrol the area but had not promised, let alone permitted, any female labor in the community fields of San Luis because of the rising numbers of slave raids.[87] He then tried repeatedly to explain to the new lieutenant governor that it was unsafe to allow Apalachee women to go "searching for it [seed]" or planting it in such an exposed setting.[88]

It is striking how differently Matheo Chuba and Doña Juana recalled the same event. She spoke of his time in jail to highlight her family's power to save him; he contextualized his imprisonment as part of Spanish efforts to circumvent Apalachee mobility, safety, and freedom. Matheo Chuba took this opportunity to school Spanish officials on how Apalachee leadership actually worked. He explained that he had no seeds or additional food, for "neither the Indian women or men gave him anything" simply because he was chief. On the contrary, Chief Matheo Chuba's wealth and power derived from his ability to protect his people, especially his female population.[89]

It was in the middle of his testimony about the new labor demands made on Apalachee women that Chief Matheo Chuba spoke of Doña Juana. He expressed no surprise or derision at their nighttime meeting in his cell; he simply and quickly included her in his account as he transitioned from talking about Native women working in the community fields to discussing his obligations as cacique of San Luis. As Matheo Chuba described an Apalachee world in turmoil, he pointed to the two Criolla women who came to rescue him. Translated and transcribed, the chief's words are mediated by many voices, and though it is not clear why he mentioned Doña Juana when he did, her mobility and power contrasted sharply with the Apalachee women that otherwise populated his testimony.

Chief Matheo Chuba's implicit comparison between the unnamed Native women in his testimony and the Florencia women in his cell revealed more than an Apalachee world under threat; it showed how Apalachee leaders registered those threats in 1687. Doña Juana was tangential to his story, as he was to hers, yet she offered a simple and tangible way for him to articulate a gendered violence that threaten his town. The women Matheo Chuba depended on were increasingly unsafe, harassed and enslaved by an enemy he left unmentioned. He focused on their safety and needs in order to explain the larger threats that Apalachees now faced. Matheo Chuba also pointed to the lieutenant governor, who had basically imprisoned him on a whim and shown that, although long-standing, the Apalachee-Spanish alliance was fraught. Doña Juana and her husband had freed Matheo Chuba this time, but their actions revealed more about the reach and arbitrariness of Spanish power than about meaningful efforts to safeguard Apalachee relations or protect Apalachee interests. Where Doña Juana saw the influence and power of her family, the Apalachee chief saw cracks in the foundation.

Almost twelve years later, Doña Juana left another archival mark that also involved an Apalachee chief, but one she assaulted rather than helped. In broad daylight and for everyone to see, Doña Juana "gave two slaps in the face to the cacique of San Luis because he had not brought her fish on one Friday," or so Don Patricio, cacique of Ivitachuco, and Don Andrés, cacique of San Luis, recounted in their letter. Their epistle was not specifically about Doña Juana. It was instead a careful letter that balanced loyalty-affirming praise for Florida officials with formal complaints about the egregious labor conditions in Apalachee, the daily interferences of the Franciscans, and concerns about land lost to cattle ranching.[90] Don Patricio and Don Andrés wrote in broad terms about the threats facing Apalachee, but their strategic political rhetoric lost some of its nuance and became rather candid when they addressed the "injuries as committed by Juana Caterina, wife of the said deputy."[91]

In the years since Matheo Chuba's release from jail, Apalachee had changed. The power of the Florencia family had expanded while Native leaders had struggled to preserve their influence. Confronted by rising violence both within and beyond their lands, the caciques of Ivitachuco and San Luis pointed to Doña Juana as a particularly dangerous threat. Her demands, rooted in her entitled sense of class power and Spanish authority, were built on profoundly destabilizing gendered forms of violence. With her "two slaps," Doña Juana was communicating more than a hunger for fish.

> [She] obliged the village to furnish six Indian women for the grinding every day without payment for their work; and although this was [contrary to] an order of the inspector, it is not observed, and notwithstanding, [they] continue doing it. And also that she be given an Indian to go and come every day with a pitcher of milk for the house.[92]

The "injuries" caused by Doña Juana were detestable. She abused Indian women. She expected work and food "without payment," and even though the laws strictly forbade this kind of behavior, she acted as she pleased. The Spanish enslavement of Native women in San Luis was a well-documented problem. Don Patricio and Don Andrés were by no means claiming that Doña Juana was exceptional in her actions, but she seemed exceptional in her immunity. They argued that she should not be beyond the reproach of the law.[93]

Don Patricio and Don Andrés wanted to hold her accountable. They went after her. They mentioned her by name. The caciques insisted that Doña Juana's demands and attack were about more than one Spanish woman acting badly. Her actions exemplified everything that was wrong in Spanish Apalachee: the abuse, the corruption, and the Spanish institutions that promised protection but ended by exposing Native people to more harm than good. While Doña Juana's 1709 petition complains about her hardships in Apalachee, the 1699 letter from the Apalachee chiefs describes the labor and exploitation of Native women that underwrote and made possible Spanish life in

San Luis. As Matheo Chuba had done a decade earlier, Don Patricio and Don Andrés pointed to Doña Juana to critique the gendered nature of colonial violence.

Perhaps the clearest expression of that violence and power came not from an elite Apalachee man discussing the struggles of Apalachee women, but from an Apalachee woman herself. The final Apalachee story about Doña Juana begins with the testimony of an Apalachee mother separated from her child by the capricious demands of the doña.

> One afternoon while this Indian woman was at the door of the house of the lieutenant [Jacinto] with a little daughter in her arms who was still nursing and was not walking on her own, but crawled on all fours, the lieutenant's wife [Juana] ordered her to go gather some chestnuts that she was craving for. And the Indian woman replied to her that she would have to go with that little one. And [Juana] again said that she should go and that she should leave her there and that they would [take] care of her. With that the poor Indian woman had to put the child on the ground and go to gather the chestnuts because of the fear that they had.[94]

Manuel de Quiñones, who wrote down this woman's words, was a relatively new arrival to La Florida. Traveling to Apalachee Native towns was one of his first assignments, if not his very first one. He had been appointed as secretary or notary to Captain Juan de Ayala y Escobar, the official surveyor and visitador of Apalachee.[95] Ayala had close familial ties and economic interests in Apalachee, and he was intimately connected to the powerful Florencia family who controlled much of the land, ranches, and trade in the region.

Apalachee leaders rightly viewed Ayala's close affiliations with the Florencia family with suspicion and apprehension. If any Apalachee leader approached the visitador with complaints or recommendations, Ayala never wrote them down. But Quiñones could not stand idly by. Shocked by the blatant abuse of power he witnessed, the secretary organized covert meetings to record Apalachee complaints without interference from Ayala or the Florencia family. Quiñones never explained how he managed to convince the Apalachee leadership that he was trustworthy or why he decided to take on this endeavor in the first place, but the devastating stories he heard and the bruises on their bodies that the Apalachee men showed him, left the secretary in a deep state of sadness: "Lastimeras que a mi me con tristaban" (pains that aggrieved me).[96]

The Apalachee woman who approached Quiñones early one morning did so without hesitation. She knew exactly who he was, and she demanded he listen to her. Though separating this woman's words from Quiñones's later recollections and writings is nearly impossible, it is important to note the individual details the woman provided to situate the story: she was nursing and holding her little baby when Doña Juana de Florencia approached. Immediately, what was personal and intimate became consumed by a profound and communal fear: "fear that *they* had."[97] The Apalachee woman's motherhood was personal. Her apprehension about the Spanish matriarch was widely shared. Despite the profound imbalance between Doña Juana, who was well known and well documented, and this Apalachee mother, who was not even given a name, this woman was not alone. She was the voice of and for so many other silenced and injured Native women.

The Apalachee woman had begrudgingly left her child and gone to gather chestnuts for Doña Juana. Although Doña Juana had promised to watch the Apalachee child left in her care, "after the Indian woman went [Juana] paid no more attention to the little child than if she had been a little dog."[98] The result was catastrophic. "The little girl, as she was missing her mother, while crawling along and crying, rolled away," and fell into a small hole with water. "And the little girl drowned in effect without anyone seeing her fall in and without anyone thinking about her until her mother came around." When she returned, the Apalachee woman first gave Doña Juana the chestnuts and then "she asked for her little daughter." No one knew where her child was. Her frantic survey of the area began, "searching for her here and searching for her there," until "an Indian man went into the spring and pulled the little drowned girl out."[99]

The Native woman, in telling, re-telling, and processing these horrendous events, thought about what had happened to her daughter after Juana had sent her away on a trivial errand. Had her daughter tried to crawl away from abuse and disdain? Had she tried to get back to her mother? Quiñones does not portray the little girl's crawling as careless or mistaken. This child's only crime "was missing her mother." Her death was on Juana's hands.

The Apalachee woman's deep anger and sorrow is evident in her reproach that her child died "without anyone seeing her" and "without anyone thinking about her." Doña Juana never mentions this horrific incident but instead spends time bemoaning the theft of her jewelry chest. The Apalachee woman had endured a loss that was clearly, exponentially, and incomparably more profound. Yet more people remarked on Doña Juana's *vaulito* than on the missing Apalachee girl. It took her mother's return, after hours of forced labor, to question her daughter's absence. Where was she? Had no one noticed her gone? Had no one cared?

This death was not merely an accidental drowning. It was part of a pattern of abuse, neglect, and personal violence inflicted by the Spaniards and especially the Florencia family. Quiñones concluded the account by asking his intended reader, the governor of Florida, to empathize with this distraught Native mother: "What this poor mother must have felt!" For Quiñones, this child's death was yet another example of the many abuses perpetrated by the Florencia family. For the Apalachee woman, the drowning was more than an item on a long list. It was the list. It was her daughter. It was a future taken.

Only Don Patricio Hinachuba, chief of Ivitachuco, managed to save his town in Apalachee from the violence of Queen Anne's War. In a remarkable feat, Don Patricio went out of his town and confronted Colonel Moore's army, which had come to raid Ivitachuco and raze Apalachee to the ground. Don Patricio knew the fate that had befallen his neighbors. He saw Doña Juana and her husband planning the evacuation of San Luis. And he knew the army before him would have few qualms about burning his town to the ground and carrying away with them any women and children they could apprehend. The chief's decision to ride out by himself to meet the sizeable army surprised the English colonel. Don Patricio contended that Ivitachuco was a formidable town, and though it would probably fall to the invading forces, the effort would take more men and resources than Moore probably wanted to deploy.

Don Patricio manipulated Moore's fears of repeating his failed 1702 campaign and offered instead an exchange: he would give the Native-English forces all the goods and silver in his town, and, in return, they would leave Ivitachuco unharmed.

The cacique of Ivitachuco succeeded. His deeds are only recounted in English sources; it seems that Don Patricio did not tell Spanish officials he had readily given up costly church furnishings to a Protestant invader in order to save his town.[100] Ever the experienced leader, Don Patricio knew that the safety he had secured was temporary. As violence ripped Apalachee apart in 1704, Don Patricio Hinachuba requested to move his family and community farther west, to a safer location.[101] Although his initial letter asking to relocate Ivitachuco is lost, Governor Zúñiga y Cerda's response gives insight into the chief's deeply personal request. Don Patricio "has asked me," the governor explained, "for permission so that his wife and children might travel to Pensacola for a short time until this province's condition changes in some way."[102] Don Patricio vowed that the move would be temporary and that he and his elder son would stay in the area and fight against English advances. But to truly save Apalachee, he had to protect "his wife and children," emphasizing the need to care for those who made and sustained Apalachee communities.[103]

Governor Zúñiga y Cerda refused the chief's petition, fearing a chain reaction that would leave all of Apalachee depopulated. The governor clarified: "My not having granted this petition has not been because I fail to recognize the adequate reasons you have, but rather because of the rumors that have come to my attention that their absence would be a source of affliction to you."[104] It is clear, however, that Zúñiga y Cerda was not actually concerned about how much Don Patricio would miss his wife and children; he was worried about what Apalachee men would do if their women and children moved elsewhere. Would Don Patricio stay and fight for the Spaniards if his wife and children were relocated to safety? The governor thought not. Don Patricio's gendered request for the safety of his people was met with an equally gendered rebuttal. Zúñiga y Cerda used the growing threat to Native women and children to galvanize Apalachee. Don Patricio's wife would remain in Ivitachuco to force Don Patricio to do the same. The governor made a calculated decision about the cost of Native women's lives vis-à-vis the protection afforded by their male kin. Don Patricio Hinachuba made very different calculations.

Defying the governor's orders, Don Patricio decided that his people's safety was paramount, and he moved his entire town to Abosaya, farther east in Timucua lands.[105] Ivitachuco at Abosaya became a town of refugees, home for displaced Apalachee people as well as Yguajas, Chiluques, and most likely Timucuas and Chacatos.[106] The safety Don Patricio so desperately wanted for his people proved elusive, however, and soon slave raiders began targeting his new town. Though these attacks on Ivitachuco at Abosaya in 1705 and 1706 are not as well documented as those in the main Apalachee towns, they show the centrality of Native initiative and power in the southern fronts of Queen Anne's War. Neither Moore nor any other leading English officer accompanied these later raids into Apalachee and Timucua. Florida officials took more than twenty-one days to send reinforcements to the area, and when Captain Don Joseph de Begambre finally reached Ivitachuco at Abosaya he thought he had arrived too late.

The town looked tattered and beaten, but Don Patricio Hinachuba and the people under his care were still fighting. Realizing that the enemy was still within reach, the Spanish captain rode after the slavers "with a group of infantry and Christian Indians with their arms." Begambre pursued "the enemy Indians that carried off as captives *all the women* with *all their children* and others of minor age."[107] In a rare moment of triumph for the Spanish-Native forces, they managed to surprise and overtake the Indian slavers. "Succeeding in having taken from the enemy the booty from the village and other slaves and people whom they carried off from this city," Begambre's army managed to "free from captivity so many women . . . except for a few they were holding in stocks, [whom] they [the slavers] killed during the skirmishes."[108]

Perhaps most striking, the attack on Ivitachuco at Abosaya exposed the logistics of taking and transporting Indian slaves, a seldom visible aspect of Indian slavery. Begambre noted the binds, the guards, and even the holding cells needed to keep Native women enslaved. He also pointed out that when Spanish forces surprised the Indian slavers, these English-armed Indians had killed the

Native women in the cells or simply refused to move them to safety during the fighting.[109] Indian slavery had particularly targeted Native women, something Begambre clearly observed in the makeshift cells in the slavers' camp and in the bodies killed in the crossfire. But this gendered violence had a much more profound and systemic impact than Begambre or any other Spanish colonial officer was likely to recognize, one that plays a central role in each of the three Apalachee accounts about Doña Juana.

Indian slavery and the violence of Queen Anne's War undid Don Patricio Hinachuba's efforts at Ivitachuco at Abosaya, forcing his people to move to San Agustín and end their time as an independent community. The residents of Ivitachuco at Abosaya discovered they were in good company, as most other Timucua and Apalachee suffered similar fates. Spanish officials noted the influx of Apalachees, Chacatos, Talapoosas, and Apalachicolas near Pensacola. Some of these Native refugees stayed, but many continued west toward Mobile.[110] Florida officials were not pleased, and they attempted to keep the remaining Apalachee communities within Spanish jurisdictions.

> [T]he governor of Pensacola offered very considerable presents to the chiefs . . . to make them return which they refused saying that the French assisted their allies better than did the Spaniards[;] the French furnished arms, in addition to the fact that they were not masters of their wives among the Spanish and that among the French they were at rest as to that.[111]

The Apalachee chiefs found Mobile safer, for them and for their families. In French lands, their wives were beyond the immediate reach of Indian slavery and the control of abusive Spanish haciendas and households, like Doña Juana's. The physical and sexual exploitation that their women had suffered in Spanish lands gave Native people a greater motivation to leave Florida than the offer of "very considerable presents" gave them to stay. But the chiefs' insistence that they, not the Spaniards, were now "masters of their wives" hints at a shift in matrilineal practices and values. Like Don Patricio's initial request to the governor that tried to use Spanish gender norms to his advantage, these efforts to protect Native women in the context of a deeply patriarchal European colonial society encouraged Apalachee men to assume more control over women's mobility, bodies, and labor.

Queen Anne's War tested the flexibility and power of existing gender norms. If Doña Juana entered the Spanish archive to win, Native women, like the ones captured from Ivitachuco, seemed to enter it to die. Native women were most visible in moments of violence and trauma, creating an almost unbendable historical arc that tied female Native bodies to loss, erasure, and death. But Native women were clearly so much more. They were what the Indian slavers wanted. They were what the town of Ivitachuco had lost and most desperately wanted returned. They were the people Matheo Chuba worried about and the ones Don Patricio and Don Andrés sought to protect. Native women were, as the grieving Apalachee mother asserted, the most valuable and, at the same time, the most vulnerable resources for their community.[112] Doña Juana had exploited the reproductive and productive labor of Native women; but Apalachees pushed back, linking Native women, as well as their knowledge and labor, to Apalachee sovereignty and survival. On the front lines of Queen Anne's War, Native women reframed Doña Juana's story of empire and power: they spoke instead of a vibrant Native world adapting, bending, and fighting for a future still within their grasp.

Epilogue

for what we choose and what we neglect to choose
for what we wish we'd known
for each hand unclasped tongue unbridled
one whisper falling short of heard

until they're home, until they are all home.

—ANNA MARIE SEWELL, "Washing the World"

THE NUMBER OF MURDERED and missing Native women and girls is astonishing in the worst possible meaning of that word. Since 2016, close to 6,000 American Indian and Alaska Native women and girls have been killed or disappeared, with less than 1 percent of that number ever reported to the Department of Justice. "Homicide is the third leading cause of death among Native girls and women aged 10 to 24, and the fifth leading cause of death for Native women aged 25 to 34."[1] The incomplete investigations, the lack of prosecution, and the many unresolved cases show a general disregard for the lives and struggles of Native women.

Native families, friends, communities, and activists have demanded the return of their loved ones and have deployed a variety of strategies to draw attention to the violence Native women and girls face, from data gathering to political lobbying; from official reports to twitter hashtags that list the names of Indigenous women who have yet to be found; and from the Native Women's Association of Canada's Faceless Dolls Project to the REDress project originated by Jaime Black, which displays brightly colored, disembodied gowns as haunting symbols of the emptiness left by murdered and missing Native women. The efforts to counter this epidemic of violence are as varied as they are evocative. Most share an underlying drive: make Native women visible.

That argument hardly seems revolutionary. After all, who would contest that Native women should appear in contemporary as well as historical accounts? Who would deny that they matter? At best, it seems like a straw-man argument. And yet, where are the Native women? Why has their disappearance, both today and in the archive, remained a common, normalized occurrence? In her poem "Trigger Warning or Genocide Is Worse Than Racism," Marcie Rendon writes: "don't tell me you don't see indians here / your only wish / is that we would / silently disappear."[2]

When we try to draw attention to the deaths disproportionately affecting contemporary Native communities, a longer history of abuse and neglect comes to the surface. The struggles facing Native women today are nothing new, and, as Sarah Deer has powerfully demonstrated, they are rooted in a long history of colonialism, oppression, and dispossession.[3] In this book I have tried to unearth some of these roots. On the one hand, the colonial past proves distant and foreign from anything taking place today; on the other hand, it bears some uncanny resemblances to the ways women, especially Native women, have to contend with rampant, systemic violence, an often aggressive indifference toward their livelihoods and lives, and even outright erasure from the worlds they inhabit and the narratives they produce.[4] But if this violence is historical, then so are Native women's survival, resistance, strength, and hope.

We need this whole history now more than ever. Native women and their stories help challenge core assumptions about who mattered in the early American world; they show the centrality, impact, and significance of gender in the dynamic adaptability of Native peoples; and they offer a new way of framing the wars and violence that shattered the region. By focusing mainly on Native women's absences and on the minimal role they seem to play in colonial sources that spend more time downplaying their importance, questioning their actions, and trivializing their contributions than they do recording their words, however, we have emphasized questions and uncertainties over Native women's knowledge and deeds. We have repeated and replicated colonial silences, not addressed them.

It becomes clear, then, that Native women's long historical shadows are not cast solely by their absences but also by our continued and repeated denial of their presence (and present). Today's ravaging epidemic of murdered and missing Indigenous women is perhaps the most devastating extension of that denial. The violence used to keep Native women silent and silenced, now as well as in the colonial era, has created very peculiar narratives that center those who murder and kill, while utterly neglecting those who perished, escaped, endured, or resisted. This silence, in both life and death, is not the whole story, and it must not be the only story we tell of Native women.

This book began with Timucua Eve demanding more. She did not simply want the knowledge that the forbidden apple would grant; she wanted to be equal to or perhaps even more commanding than her husband. Timucua Eve spoke of a power that the Yndia Chacata carried as she fled slavery and searched for safety. Her murder story can certainly be read as one about violence and suffering, but it is also a story of hope and possibilities. The Yndia Chacata constructed, inhabited, and strove to continue building the world around her. Echoes of her efforts can be found in the demands made by Ychu Francisca, Afac Gabriela, and the many other unnamed women petitioners in Timucua and Apalachee. Clear articulations of the central place of Native women's work and standing in their matrilineal communities can also be heard from María Magdalena and her son Benito of Machava, Chief Diocsale of San Carlos de Achercatane, and the Guale chief Juan Chicasle of Santa María. The important roles and responsibilities of women even came into focus in settings like San Agustín and San Luis; the experiences of Black women like Isavel de los Ríos and the conceits of Criolla women like Doña Juana de Florencia show how gender was central to expressions and assertions of power in this colonial context.

Stories of Native women are often buried in colonial documents, but sometimes they are simply right there. To find them requires a careful eye as well as a discerning ear that listens and believes their experiences. It requires legitimizing their knowledge and practices. It requires privileging what Native women did, made, and defended. And it requires reading many colonial documents, often in non-European languages, and seeing them for all their possibilities, not simply for their limitations and absences. After all, women in the early South were more than the archival fragments that documented their struggles. They had full and complicated lives, and they were neither absent nor silent. They were loud, sometimes overwhelmingly so. Nocotosibonihabela, Nenesibonihabela. They must be heard. They must be seen.

Notes

Introduction

1. Francisco Pareja, *Catecismo en Lengua Timuquana y Castellana* . . . (Mexico City: Imprenta de Ioan Ruyz [1627]), folios 54–66.
2. Charles Hudson, *Knights of Spain, Warriors of the Sun: Hernando De Soto and the South's Ancient Chiefdoms* (Athens: University of Georgia Press, 1997), 174–175, 181–192. For an overview of Native women as leaders, see Ruth Trocolli, "Elite Status and Gender: Women Leaders in Chiefdom Societies of the Southeastern U.S." (PhD diss., University of Florida, 2006), 90–124. Stephen Edward Reilly, "A Marriage of Expedience: The Calusa Indians and Their Relations with Pedro Menéndez De Avilés in Southwest Florida, 1566–1569," *Florida Historical Quarterly* 59, no. 4 (1981): 395–421. Jeanne L. Gillespie, "Amerindian Women's Influence on the Colonial Enterprise of Spanish Florida," *Southern Quarterly* 51, no. 4 (2014): 84–102, 85–86.
3. To read the Timucua language George Aaron Broadwell has built a database of Timucua texts: https://www.webonary.org/timucua/. For more on the Timucua language, see Alejandra Dubcovsky and George Aaron Broadwell, "Writing Timucua: Recovering and Interrogating Indigenous Authorship," *Early American Studies: An Interdisciplinary Journal* 15, no. 3 (2017): 409–441. Alejandra Dubcovsky, Georga Aaron Broadwell, Robert Clark, Doug Henning, Carly Tozian, and Seth Katenkamp, "Hebuano: Open Access Materials and Lessons for Learning the Timucua Language," https://hebuano.wordpress.com/. Timucua language work is done in consultation with Timucua descendants, Seminole Tribe of Florida Historic Preservation Office, Seminole Nation Historic Preservation Office, and the Muscogee Nation Historic and Cultural Preservation Department. For more on the Timucua language, see Jerald T. Milanich

and William C. Sturtevant, *Francisco Pareja's 1613 Confessionario: A Documentary Source for Timucuan Ethnography* (Tallahassee: Florida Division of Archives, History, and Records Management, 1972), 1–21; Jerald T. Milanich, *The Timucua* (Cambridge: Blackwell Publishers, 1996), 172–173. James M. Crawford, "Timucua and Yuchi: Two Language Isolates of the Southeast," in *The Languages of Native America: Historical and Comparative Assessment*, ed. Lyle Campbell and Marianne Mithun (Austin: University of Texas Press, 1979); Ives Goddard, "The Description of the Native Languages of North America Before Boas," in *The Handbook of North American Indians*, vol. 17 (Washington, D.C.: Smithsonian Institution, 1996), 17–42.

4. Pareja, *Catecismo* (1627), folio 55. Special thanks to George Aaron Broadwell, Doug Henning, and Seth Katenkamp for helping with this translation. This new translation is made through interlinear glossing, a standard linguistic method that breaks each word in a sentence into its constituent morphemes, lists the meaning of each morpheme, and demonstrates how the meaning of the entire sentence is related to the meaning of its parts.
5. LeAnne Howe, *Choctalking and Other Realities* (San Francisco: Aunt Lute Books, 2013), 8–9. Dubcovsky and Broadwell, "Writing Timucua," (2017): 409–441.
6. For the importance of working with Native language texts, see David A. Chang, *The World and All the Things upon It: Native Hawaiian Geographies of Exploration* (Minneapolis: University of Minnesota Press, 2016), x–xii. Chris Pexa, *Translated Nation: Rewriting the DakhóTa OyáTe* (Minneapolis: University of Minnesota Press, 2019), 1–15. See also a special issue on "A Language of Empire, a Quotidian Tongue: The Uses of Nahuatl in New Spain," *Ethnohistory* 59, no. 4 (2012), which features articles by Yanna Yannakakis, John F. Schwaller, Mark Z. Christensen, Robert C. Schwaller, Laura E. Matthew and Sergio F. Romero, Martin Nesvig, and Caterina Pizzigoni.
7. "Juan Márquez Cabrera to Antonio Matheos, n.d. [December 1685]," Archivo General de India (hereafter, AGI) Mexico 56, cited also in John H. Hann, "Cloak and Dagger in Apalachicole Province in Early 1686," *Florida Historical Quarterly* 78, no. 1 (1999): 74–93, 80.
8. Theda Perdue, *Cherokee Women: Gender and Culture Change, 1700–1835* (Lincoln: University of Nebraska Press, 1998), 3. See also Rebecca Kugel and Lucy Eldersveld Murphy, *Native Women's History in Eastern North America before 1900: A Guide to Research and Writing* (Lincoln: University of Nebraska Press, 2007). For an overview of the field, see Michelle LeMaster, "Pocahontas Doesn't Live Here Anymore: Women and Gender in the Native South Before Removal," *Native South* 7 (2014): 1–32. Brooke Bauer, *Becoming Catawba* (Tuscaloosa: University of Alabama Press, forthcoming).

9. *The Narrative of Cabeza de Vaca*, ed. Rolena Adorno and Patrick Charles Pautz (Lincoln: University of Nebraska Press, 2003). Andrés Reséndez, *A Land So Strange: The Epic Journey of Cabeza de Vaca* (New York: Basic Books, 2007). Mariah Wade, "Go-between: The Roles of Native American Women and Alvar Núñez Cabeza de Vaca in Southern Texas in the 16th Century." *Journal of American Folklore* 112, no. 445 (1999): 332–342. For women's presence in early English narratives, see Helen C. Rountree, "Powhatan Indian Women: The People Captain John Smith Barely Saw," *Ethnohistory* 45, no. 1 (1998): 1–29.
10. For the need to interrogate rather than replicate the archive, see Alyssa Mt. Pleasant, Caroline Wigginton, and Kelly Wisecup, "Materials and Methods in Native American and Indigenous Studies: Completing the Turn," *William and Mary Quarterly* 75, no. 2 (2018): 207–236. Jim Downs, "When the Present Is Past: Writing the History of Sexuality and Slavery," in *Sexuality and Slavery: Reclaiming Intimate Histories in the Americas*, ed. Daina Ramey Berry and Leslie M. Harris (Athens: University of Georgia Press, 2018), 189–204.
11. For works by Native women that try to center or highlight Native women, see Patricia Albers and Beatrice Medicine, *The Hidden Half: Studies of Plains Indian Women* (Washington, D.C.: University Press of America, 1983); Lisa Tanya Brooks, *Our Beloved Kin: A New History of King Philip's War* (New Haven: Yale University Press, 2018); Brenda J. Child, *Holding Our World Together: Ojibwe Women and the Survival of Community*, Penguin Library of American Indian History (New York: Viking, 2012); Sarah Deer, *The Beginning and End of Rape: Confronting Sexual Violence in Native America* (Minneapolis: University of Minnesota Press, 2015); Mishuana Goeman, *Mark My Words: Native Women Mapping Our Nations* (Minneapolis: University of Minnesota Press, 2013); LeAnne Howe, "Embodied Tribalography: Mound Building, Ball Games, and Native Endurance in the Southeast," *Studies in American Indian Literatures* 26, no. 2 (2014): 75–93; Rebecca Kugel, *To Be the Main Leaders of Our People: A History of Minnesota Ojibwe Politics, 1825–1898* (East Lansing: Michigan State University Press, 1998); Michelene E. Pesantubbee, *Choctaw Women in a Chaotic World: The Clash of Cultures in the Colonial Southeast* (Albuquerque: University of New Mexico Press, 2005); Audra Simpson, *Mohawk Interrupts: Political Life Across the Borders of Settler States* (Durham: Duke University Press, 2014). For other works that center Native women, see Juliana Barr, *Peace Came in the Form of a Woman: Indians and Spaniards in the Texas Borderlands* (Chapel Hill: University of North Carolina Press, 2007); Gunlög Maria Fur, *A Nation of Women: Gender and Colonial Encounters Among the Delaware Indians* (Philadelphia: University of Pennsylvania Press, 2009); Tiya Miles, "The Narrative of Nancy, a Cherokee Woman," *Frontiers: A Journal of Women Studies* 29, no. 2-3 (2008): 59–80; Theda Perdue, *Cherokee Women* (1998); Susan Sleeper-Smith, *Indigenous Prosperity*

and American Conquest: Indian Women of the Ohio River Valley, 1690–1792 (Chapel Hill: University of North Carolina and Omohundro Institute of Early American History and Culture, 2018).

12. For an overview of the field, see Terri L. Snyder, "Refiguring Women in Early American History," *William and Mary Quarterly* 69, no. 3 (2012): 421–450, and Nancy A. Hewitt, "Introduction," in *A Companion to American Women's History* (Malden: Blackwell, 2008): xii–xviii. For approaches in women's history: Erica Ball, Tatiana Seijas, and Terri L. Snyder, eds., *As If She Were Free: A Collective Biography of Women and Emancipation in the Americas* (Cambridge: Cambridge University Press, 2020); Juliana Barr, *Peace Came in the Form of a Woman* (2007); Steven C. Hahn, *The Life and Times of Mary Musgrove* (Gainesville: University Press of Florida, 2012); Jessica Marie Johnson, *Wicked Flesh: Black Women, Intimacy, and Freedom in the Atlantic World* (Philadelphia: University of Pennsylvania Press, 2020); Gina M. Martino, *Women at War in the Borderlands of the Early American Northeast* (Chapel Hill: University of North Carolina Press, 2018); Theda Perdue, *Cherokee Women* (1998); Susanah Shaw Romney, *New Netherland Connections: Intimate Networks and Atlantic Ties in Seventeenth-Century America* (Chapel Hill: University of North Carolina Press and Omohundro Institute of Early American History and Culture, 2014); Nancy Shoemaker, *Negotiators of Change: Historical Perspectives on Native American Women* (New York: Routledge, 1995); Susan Sleeper-Smith, *Indian Women and French Men: Rethinking Cultural Encounter in the Western Great Lakes* (Amherst: University of Massachusetts Press, 2001); Jennifer M. Spear, *Race, Sex, and Social Order in Early New Orleans* (Baltimore: Johns Hopkins University Press, 2009); Sophie White, *Voices of the Enslaved: Love, Labor, and Longing in French Louisiana* (Chapel Hill: University of North Carolina Press and Omohundro Institute of Early American History and Culture, 2019); *Women's Negotiations and Textual Agency in Latin America, 1500–1799*, Women and Gender in the Early Modern World, ed. Mónica Díaz and Rocío Quispe-Agnoli (London: Routledge, 2017).

13. John H. Hann, "Evidence Pertinent to the Florida Cabildo Controversy and the Misdating of the Juan Márquez Cabrera Governorship," *Florida Historical Quarterly* 79, no. 1 (2000): 68–83. Amy Bushnell, *The King's Coffer: Proprietors of the Spanish Florida Treasury, 1565–1702* (Gainesville: University of Florida Press, 1981): 107, 115–116.

14. For the only bishop's visit, see "A 17th Century Letter of Gabriel Diaz Vara Calderon, Bishop of Cuba, Describing the Indians and Indian Missions of Florida," ed. Lucy L. Wenhold, Smithsonian Miscellaneous Collections, vol. 95, no. 16 (Washington, D.C.: Smithsonian Institution Press, 1936), 12–14.

15. For different chronologies of Native history, see James F. Brooks, "Women, Men, and Cycles of Evangelism in the Southwest Borderlands,

A.D. 750 to 1750," *American Historical Review* 118, no. 3 (2013): 738–764; Juliana Barr, "There's No Such Thing as 'Prehistory': What the Longue Durée of Caddo and Pueblo History Tells Us About Colonial America," *William and Mary Quarterly* 74, no. 2 (2017): 203–240.

16. "The Account by a Gentleman from Elvas," in *The de Soto Chronicles: The Expedition of Hernando de Soto to North America in 1539–1543*, vol. 1, ed. Lawrence A. Clayton, Vernon James Knight, Jr., and Edward C. Moore, trans. James Alexander Robinson (Tuscaloosa: University of Alabama Press, 1993): 85–86. Christina Snyder, "The Lady of Cofitachequi: Gender and Political Power Among Native Southerners," in *South Carolina Women: Their Lives and Times*, ed. Marjorie J. Spruill, Valinda W. Littlefield, and Joan Marie Johnson (Athens: University of Georgia Press, 2009): 11–25. For a good overview of Native women leaders, see *Cacicas: The Indigenous Women Leaders of Spanish America, 1492-1825*, ed. Margarita R. Ochoa and Sara Vicuña Guengerich (Norman: University of Oklahoma Press, 2021), 9–42.
17. Ruth Trocolli, "Elite Status and Gender: Women Leaders in Chiefdom Societies of the Southeastern U.S.," 78–117.
18. "Petition from Juan and Agustín, Timucua Indians," July 6, 1636, AGI SD 27B, accessed Jeannette Thurber Connor Collection, Reel 2, P.K. Yonge Library, University of Florida, Gainesville (hereafter, PKY). John H. Hann, *A History of the Timucua Indians and Mission* (Gainesville: University Press of Florida, 1996), 26.
19. "Testimony of Manuel Calderón," May 7, 1660, part of the Residencia of Diego de Rebolledo, AGI Contaduría 964, folios 182–194. For a transcription of this testimony and many others, see John Worth, "The Timucua Missions of Spanish Florida and the Rebellion of 1656" (PhD diss., University of Florida, 1992), 356–480. "Auto Zalamototo," January 13, 1678, transcribed and translated in John Hann, *Visitations and Revolts in Florida, 1657–1695*, in *Florida Archaeology* 7 (1993), 141.
20. For the problems of privileging European perspective, see Michael J. Witgen, *An Infinity of Nations: How the Native New World Shaped Early North America* (Philadelphia: University of Pennsylvania Press, 2012), 15.
21. Jean M. O'Brien, *Firsting and Lasting: Writing Indians out of Existence in New England*, Indigenous Americas (Minneapolis: University of Minnesota Press, 2010). Zeb Tortorici, "Archival Seduction: Indexical Absences and Historiographical Ghosts," *Archive Journal*, 2015, http://www.archivejournal.net/essays/archival-seduction. Rather than replicate the archive, see Jim Downs, "When the Present Is Past."
22. Marilou Awiakta, *Selu: Seeking the Corn-Mother's Wisdom* (Golden, Colo.: Fulcrum Publishing, 1993), 35, emphasis in the original. Sarah Hill, *Weaving New Worlds: Southeastern Cherokee Women and Their Basketry* (Chapel Hill: University of Chapel Hill, 1987). See also Sarah H. Hill,

Weaving New Worlds: Southeastern Cherokee Women and Their Basketry (Chapel Hill: University of North Carolina Press, 1987).

23. Jean M. O'Brien, "Historical Sources and Methods in Indigenous Studies: Touching on the Past, Looking to the Future," in *Sources and Methods in Indigenous Studies*, ed. Chris Andersen and Jean M. O'Brien (London: Routledge, 2017), 15–22. Alyssa Mt. Pleasant, "Salt, Sand, and Sweetgrass: Methodologies for Exploring the Seasonal Basket Trade in Southern Maine," *American Indian Quarterly* 38, no. 4 (Fall 2014): 411–426. Audra Simpson, "On Ethnographic Refusal: Indigeneity, 'Voice' and Colonial Citizenship," *Junctures*, no. 9 (2007): 67–80. For contemporary scholarship on how to think through women's voices in the archive, see Marisa J. Fuentes, *Dispossessed Lives: Enslaved Women, Violence, and the Archive* (Philadelphia: University of Pennsylvania Press, 2016). Jessica Marie Johnson, *Wicked Flesh: Black Women, Intimacy, and Freedom in the Atlantic World.* Sophie White, *Voices of the Enslaved: Love, Labor, and Longing in French Louisiana.*
24. For good overviews, see Alan Gallay, *The Indian Slave Trade: The Rise of the English Empire in the American South, 1670–1717* (New Haven: Yale University Press, 2002); Christina Snyder, *Slavery in Indian Country: The Changing Face of Captivity* (Cambridge: Harvard University Press, 2010).
25. Verner W. Crane, "The Southern Frontier in Queen Anne's War." *American Historical Review* 24 (1919): 379–395.
26. For thinking through violence in colonial sources, see Ned Blackhawk, *Violence over the Land: Indians and Empires in the Early American West* (Cambridge: Harvard University Press, 2006). Matthew Jennings, *New Worlds of Violence: Cultures and Conquests in the Early American Southeast* (Knoxville: University of Tennessee Press, 2011).

Chapter One. An Yndia Chacata Guide

1. "Declaración de Santiago," March 2, 1695. Autos Hechos de Oficio de la Justicia, por el Ayudante Andrés García, Teniente de la Provincia de Timucua, contra Santiago, natural del Pueblo de San Pedro, año 1695. Archivo General de India (AGI), Escribanía de Cámara (hereafter EC), 157, 176. The bulk of the trial has been translated in John Hann, *Visitations and Revolts in Florida, 1657–1695*, in *Florida Archaeology* 7 (1993). I will use his translations. Hann, *Visitations*, 281. For the importance and value of investigating these cases, see Nicole Eustace, *Covered with Night : A Story of Murder and Indigenous Justice in Early America*. (New York: Liveright Publishing Corporation, 2021).
2. Virginia Moore Carney, *Eastern Band Cherokee Women: Cultural Persistence in Their Letters and Speeches* (Knoxville: University of Tennessee Press, 2005), 35. Zoe Todd, "An Indigenous Feminist's Take on the Ontological Turn: 'Ontology' Is Just Another Word for Colonialism," *Journal of Historical Sociology* 29, no. 1 (2016): 4–22. Leila K. Blackbird and Caroline

Dodds Pennock, "How Making Space for Indigenous People Changes History," in *What Is History, Now? How the Past and Present Speak to Each Other*, ed. Helen Carr and Suzannah Lipscomb (London: Weidenfeld and Nicolson: 2021), 265–380.

3. Kathleen DuVal, *The Native Ground: Indians and Colonists in the Heart of the Continent* (Philadelphia: University of Philadelphia Press, 2006), 1–12.
4. AGI EC 157A Cuaderno I. See also John H. Hann, "Apalachee Counterfeiters in St. Augustine," *Florida Historical Quarterly* 67, no. 1 (1988): 52–68.
5. "The Origin of Corn," in John Reed Swanton, *Myths and Tales of the Southeastern Indians* (Washington, D.C.: Government Printing Office, 1929), 9–10.
6. These oral stories also contain many more subtle messages, including lessons about balanced gender norms, about the power of land and preservation, and even about the taboos surrounding food preparation and consumption. Daniel Heath Justice, *Why Indigenous Literatures Matter* (Waterloo, ON: Wilfrid Laurier University Press, 2020): 5–6, 24–31. Colonial officials recognized and relied on women's knowledge about subsistence and foodways; see "Testimony of Teresa Martín, an Yndia natural" and "Luisa Mendez, india" February 4, 1600, AGI SD 224. Accessed from John Tate Lanning Collection, Collection #266. St. Louis Mercantile Library, University of St. Louis, Missouri.
7. Thomas King, *The Truth About Stories: A Native Narrative*, Massey Lectures Series (Toronto, ON: House of Anansi Press, 2003), 24.
8. Marilou Awiakta, *Selu: Seeking the Corn-Mother's Wisdom* (Golden, Colo.: Fulcrum Publishing, 1993), 208.
9. King, *The Truth About Stories*, 2. For the value of including Native women's stories, see Kelly Julianna Morgan, "Dakotapi Women's Traditions: A Historical and Literary Critique of Women as Culture Bearers" (PhD diss., University of Oklahoma, 1997), 44–78. Craig S. Womack, *Red on Red: Native American Literary Separatism* (Minneapolis: University of Minnesota Press, 1999), 15. Deena Rymhs, "But the Shadow of Her Story: Narrative Unsettlement, Self-Inscription, and Translation in Pauline Johnson's Legends of Vancouver," *Studies in American Indian Literatures* 13, no. 4 (2001): 51–78. For how to think about women's presence, see Edward Anthony Polanco, " 'I Am Just a *Tiçitl*': Decolonizing Central Mexican Nahua Female Healers, 1535–1635," *Ethnohistory* 65, no. 3 (2018): 441–463. For thinking through mutilated bodies as evidence, see Sylvia Sellers-García, *The Woman on the Windowsill* (New Haven: Yale University Press, 2020), 194; and Ninna Nyberg Sørensen, "Governing Through the Mutilated Female Body: Corpse, Bodypolitics, and Contestation in Contemporary Guatemala in Governing the Dead," in *Governing the Dead*, ed. Finn Stepputat (Manchester: Manchester University Press, 2016): 203–225.
10. For the long history of violence against Native women, see Sarah Deer, *The Beginning and End of Rape: Confronting Sexual Violence in Native*

America (Minneapolis: University of Minnesota Press, 2015), 16–30, 60–79; Sarah Deer, "Heeding the Voice of Native Women: Toward an Ethic of Decolonization," *North Dakota Law Review* 81 (2005): 807–822; and Karen Anderson, *Chain Her by One Foot: The Subjugation of Women in Seventeenth-Century New France* (New York: Routledge, 1991). For contemporary comparison, see "The Missing and Murdered Indigenous Women Database," https://www.mmiwdatabase.com.

11. Charles M. Hudson, *The Southeastern Indians* (Knoxville: University of Tennessee Press, 1976): 251–257.
12. AGI EC 157. Hann, *Visitations*, 276.
13. Ibid.
14. "Diego's Testimony in San Matheo," February 20, 1695. AGI EC 157, folio 174. Hann, *Visitations*, 278. "Lázaro's Testimony," February 19, 1695. AGI EC 157, folios 173–174. Hann, *Visitations*, 277.
15. Ibid.
16. "Diego's Testimony in San Matheo," February 20, 1695. AGI EC 157, folio 174. Hann, *Visitations*, 278.
17. For the importance of paths, see Joshua A. Piker, " 'White & Clean' & Contested: Creek Towns and Trading Paths in the Aftermath of the Seven Years' War," *Ethnohistory* 50, no. 2 (2003): 315–347; and Angela Pulley Hudson, *Creek Paths and Federal Roads: Indians, Settlers, and Slaves and the Making of the American South* (Chapel Hill: University of North Carolina Press, 2010), 11–36.
18. "Testimony of Chucuta Antonio," February 29, 1695, in San Matheo, AGI EC 157, folio 175. Hann, *Visitations*, 279.
19. Ibid.
20. "Lázaro's Testimony," February 19, 1695, AGI EC 157, folios 173–174. Hann, *Visitations*, 277. For clothing, space, and female presentation in a slightly different context, see Amanda Flather, *Gender and Space in Early Modern England* (New York: Boydell Press, 2007), 27.
21. For Spanish efforts in Timucua territory see Jerald T. Milanich, *The Timucua* (Cambridge: Blackwell Publishers, 1996); John Worth, "Spanish Missions and the Persistence of Chiefly Power," in *The Transformation of the Southeastern Indians, 1540–1760*, ed. Robbie Ethridge and Charles Hudson (Jackson: University Press of Mississippi, 2002): 39–65; and Paul Kelton, *Epidemics and Enslavement: Biological Catastrophe in the Native Southeast, 1492–1715* (Lincoln: University of Nebraska Press, 2007), 101–159. For the Timucua Rebellion see John E. Worth, *The Timucuan Chiefdoms of Spanish Florida*, vol. 2, *Resistance and Destruction* (Gainesville: University Press of Florida, 1998), 38–65; Justin B. Blanton, "The Role of Cattle Ranching in the 1656 Timucuan Rebellion: A Struggle for Land, Labor, and Chiefly Power," *Florida Historical Quarterly* 92, no. 4 (2014): 667–684; and Alejandra Dubcovsky, *Informed Power: Communication in the Early American South* (Cambridge: Harvard University Press, 2016), 68–96.

22. "Testimony of Chucuta Antonio," February 29, 1695, in San Matheo, AGI EC 157, folio 175. Hann, *Visitations*, 278.
23. Chucuta Antonio gave his testimony in Apalachee, which went through two interpreters, first translated into Timucua by Francisco, an Indian leader from Asile, and then into Spanish by Juan Bautista Martínez, a Timucua Indian from Santa Fé.
24. "Conde de Galve to His Majesty," May 15, 1693, in Irving A. Leonard, *Spanish Approach to Pensacola, 1689–1693* (Albuquerque: The Quivira Society, 1939), 123–131. John Reed Swanton, *Early History of the Creek Indians and Their Neighbors* (Washington, D.C.: Government Printing Office, 1922), 95, 119. That being said, during the Spanish investigation into the so-called Chacato revolt of 1675, Chata Alonso was hired to translate from Apalachee to Chacato, signaling that, though related, the languages were distinct. See Governor Hita de Salazar's Investigation into Juan Fernández Diosale's Conduct in 1676, AGI EC, accessed through Stetson Collection, Reel 27, PKY. Diego de Quiroga y Losada discussing Fray Juan Paiva, San Luis 1677, April 1, 1688. AGI SD 243. John Hann, "The Chacato Revolt Inquiry," *Florida Archaeology* 7 (1997): 29–52.
25. AGI EC 157. Hann, *Visitations*, 294, footnote 10. *Tolocano*, as it is more commonly spelled, was comprised of "parched maize, flour, alone or mixed with nut-meat flour and persimmons or berries, that was carried."
26. "Lázaro's Testimony," February 19, 1695. AGI EC 157, folios 173–174. Hann, *Visitations*, 277.
27. Bernard Romans, *A general map of the southern British colonies in America, comprehending North and South Carolina, Georgia, East and West Florida, with the neighboring Indian countries, from the modern surveys of Engineer de Brahm, Capt. Collet, Mouzon, & others, and from the large hydrographical survey of the coasts of East and West Florida* (London: Printed for R. Sayer and J. Bennett, map, chart, and printsellers, 1776). https://www.loc.gov/item/gm71005467/. For Native women and water, see Brooke Bauer, *Becoming Catawba* (Tuscaloosa: University of Alabama, forthcoming), chapter 1.
28. For earlier materials on the Chacatos, see "Governor Damián Vega Castro y Pardo letter to the King," August 12, 1639. AGI SD 225 Reel 11. PKY. John H. Hann, "Translation of Governor Rebolledo's 1657 *Visitation of Three Florida Provinces*," *Florida Archaeology* 2 (1986). "A 17th Century Letter of Gabriel Díaz Vara Calderón, Bishop of Cuba, Describing the Indians and Indian Missions of Florida," ed. Lucy L. Wenhold, Smithsonian Miscellaneous Collections (Washington, D.C.: Smithsonian Institution Press, 1936), 8–9. Governor Pablo Hita y Salazar, Letter to the Queen, August 24, 1675. AGI SD 839. John E. Worth, *The Timucuan Chiefdoms of Spanish Florida*, vol. 1, *Assimilation* (Gainesville: University Press of Florida, 1998), 18. John H. Hann, *Apalachee: The Land Between the Rivers* (Gainesville: University of Florida Press, 1988), 28–29. For the so-called

Chacato revolt, see AGI EC 156A. Translated in John Hann, *Visitations*, 31–76.

29. "Carta del Gobernador Don Laureano de Torres Ayala a SM," March 1, 1695, in Manuel Serrano y Sanz, *Documentos Historicos De La Florida y La Luisiana* (Madrid: Librería General de Victoriano Suárez, 1912), 224–226.

30. Patricia Galloway, "Where Have All the Menstrual Huts Gone? The Invisibility of Menstrual Seclusion in the Late Prehistoric Southeast," in *Women in Prehistory: North America and Mesoamerica*, ed. Cheryl Claasen and Rosemary A. Joyce (Philadelphia: University of Pennsylvania Press, 1997): 47–62. Gregory A. Waselkov and Philip J. Carr, "Avoidance Strategies of a Displaced Post-Mississippian Society on the Northern Gulf Coast, Circa 1710," in *Contact, Colonialism, and Native Communities in the Southeastern United States*, ed. Edmond A. Boudreaux, Maureen Meyers, and Jay K. Johnson (Gainesville: University Press of Florida, 2020): 126–139. James Adair, *The History of the American Indians, Particularly Those Nations Adjoining to the Mississippi, East and West Florida, Georgia, South and North Carolina, and Virginia* (London: Printed for Edward and Charles Dilly, 1775), 424. John Reed Swanton, *The Indians of the Southeastern United States*, [United States] Bureau of American Ethnology Bulletin 137 (Washington, D.C.: Government Printing Office, 1946), 554. Paul Kelton, *Epidemics and Enslavement: Biological Catastrophe in the Native Southeast, 1492–1715* (Lincoln: University of Nebraska Press, 2007), 18. For a contemporary reading, see Kim Anderson, Barbara Clow, and Margaret Haworth-Brockman, "Carriers of Water: Aboriginal Women's Experiences, Relationships, and Reflections," *Journal of Cleaner Production* 60 (2013): 11–17. Joanne Barker, "Confluence: Water as an Analytic of Indigenous Feminisms," *American Indian Culture and Research Journal* 43, no. 3 (2019): 1–40.

31. John Lawson, *A New Voyage to Carolina; Containing the Exact Description and Natural History of That Country: Together with the Present State Thereof. And a Journal of a Thousand Miles, Travel'd Thro' Several Nations of Indians. Giving a Particular Account of Their Customs, Manners, &c.* (London: [s.n.], 1709). 15–37, 151. C. Margaret Scarry and John F. Scarry, "Native American 'Garden Agriculture' in Southeastern North America," *World Archaeology* 37 (2005): 262. Melanie Yazzie and Cutcha Risling Baldy, "Introduction: Indigenous Peoples and the Politics of Water," *Decolonization: Indigeneity, Education & Society* 7, no. 1 (2018): 1–18.

32. "Lázaro's Testimony," February 19, 1695. AGI EC 157, folios 173–174. Hann, *Visitations*, 277. *Tocalito* is neither a Timucuan nor Muskogean word; from its context, it refers to a sack or satchel to transport food. The word is perhaps a corruption of the Nahualt word *itacatl*, meaning "provisions for the road." It is possible that the scribe and/or translator used that word, since it would not be the only borrowed Nahuatl word in

the trial. For thinking through female mobility in colonial spaces, see Marisa J. Fuentes, *Dispossessed Lives: Enslaved Women, Violence, and the Archive*, 28–30, 37–45; and Shauna J. Sweeney, "Market Marronage: Fugitive Women and the Internal Marketing System in Jamaica, 1781–1834," *William and Mary Quarterly* 76, no. 2 (2019): 197–222. For food and survival, see Tiya Miles, *All That She Carried: The Journey of Ashley's Sack, a Black Family Keepsake* (New York: Random House, 2021), 193–221.

33. I am very thankful to Dr. Ian Thompson, Tribal Historic Preservation Officer of the Choctaw Nation, Dave Scheidecker, Research Coordinator in the Tribal Historic Preservation Office of the Seminole Nation, and Rene Bennett of the Apalachee Nation for the local and profound knowledge they shared as I tried to re-create the Yndia Chacata's journey. John H. Hann, "The Use and Processing of Plants by Indians of Spanish Florida," *Southeastern Archaeology* 5, no. 2 (1986): 91–102.
34. "Lázaro's Testimony," February 19, 1695. AGI EC 157, folios 173–174. Hann, *Visitations*, 277.
35. Kate Driscoll Derickson, Lorraine Dowler, and Nicole Laliberte, "Advances in Feminist Geography," *Oxford Research Encyclopedia of International Studies* (2010): 1–32. Robbie Ethridge, "Creating the Shatter Zone: Indian Slave Traders and Collapse of Southeastern Chiefdoms," in *Light on the Path: The Anthropology of the Southeastern Indians*, ed. Robbie Ethridge and Thomas J. Puckhahn (Tuscaloosa: University of Alabama Press, 2006), 208–219. For more on Native women's mobility see Nathaniel Holly, " 'The Indian Woman Peggy': Mobility, Marriage, and Power in an Early American City," *Early Modern Women: An Interdisciplinary Journal* 14 (2019): 85–94.
36. "Lázaro's Testimony," February 19, 1695. AGI EC 157, folios 173–174. Hann, *Visitations*, 277.
37. "Diego's Testimony" in San Matheo, February 20, 1695. AGI EC 157, folio 174. Hann, *Visitations*, 278.
38. For historizing and working against violence against Native women see Deer, *The Beginning and End of Rape*, 16–30, 60–79; Karen Anderson, *Chain Her by One Foot*; Kim Anderson, *A Recognition of Being: Reconstructing Native Womanhood* (Toronto: Canadian Scholars' Press, 2001), 57–78; Rosemary Georgeson and Jessica Hallenbeck, "We Have Stories: Five Generations of Indigenous Women in Water," *Decolonization: Indigeneity, Education & Society* 7, no. 1 (2018): 20–38. Daniel Maltz and JoAllyn Archambault, "Gender and Power in Native North America," in *Women and Power in Native North America*, ed. Laura F. Klein and Lillian A. Ackerman (Norman: University of Oklahoma Press, 1995), x, 294.
39. For the escape and flight of a Tawasa Indian named Lamhatty in 1708, see Gregory A. Waselkov, "Indian Maps of the Colonial Southeast," in *Powhatan's Mantle*, ed. Gregory A. Waselkov, Peter H. Wood, and Tom Hatley (Lincoln: University of Nebraska, 1989), 462–469.

40. New and upcoming work by Beck Goetz, Andrew Johnson, Hailey Negrin, and Honor Sachs attempts to recover the experiences of enslaved Native people in the Southeast.
41. Thomas Nairne, *A Letter from South Carolina* . . . (London: Printed for A. Baldwin, 1710), 34–35. For the idea of the "Spanish Indian" in English sources, see Kirsten Silva Gruesz, *Cotton Mather's Spanish Lessons: A Story of Language, Race, and Belonging in the Early Americas*. (Cambridge, Mass.: The Belknap Press of Harvard University Press, 2022), 101–120.
42. Christina Snyder, *Slavery in Indian Country: The Changing Face of Captivity* (Cambridge: Harvard University Press, 2010), and Robbie Ethridge, *From Chicaza to Chickasaw: The European Invasion and the Transformation of the Mississippian World, 1540–1715* (Chapel Hill: University of North Carolina Press, 2010). For these patterns in a different context, see Brett Rushforth, "A Little Flesh We Offer You": The Origins of Indian Slavery in New France." *William and Mary Quarterly* 60, no. 4 (2003): 777–808.
43. *Mapping the Mississippian Shatter Zone: The Colonial Indian Slave Trade and the Regional Transformation in the American South*, ed. Robbie Ethridge and Sheri M. Shuck-Hall (Lincoln: University of Nebraska Press, 2009). For centering Native stories, see Margaret Kovach, *Indigenous Methodologies: Characteristics, Conversations, and Contexts* (Toronto: University of Toronto Press, 2009), 94–108.
44. Governor José de Zúñiga y Cerda, "Primera, y breve relación de las favorables noticias" (Madrid, 1703), JCB. For visual representation of the slaving raids, see Hammerton's "Map of the Southeastern Part of North America" (1721), Yale Center for British Art, New Haven, Connecticut. For mentions of small raids, see "Antonio Matheos to Juan Marquez Cabrera," San Luis, May 19, 1686, AGI SD 839, in John H. Hann, "Cloak and Dagger in Apalachicole Province in Early 1686," *Florida Historical Quarterly* 78, no. 1 (1999): 81–88. Hann, *Apalachee*, 264–283. "Francisco de Córcoles y Martínez about siege of Abosaya," January 30, 1706, AGI SD 858, folios 285–287 [1115] Hann HC-Comps_2004 [36]. John E. Worth, "Razing Florida: The Indian Slave Trade and the Devastation of Spanish Florida, 1659–1715," in Ethridge and Shuck-Hall, *Mapping the Mississippian Shatter Zone*, 295–311. For attacks against women, see Bauer, *Becoming Catawba*, chapter 4, and Theda Perdue, *Cherokee Women: Gender and Culture Change, 1700–1835* (Lincoln: University of Nebraska Press, 1998), 86–87.
45. For a longer rendition of the attack on Ayubale, see Alejandra Dubcovsky, " 'All of Us Will Have to Pay for These Activities': Colonial and Native Narratives of the 1704 Attack on Ayubale," *Native South* 10 (2017): 1–18. "Zúñiga y Cerda to the King," October 6, 1704, AGI SD 858. James Moore, "An Account of What the Army Did, under the Command of Col. Moore, in His Expedition Last Winter, against the Spaniards and the Spanish Indians," in *Historical Collections*, ed. B. R. Carroll (New York: Harper & Brothers, 1836), 576. Hann, *Apalachee*, 233.
46. The trial concerning the murder of the Yndia Chacata also placed inter-Indian rivalries front and center. Santiago had hunted two bears in Ivita-

chuco-claimed land and returned home to San Pedro with the spoils. Don Patricio, chief of Ivitachuco, had tried to punish Santiago for his earlier transgressions, but failed. The Yndia Chacata offered the perfect opportunity for Don Patricio to rally his "vassals" against Santiago, or so Santiago's lawyer argued. AGI EC 157. Hann, *Visitations*, 283. John Hann and Amy Bushnell, the two scholars who have examined the case, strongly disagree on the veracity of this claim. Bushnell blames Don Patricio for falsely incriminating Santiago, and Hann argues that Santiago merely had a good lawyer. Though there is evidence that supports both claims, what is truly evident are the complex relations among Chacatos, Apalachees, and Timucuas. Amy Bushnell, "Patricio De Hinachuba: Defender of the Word of God, the Crown of the King, and the Little Children of Ivitachuco," *American Indian Culture and Research Journal* 3, no. 3 (1979): 1–21. AGI EC 157. For discussions of territoriality in other borderlands, see Sol Lanteri, Silvia Ratto, Ingrid de Jong, and Victoria Pedrotta, "Territorialidad Indígena Y Políticas Oficiales De Colonización: Los Casos De Azul Y Tapalqué En La Frontera Sur Bonaerense (Siglo Xix)," *Antíteses* 4, no. 8 (2011): 729–752.

47. Christina Snyder, *Slavery in Indian Country*, 36–37, 92–110. See Kirsten Fischer, "The Imperial Gaze: Native American, African American, and Colonial Women in European Eyes," in *A Companion to American Women's History*, ed. Nancy Hewitt (Maiden, Mass.: Blackwell, 2002). "Carta del Gobernador Don Laureano de Torres Ayala a SM," March 1, 1695, in Manuel Serrano y Sanz, *Documentos Históricos*, 224. Alan Gallay, *The Indian Slave Trade: The Rise of the English Empire in the American South, 1670–1717* (New Haven: Yale University Press, 2003). Hayley Negrin, "Possessing Native Women and Children: Slavery, Gender, and English Colonialism in the Early American South, 1607–1730" (PhD diss. [in progress], New York University). D. Andrew Johnson, "Displacing Captives in Colonial South Carolina: Native American Enslavement and the Rise of the Colonial State After the Yamasee War," *Journal of Early American History* 7, no. 2 (Summer 2017): 115–140.
48. Waselkov and Carr, "Avoidance Strategies," in Boudreaux et al., *Contact, Colonialism, and Native Communities in the Southeastern United States*, 126–139.
49. "Journal of Don Laureano de Torres y Ayala," August 5, 1693, in Leonard, *Spanish Approach to Pensacola*, 228–254, especially 230.
50. "Carta del Gobernador Don Laureano de Torres Ayala a SM," March 1, 1695, in Manuel Serrano y Sanz, *Documentos Históricos*, 224–228.
51. Ibid., 207–224.
52. Mishuana Goeman, "Ongoing Storms and Struggles: Gendered Violence and Resource Exploitation," in *Critically Sovereign: Indigenous, Gender, Sexuality, and Feminist Studies*, ed. Joanne Barker (Durham: Duke University Press, 2017), 99–126, 114.
53. "Auto Pablo Hita y Salazar," June 8, 1675. AGI SD 839. Stetson Collection Reel 14, PKY.

54. "Expedición Contra los Chiscas, 1677," in Manuel Serrano y Sanz, *Documentos Históricos*, 207.
55. Ibid., 205–216. Baszile, "Apalachee Testimony in Florida: A View of Slavery from the Spanish Archives," in *Indian Slavery in Colonial America*, ed. Alan Gallay (Lincoln: University of Nebraska Press, 2009), 189–205.
56. "Expedición Contra los Chiscas, 1677," in Manuel Serrano y Sanz, *Documentos Históricos*, 209. Marching under the banner of the Virgin was not an unusual sight, and historians like Juliana Barr have documented many examples in the late eighteenth-century southwest; however, in Florida the 1676 Apalachee attack against the Chiscas is one of the few recorded accounts of this practice. Amy Turner Bushnell, *Situado y Sabana: Spain's Support System for the Presidio and Mission Provinces of Florida*, Anthropological Papers of the American Museum of Natural History, vol. 3 (1994), 144.
57. George E. Lankford, "Chacato, Pensacola, Tohomé, Naniaba, and Mobila," in *Handbook of North American Indians: Southeast*, ed. Raymond D. Fogelson and William C. Sturtevant (Washington, D.C.: Smithsonian Institution, 2004), 664–668. For the political strategies of small nations, see Elizabeth N. Ellis, *The Great Power of Small Nations: Indigenous Diplomacy in the Gulf South* (Philadelphia: University of Pennsylvania Press, 2022).
58. For thinking through how smaller groups develop and sustain alliances, see Elizabeth Ellis, "The Natchez War Revisited: Violence, Multinational Settlements, and Indigenous Diplomacy in the Lower Mississippi Valley," *William and Mary Quarterly* 77, no. 3 (2020): 441–472. Elizabeth Ellis. *The Great Power of Small Nations: Indigenous Diplomacy in the Gulf South* (Philadelphia: University of Pennsylvania Press, 2022).
59. Bushnell, *Situado y Sabana*, 175. "The junta de Guerra that Governor Torres called in St. Augustine approved the expedition, endorsed the choice of the cacique Matheo Chuba to lead it, and asked that the number of participants be limited to 400, including leaders. They instructed Captain Perez to issue 4 peruleras of gunpowder and 2000 musketballs to the Apalaches, and 6 Spanish soldiers, if they wanted to take the chance of the '*mala union*' that might result from putting Spanish soldiers under Indian command." See also Jennifer Baszile, "Apalachee Testimony in Florida," 189–190.
60. For discussions on Native movement and agency, see Stephen Warren, *The Worlds the Shawnees Made: Migration and Violence in Early America* (Chapel Hill: University of North Carolina Press, 2014), 1–25. Denise I. Bossy, "Introduction: Recovering Yamasee History," in *The Yamasee Indians: From Florida to South Carolina*, ed. Denise I. Bossy (Lincoln: University of Nebraska Press, 2018), 1–24. For gender and mobility in a different context, see Jennifer L. Morgan, *Laboring Women: Reproduction and Gender in New World Slavery* (Philadelphia: University of Pennsylvania Press, 2004), 169; and Amélie Allard, "Gendered Mobilities: Performing Masculinities in the Late Eighteenth-Century Mobile Fur Trade Community," *Ethnohistory* 65, no. 1 (2018): 75–99.

61. "Nos matan a nuestros parientes, y lo que mas es de sentie es los exclavos que se lleban y las mosas que con ellos ban hacienzo." Expedición Contra los Chiscas, 1677," in Manuel Serrano y Sanz, *Documentos Históricos*, 207.
62. Ibid.
63. For thinking about the gendered violence of colonialism, see Maile Arvin, Eve Tuck, and Angie Morrill, "Decolonizing Feminism: Challenging Connections between Settler Colonialism and Heteropatriarchy," *Feminist Formations* Vol. 25, No. 1 (2013), 8–34. For the specific erasures in narratives about enslavement, I consulted with Dr. Ian Thompson, Historic Preservation Department, April 2020. And with the Tribal Historic Preservation Office, Seminole Tribe Florida, March 2020.
64. Recorded by Dr. A. S. Gatschet from Judge George W. Stidham, in John Reed Swanton, *Myths and Tales of the Southeastern Indians*, 115–116. "Gatschet attributes much credit for his work to Judge George W. Stidham of Eufaula, Indian Territory. Stidham was born in 1817 in Alabama of Scotch-Irish and Creek parents. His family settled at Choska, south of Coweta in Oklahoma, following removal from Alabama. . . . He served the Creek Nation as chief judge on the Creek Supreme Court, helped to draft the Okmulgee constitution for the Creek Nation, and in the 1870s served on at least fifteen tribal delegations to Washington, D.C."; see Bill Grantham, *Creation Myths and Legends of the Creek Indians* (Gainesville: University Press of Florida, 2002), 280.
65. Craig S. Womack, *Red on Red*, 191.
66. Daniel Heath Justice, *Our Fire Survives the Storm: A Cherokee Literary History*. Indigenous Americas (Minneapolis: University of Minnesota Press, 2006), 49.
67. For the concept of "survivance," see Gerald Vizenor, "Aesthetics of Survivance: Literary Theory and Practice," in *Survivance: Narratives of Native Presence*, ed. Gerald Vizenor (Lincoln: University of Nebraska Press, 2008), 1–24.
68. "Visitation, 1694–1695," Joaquín de Florencia. AGI EC 157. Hann, *Visitations*, 188. For a longer discussion of tribute, vassals, and *vasallo* see Bradley J. Dixon, " 'His One Netev Ples': The Chowans and the Politics of Native Petitions in the Colonial South," *William and Mary Quarterly* 76, no. 1 (2019): 41–74.
69. "Visitation, 1694–1695," Joaquín de Florencia. AGI EC, 157. Hann, *Visitations*, 187. Fred Lamar Pearson, Jr., "The Florencia Investigation of Spanish Timucua," *Florida Historical Quarterly* 51, no. 2 (1972): 166–176. For discussions of community building in borderland regions, see Cynthia Radding, "Colonial Spaces in the Fragmented Communities of Northern New Spain," in *Contested Spaces of Early America*, ed. Juliana Barr and Edward Countryman (Philadelphia: University of Pennsylvania Press, 2014), 115–141.
70. "Visitation, 1694–1695," Joaquín de Florencia AGI EC 157. Hann, *Visitations*, 187. On Chacato refugees see Ann S. Cordell, *Continuity and Change*

in Apalachee Pottery Manufacture: A Technological Comparison of Apalachee-Style and Colono Ware Pottery from French Colonial Old Mobile and Mission San Luis de Talimali. Archaeological Monograph, 1 (Mobile: University of South Alabama Press, 2001), 29–30. Gregory A. Waselkov and Bonnie Gums, *Plantation Archaeology at Riviere aux Chien, ca. 1725–1848* (Mobile: University of South Alabama Press, 2000), 184.

71. Miller Shores Wright, "The Development of Slaving Societies in the Americas: Marginal Native and Colonial Slavers in Sao Paulo and Carolina, 1614–1715" (PhD diss., Rice University, 2021), 272–282.
72. Kim Tallbear, "Standing With and Speaking as Faith: A Feminist-Indigenous Approach to Inquiry," *Journal of Research Practice* 10, no. 2 (2014): 1–7.
73. Justice, *Our Fire Survives the Storm*, 53.
74. Deer, *The Beginning and End of Rape*, 18–20. Theda Perdue, *Cherokee Women: Gender and Culture Change, 1700–1835* (Lincoln: University of Nebraska Press, 1998), 3. For a general overview see Laura F. Klein and Lillian A. Ackerman, *Women and Power in Native North America* (Norman: University of Oklahoma Press, 1995).

Chapter Two. Standing in Place, Not Standing Still

1. John E. Worth, *The Timucua Chiefdoms of Spanish Florida*, vol. 2, *Resistance and Destruction* (Gainesville: University Press of Florida, 1998), 1–26, quote on 13. For a longer history of attacks on women's crops in the area, see John H. Hann, *A History of the Timucua Indians and Mission* (Gainesville: University Press of Florida, 1996), 56. For the importance of women's agricultural knowledge see Susan Sleeper-Smith, *Indigenous Prosperity and American Conquest: Indian Women of the Ohio River Valley, 1690–1792* (Chapel Hill: University of North Carolina Press and Omohundro Institute of Early American History and Culture, 2018). For discussions of hunger in early America, see Rachel B. Herrmann, *No Useless Mouth: Waging War and Fighting Hunger in the American Revolution* (Ithaca: Cornell University Press, 2019), chapter 1.
2. "Junta in Santa María in Guale," February 10, 1695, AGI EC 157 A. Cuaderno 1. Folios 131–132, cited in John Hann, *Visitations and Revolts in Florida, 1657–1695*, in *Florida Archaeology* 7 (1993), 235. Hann, *A History of the Timucua Indians and Mission*, 95.
3. "Junta in Santa María in Guale," February 10, 1695, AGI EC 157 A. Cuaderno 1. Folios 131–132, cited in Hann, *Visitations*, 235.
4. For Native women as targets of assaults, see Maeve Kane, " 'She Did Not Open Her Mouth Further': Haudenosaunee Women as Military and Political Targets During and After the American Revolution," in *Women in the American Revolution: Gender, Politics, and the Domestic World*, ed. Barbara Oberg (Charlottesville: University of Virginia Press, 2019): 83–102.

5. "Diego de Jaén Responds to Charges," April 1695, AGI EC 157 A. Cuaderno 1. Folios 143–145, cited in Hann, *Visitations*, 253.
6. For more information on Salish environmental and scientific practices, beautifully depicted by Molly Murphy Adams in figure 4, see Mitchell Rose Bear Don't Walk, "Recovering Our Roots: The Importance of Salish Ethnobotanical Knowledge and Knowledge and Traditional Food Systems to Community Wellbeing on the Flathead Indian Reservation in Montana" (MA thesis, University of Montana, 2019); Adam N. Johnson, Regina Sievert, Michael Durglo, Sr., Vernon Finley, Louis Adams, and Michael H. Hofmann, "Indigenous Knowledge and Geoscience on the Flathead Indian Reservation, Northwest Montana: Implications for Place-Based and Culturally Congruent Education," *Journal of Geoscience Education* 62, no. 2 (2014): 187–202; and the Salish–Pend d'Oreille Culture Committee, the Elders Cultural Advisory Council, and the Confederated Salish and Kootenai Tribes, *The Salish People and the Lewis and Clark Expedition* (Lincoln: University of Nebraska Press, 2005).
7. "Diego de Jaén Responds to Charges," April 1695, AGI EC 157 A. Cuaderno 1. Folios 143–145, cited in Hann, *Visitations*, 253.
8. Ibid.
9. John H. Hann, "Translation of Alonso de Leturiondo's Memorial to the King of Spain," *Florida Archaeology* 2 (1986): 165–225. "Alonso de Leturiondo to His Majesty," April 29, 1697. AGI SD 235, no 143. See also John H. Hann, "The Use and Processing of Plants by Indians of Spanish Florida," *Southeastern Archaeology* 5, no. 2 (1986): 91–102.
10. "Petition by María, cacica of San Francisco," January 25, 1678, April 1695, AGI EC 156 B. Folios 528–530; Hann, *Visitations*, 138. Amy Turner Bushnell, "Ruling 'the Republic of Indians' in Seventeenth-Century Florida," in *Powhatan's Mantle*, ed. Gregory A. Waselkov, Peter H. Wood, and Tom Hatley (Lincoln: University of Nebraska Press, 1989), 195–214. For the role of cacicas in other borderlands, see Florencia Roulet, "Mujeres, Rehenes Y Secretarios: Mediadores Indígenas En La Frontera Sur Del Río De La Plata Durante El Período Hispánico," *Colonial Latin American Review* 18, no. 3 (2009): 303–337.
11. Daniel Heath Justice, *Our Fire Survives the Storm: A Cherokee Literary History*. Indigenous Americas (Minneapolis: University of Minnesota Press, 2006), 27–34. Mishuana Goeman, *Mark My Words: Native Women Mapping Our Nations* (Minneapolis: University of Minnesota Press, 2013): 1–40, especially 15. Kathryn E. Holland Braund, "Guardians of Tradition and Handmaidens to Change: Women's Roles in Creek Economic and Social Life During the Eighteenth Century," *American Indian Quarterly* 14, no. 3 (1990): 239–258, and *Deerskins and Duffels: The Creek Indian Trade with Anglo-America, 1685–1815* (Lincoln: University of Nebraska Press, 1993). Clara Sue Kidwell, "Choctaw Women and Cultural Persistence in Mississippi," in *Negotiators of Change: Historical Perspectives on Native American Women*, ed. Nancy Shoemaker (New York: Routledge,

1995), 115–134. For the adaptability of Native women's practices, see Sarah H. Hill, *Weaving New Worlds: Southeastern Cherokee Women and Their Basketry* (Chapel Hill: University of North Carolina Press, 1997); James Taylor Carson, "From Corn Mothers to Cotton Spinners: Continuity in Choctaw Women's Economic Life, a.d. 950–1830," in *Women of the American South: A Multicultural Reader*, ed. Christie Anne Farnham (New York: New York University Press, 1997), 8–25. For Latin American context, see Magali Barreto Ávila, "La Lucha De Las Mujeres Indígenas Por El Territorio. La Producción Del Espacio Del Tianguis Campesino En La Ciudad De Ocosingo, Chiapas," in *Des/Posesión: Género, Territorio Y Luchas Por La Autodeterminación*, ed. Marisa Belausteguigoitia Rius and María Josefina Saldaña-Portillo (México: Universidad Nacional Autónoma de México, 2015), 101–124.

12. "Cacique of Machava, 1674," AGI SD 234. Cited translation from Appendix B, Worth, *The Timucua Chiefdoms*, vol. 2. 192–197.
13. For more on the so-called Timucua Rebellion see, Worth, *The Timucua Chiefdoms*, vol. 2, 48–65. Justin B. Blanton, "The Role of Cattle Ranching in the 1656 Timucua Rebellion: A Struggle for Land, Labor, and Chiefly Power," *Florida Historical Quarterly* 92, no. 4 (2014): 667–684.
14. "Cacique of Machava, 1674," AGI SD 234. Cited translation from Appendix B, Worth, *The Timucua Chiefdoms*, vol. 2, 196.
15. "Cacique of Machava, 1674," AGI SD 234. Cited translation from Appendix B, Worth, *The Timucua Chiefdoms*, vol. 2, 194.
16. Worth, *The Timucua Chiefdoms*, vol. 2, 196.
17. The letters were probably written in Timucua since Benito and Gregorio spoke through interpreters. For more on Timucua literacy, see Alejandra Dubcovsky and George Aaron Broadwell, "Writing Timucua: Recovering and Interrogating Indigenous Authorship," *Early American Studies: An Interdisciplinary Journal* 15, no. 3 (2017): 409–441; and Alejandra Dubcovsky and George Aaron Broadwell, "Chief Manuel's 1651 Timucua Letter: The Oldest Letter in a Native Language of the United States," *Proceedings of the American Philosophical Society* 164, no. 4 (2020).
18. "Francisco de Pareja to the king," March 8, 1599, Reel 7, Stetson Collection, PKY, as quoted in Daniel Stowell, *Timucuan Ecological and Historic Preserve: Historic Resource Study* (Atlanta: National Park Service, 1996); Jerald T. Milanich, *The Timucua* (Cambridge: Blackwell Publishers, 1996), 109–110.
19. For discussions of abandoned towns and population loss, see "Council in San Pedro de Potohiriba," December 7, 1694, in Joaquín de Florencia, Visitation, 1694–1695. AGI EC 157. Hann, *Visitations*, 200. [Visitation of the Tocopaca of Vacissa at Ivitachuco], December 3, 1694, Hann, *Visitations*, 172. John H. Hann, *Apalachee: The Land Between the Rivers* (Gainesville: University of Florida Press, 1988), 15–20.
20. "Cacique of Machava, 1674," AGI SD 234. Cited translation from Appendix B, Worth, *The Timucua Chiefdoms*, vol. 2, 196.

21. Council houses were similar to most Timucua houses in their palm thatch and wooden pole construction and in their lack of Spanish construction hardware like nails, iron, or spikes. As Allison Bigelow has shown in the Taino context, the "circular structure reflected and refracted . . . cosmologies, communicating symbolic registers of cultural value"; Allison Margaret Bigelow, *Mining Language: Racial Thinking, Indigenous Knowledge, and Colonial Metallurgy in the Early Modern Iberian World* (Chapel Hill: University of North Carolina Press and Omohundro Institute of Early American History and Culture, 2020), 64–65. Christopher B. Rodning, "Mounds, Myths, and Cherokee Townhouses in Southwestern North Carolina," *American Antiquity* 74, no. 4 (2009): 627–663.
22. John H. Hann, "1630 Memorial of Fray Francisco Alonso De Jesus on Spanish Florida's Missions and Natives," *The Americas* 50, no. 1 (1993): 85–105, 94. For the importance of the council fires, see Heidi Bohaker, *Doodem and Council Fire: Anishinaabe Governance Through Alliance* (Toronto: University of Toronto Press, 2020).
23. See descriptions of cacica Doña María, in "Letter from Gonzalo Méndez de Canzo," AGI SD 224, folios 144–156. Francis J. Michael and Kathleen M. Kole, "Murder and Martyrdom in Spanish Florida: Don Juan and the Guale Uprising of 1597," *American Museum of Natural History Anthropological Papers*, vol. 95 (2011): 99. Antonio Arguelles, "Visitation to Guale and Mocama," AGI EC 156B, folios 519–530.
24. "Order to Captain Martín Alcaide de Córdoba to go to San Juan del Puerto and invest the cacique whose right it is," in the Orders of Francisco de la Guerra y Vega, January 17, 1665, included in Manuel Montiano's 1739 report on Guale, AGI SD 2584, cited in John E. Worth, *The Struggle for the Georgia Coast: An 18th-Century Spanish Retrospective on Guale and Mocama* (New York: American Museum of Natural History, 1995), 70–72. Fred Lamar Pearson, Jr., "The Arguelles Inspection of Guale: December 21, 1677–January 10, 1678," *Georgia Historical Society* 59, no. 2 (1975): 210–222.
25. "[San Juan del Puerto]," January 8, 1678; Hann, *Visitations*, 93.
26. Ibid. For more on Merenciana, see John H. Hann, "St. Augustine's Fallout from the Yamasee War," *Florida Historical Quarterly* 68, no. 2 (1989): 181–201. Ruth Trocolli, "Elite Status and Gender: Women Leaders in Chiefdom Societies of the Southeastern U.S." (PhD diss., University of Florida, 2006), 101–103.
27. Sarah Deer, *The Beginning and End of Rape: Confronting Sexual Violence in Native America* (Minneapolis: University of Minnesota Press, 2015), 25.
28. Gregorio de Movilla, *Forma breve de Administrar a los Indios y Españoles que Viven entre Ellos* (Mexico: Imprenta de Iuan Ruyz, 1635), folio 14.
29. Movilla, *Forma breve* . . . 1635 folios 15–17.

30. For a similar discussion in a different context, see Juliana Barr, *Peace Came in the Form of a Woman: Indians and Spaniards in the Texas Borderlands* (Chapel Hill: University of North Carolina Press, 2007), 121.
31. Special thanks to Robert Clark, Qibiro Ano (The Great Deer Lineage), for his insights and many exchanges about Timucua familial terms. John Reed Swanton, *Terms of Relationship in Timucua* (Washington, D.C.: [Printed at the J. W. Bryan Press], 1916).
32. Robert H. Jackson, "Una Mirada a los Patrones Demográficos de las Misiones Jesuitas de Paraguay," *Fronteras de la Historia* (Bogotá, Colombia: Instituto Colombiano de Antropología e Historia [ICANH], 2004), vol. 9, 129–178. For reducciones in Española, see Esteban Mira Caballos, "La Primera Utopía Americana: Las Reducciones De Indios De Los Jerónimos En La Española (1517–1519)," *Jahrbuch für Geschichte Lateinamerikas—Anuario de Historia de America Latina* 39, no. 1 (2013): 9–35.
33. Bonnie McEwan, "Hispanic Life on the Seventeenth-Century Florida Frontier," *Florida Anthropologist* 44, no. 2–4 (1991): 255–267. John H. Hann, "Summary Guide to Spanish Florida Missions and Visitas, with Churches in the Sixteenth and Seventeenth Centuries," *The Americas* 66, no. 4 (1990): 417–513.
34. For the incredible variability of mission experience in Florida, the better-excavated sites in Guale offer interesting comparisons. See Rebecca Saunders, *Stability and Change in Guale Indian Pottery, A.D. 1300–1702* (Tuscaloosa: University of Alabama Press, 2000). Elliot Blair, "Making Mission Communities: Population Aggregation, Social Networks, and Communities of Practice at 17th Century Mission Santa Catalina De Guale" (PhD thesis, University of California, Berkeley, 2015). Carey J. Garland, Laurie J. Reitsema, Clark Spencer Larsen, and David Hurst Thomas, "Early Life Stress at Mission Santa Catalina De Guale: An Integrative Analysis of Enamel Defects and Dentin Incremental Isotope Variation in Malnutrition," *Bioarchaeology International* 2 (2018): 75–94.
35. Amy Turner Bushnell, *Situado y Sabana: Spain's Support System for the Presidio and Mission Provinces of Florida.* Anthropological Papers of the American Museum of Natural History, vol. 3 (1994), 28.
36. "Auto Concerning Chacatos," October 3, 1675. AGI EC 156, folios 119–142. Hann, *Visitations*, 36–43. See also Lisa Brooks, *Our Beloved Kin: A New History of King Philip's War* (New Haven: Yale University Press, 2018): 7–9.
37. Sarah M. S. Pearsall, " 'Having Many Wives' in Two American Rebellions: The Politics of Households and the Radically Conservative," *American Historical Review* 118, no. 4 (2013): 1001–1028.
38. "Carlos, Principal cacique," October 5, 1675; Hann, *Visitations*, 50. Joseph Hall, "Confederacy Formation on the Fringes of Spanish Florida," *Mediterranean Studies* 9 (2000): 123–141. John H. Hann, "Cloak and Dagger in Apalachicole Province in Early 1686," *Florida Historical Quarterly* 78, no. 1 (1999): 74–93.

39. "[Report on Chacato]," September 10, 1674, AGI SD 234, *1675 Visitation*, 34–35.
40. C. Margaret Scarry and John F. Scarry, "Native American 'Garden Agriculture' in Southeastern North America," *World Archaeology* 37 (2005): 259–274. H. M. Foster II, "Optimization of Horticulture Among the Muscogee Creek Indians of the Southeastern United States," *Journal of Anthropological Archaeology* 22 (2003): 411–424.
41. Quote from John Worth, as cited in Elliot H. Blair and David Hurst Thomas, "The Guale Uprising of 1597: An Archaeological Perspective from Mission Santa Catalina De Guale (Georgia)," in *Indigenous Landscapes and Spanish Missions: New Perspectives from Archaeology and Ethnohistory*, ed. Lee M. Panich and Tsim D. Schneider (Phoenix: University of Arizona Press, 2014), 29. For the connection between Spanish missions in Florida and violence, see Charles Cobb, "Indigenous Negotiations of Missionization and Religious Conversion," in *The Routledge Handbook of the Archaeology of Indigenous-Colonial Interaction in the Americas*, ed. L. M. Panich and S. L. Gonzalez (London: Routledge, 2021), 163–179.
42. Sarah M. S. Pearsall, *Polygamy: An Early American History* (New Haven: Yale University Press, 2019), 27–38.
43. Theda Perdue, *Cherokee Women: Gender and Culture Change, 1700–1835* (Lincoln: University of Nebraska Press, 1998), 44.
44. John H. Hann, *The Native American World Beyond Apalachee: West Florida and the Chattahoochee Valley* (Gainesville: University Press of Florida, 2006), 33–44. John H. Hann, "Chacato Troubles (1674–1675)," in *Colonial Wars of North America, 1512–1763: An Encyclopedia*, ed. Alan Gallay (New York: Garland, 1996): 111–112.
45. For example, Juan Ebanjelista, who served as an interpreter for the Spaniards during the Franciscan revolt against the Chacatos, was married to an Apalachee woman from Ivitachuco and, following matrilocal practices, lived with his wife in the powerful Apalachee town. "Auto Concerning Chacatos," October 3, 1675. Hann, *Visitations*, 45.
46. For critiques of Native male stereotypes, see Louise Erdrich, *Love Medicine: A Novel* (Toronto: Bantam Books, 1985); Louise Erdrich, *The Last Report on the Miracles at Little No Horse* (New York: HarperCollins, 2001). Angela Laflen, "Unmaking the Self-Made Man: Louise Erdrich's Fictional Exploration of Masculinity," in *Women Constructing Men: Female Novelists and Their Male Characters, 1750–2000*, ed. Katharina Rennhak and Sarah S. G. Frantz (Lanham: Lexington Books, 2011), 207–226.
47. Jerald T. Milanich and William C. Sturtevant, *Francisco Pareja's 1613 Confessionario: A Documentary Source for Timucuan Ethnography* (Tallahassee: Florida Division of Archives, History, and Records Management, 1972), 1–21; Folio 184. Dubcovsky and Broadwell, "Writing Timucua," *Early American Studies* (2017): 409–441.

48. In John Reed Swanton, *Myths and Tales of the Southeastern Indians* (Washington, D.C.: Government Printing Office, 1929), 19, 62–63, 66, 91.
49. "The Owl Gets Married," and "The Huhu Gets Married," *Myths of the Cherokee* (Washington, D.C.: Government Printing Office, 1902), 292–293.
50. "Auto Concerning the Rebellion of the Chacatos," October 3, 1675. Hann, *Visitations*, 45.
51. The so-called Chacato Revolt has parallels to the Guale uprising of 1597, in which Franciscan efforts to stop polygamous practices also incited unrest. See Francis J. Michael and Kathleen M. Kole, "Murder and Martyrdom in Spanish Florida." Sarah M. S. Pearsall, " 'Having Many Wives' in Two American Rebellions: The Politics of Households and the Radically Conservative," *American Historical Review* 118, no. 4 (2013): 1001–1028.
52. "Juan Fernández de Florencia," Hann, *Visitations*, 43.
53. "Fray Rodrigo de la Barrera to Deputy Governor Andrés Peres," July 26, 1675, Hann, *Visitations*, 38.
54. "Elena, wife of Carlos," October 5, 1675, Hann, *Visitations*, 50. Clara Sue Kidwell, "Indian Women as Cultural Mediators," *Ethnohistory* 39, no. 2 (1992): 97–107. Karen L. Kilcup, " 'We Planted, Tended, and Harvested Our Corn': Native Mothers, Resource Wars, and Conversion Narratives," in *Fallen Forests: Emotion, Embodiment, and Ethics in American Women's Environmental Writing, 1781–1924* (Athens: University of Georgia Press, 2013), 21–73. Denise K. Lajimodiere, "Ogimah Ikwe: Native Women and Their Path to Leadership," *Wicazo Sa Review* 26, no. 2 (2011): 57–82, especially 58–60. Theda Purdue, "Cherokee Women and the Trail of Tears," *Journal of Women's History* 1, no. 1 (1989): 14–30.
55. "Elena, wife of Carlos," October 5, 1675, Hann, *Visitations*, 50. Another account of this interaction is in "Nicolás, witness in San Nicolas," Hann, *Visitations*, 47.
56. "Elena, wife of Carlos," October 5, 1675, Hann, *Visitations*, 50.
57. "Testimony of Juan Ebasnjestia testimony," October 3, 1675, Hann, *Visitations*, 46.
58. "Andrés Pérez to Hita y Salazar," August 2, 1676, Hann, *Visitations*, 39.
59. Robert C. Galgano, *Feast of Souls: Indians and Spaniards in the Seventeenth-Century Missions of Florida and New Mexico* (Albuquerque: University of New Mexico Press, 2005), 80–87. For more on Diocsale's story after the revolt, see Jennifer Baszile, "Apalachee Testimony in Florida: A View of Slavery from the Spanish Archives," in *Indian Slavery in Colonial America*, ed. Alan Gallay (Lincoln: University of Nebraska Press, 2009), 189–205.
60. "Visitation of San Cruz de Capole," December 4, 1694. Joaquín de Florencia, Visitation, 1694–1695. AGI EC 157. Hann, *Visitations*, 173.
61. Ibid.
62. Ibid.

63. "Visitation of San Francisco de Oconi," December 2, 1694. Joaquín de Florencia, Visitation, 1694–1695. AGI EC 157. Hann, *Visitations*, 170.
64. For more on how women petitioned in Spanish America, see Bianco Premo, "Before the Law: Women's Petitions in the Eighteenth-Century Spanish Empire," *Comparative Studies in Society and History* 53, no. 2 (2011): 261–289. Marcela Weintraub-Yadlin, "Construcciones Discursivas En Torno a La Mujer Colonial: Desde Lo Hablado a Hablar Por Sí Misma," *Centro de Estudios de la Realidad Social*, 2018, https://ongceres.cl/2018/04/20/construcciones-discursivas-en-torno-a-la-mujer-colonial-desde-lo-hablado-a-hablar-por-si-misma/. Mónica Bolufer and Isabel Morant, "Identidades Vividas, Identidades Atribuidas," in *Entre Dos Orillas: Las Mujeres En La Historia De España y América Latina*, ed. Pilar Pérez-Fuentes (Barcelona: Icaria, 2012), 317–352.
65. For definitions of the Timucua words, see https://timucua.webonary.org/; Movilla, *Explicacion de la Doctrina* (1635), the online Timucua folios, 023–025. Personal communication, George Aaron Broadwell, October 24, 2019.
66. "Visitation of Ivitachuco," December 3, 1694. Joaquín de Florencia, Visitation, 1694–1695. AGI EC 157. Hann, *Visitations*, 171.
67. "Visitation of Santa Cruz de Capole" December 5, 1694. Joaquín de Florencia, Visitation, 1694–1695. AGI EC 157. Hann, *Visitations*, 173.
68. "Visitation of San Martín Tomoli," December 7, 1694. Joaquín de Florencia, Visitation, 1694–1695. AGI EC 157. Hann, *Visitations*, 175. Emphasis mine.
69. For the centrality of Native women in farming, see Lisa Brooks, *Our Beloved Kin* (2018), 34–39. Jane Mt. Pleasant, "A New Paradigm for Pre-Columbian Agriculture in North America," *Early American Studies* 13, no. 2 (2015): 374–412. Susan Sleeper-Smith, *Indigenous Prosperity and American Conquest*, 13–66.
70. "Visitations conducted December 11–18, 1694," in Hann, *Visitations*, 197–203. "A 17th Century Letter of Gabriel Diaz Vara Calderon, Bishop of Cuba, Describing the Indians and Indian Missions of Florida," ed. Lucy L. Wenhold, Smithsonian Miscellaneous Collections, vol. 95, no. 16 (Washington, D.C.: Smithsonian Institution Press, 1936). John H. Hann, "Summary Guide to Spanish Florida Missions and Visitas, with Churches in the Sixteenth and Seventeenth Centuries," 462.
71. Bushnell, *Situado y Sabana*, 144. "Captain Fuentes to Governor Márquez Cabrera in Sápala," February 7, 1681. AGI SD 226. For a more theoretical discussion of gender and labor, see Stephanie Spencer-Wood, "Feminist Theorizing of Patriarchal Colonialism, Power Dynamics, and Social Agency Materialized in Colonial Institutions," *International Journal of Historical Archaeology* 20, no. 3 (2016): 477–491, especially 484.
72. *Tumaque* or *Tunague* seems to be a title, meaning "heir." John H. Hann, "Twilight of the Mocamo and Guale Aborigines as Portrayed in the 1695 Spanish Visitation," *Florida Historical Quarterly* 66, no. 1 (1987): 1–24.

73. "Don Joseph de la Cruz Tunaque, Cacique of Guale to Governor Márquez Cabrera," Sápala May 5, 1681. AGI SD 226.
74. Shannon Lee Dawdy, "Response to Barbara L. Voss's 'Gender, Race, and Labor in the Archaeology of the Spanish Colonial Americas,' " *Current Anthropology* 49, no. 5 (2008): 861–893. Helena Bonet Rosado and Consuelo Perfil Mata Parreño, "Las Cuentas Claras: El Rol De La Mujer En La Economía Doméstica," in *Los Trabajos De Las Mujeres En El Mundo Antiguo*, ed. Ana Delgado Hervás and Marina Picazo Gurina (Tarragona, Spain: ICAC, 2016), 37–44. For gender and politics in different contexts, see Kurt A. Jordan, "Enacting Gender and Kinship Around a Large Outdoor Fire Pit at the Seneca Iroquois Townley-Read Site, 1715–1754," *Historical Archaeology* 48, no. 2 (2014): 61–90; and Lou Ann Wurst, "The Legacy of Separate Spheres," in *Shared Spaces and Divided Places: Material Dimensions of Gender Relations and the American Historical Landscape*, ed. Deborah L. Rotman and Ellen-Rose Savulis (Knoxville: University of Tennessee Press, 2003), 225–238.
75. "Auto in Cupaica," December 29, 1677, Hann, *Visitations*, 109. For the physical toll of the repartimiento, see Dale L. Hutchinson and Clark Spencer Larsen, "Enamel Hypopolasia and Stress in La Florida, in *Bioarchaeology of Spanish Florida: The Impact of Colonialism* (Gainesville: University Press of Florida, 2001), 181–206. Christopher M. Stojanowski, Clark S. Larsen, Tiffiny A. Tung, and Bonnie G. McEwan, "Biological Structure and Health Implications from Tooth Size at Mission San Luis De Apalachee," *American Journal of Physical Anthropology* 132 (2007): 207–222.
76. Alejandra Dubcovsky, *Informed Power: Communication in the Early American South* (Cambridge: Harvard University Press, 2016), 82. Jerald T. Milanich, *Laboring in the Fields of the Lord: Spanish Missions and Southeastern Indians* (Washington, D.C.: Smithsonian Institution Press, 1999). Mark F. Boyd, "Further Consideration of the Apalachee Missions," *The Americas* 9, no. 4 (1953): 459–480.
77. "Visitation to Our Lady of la Candelaria," December 7, 1694. AGI EC 157. Hann, *Visitations*, 176.
78. Ibid.
79. For Native women's economic adaptions and decisions in other contexts, see Lucy Eldersveld Murphy, "Autonomy and the Economic Role of Indian Women of the Fox-Wisconsin Riverway Region 1763–1832," in *Negotiators of Change: Historical Perspectives on Native American Women*, ed. Nancy Shoemaker (New York: Routledge, 1995), 72–89. Roe Bubar and Pamela Jumper Thurman, "Violence Against Native Women," *Social Justice* 31, no. 4 (2004): 70–86.
80. For movement, see Stephen Warren. *The Worlds the Shawnees Made: Migration and Violence in Early America* (Chapel Hill: University of North Carolina Press, 2014), 1–25. Denise I. Bossy, "Introduction: Recovering Yamasee History," in *The Yamasee Indians: From Florida to South Carolina*,

ed. Denise I. Bossy (Lincoln: University of Nebraska Press, 2018): 1–24. For gender and mobility in a different context, see Jennifer L. Morgan, *Laboring Women: Reproduction and Gender in New World Slavery* (Philadelphia: University of Pennsylvania Press, 2004), 169.

81. "Visitation to Our Lady of la Candelaria," December 7, 1694. AGI EC 157. Hann, *Visitations*, 176.
82. Hayley Negrin, "Possessing Native Women and Children: Slavery, Gender, and English Colonialism in the Early American South, 1670–1772" (PhD diss., New York University, 2018).
83. "Visitation to Our Lady of la Candelaria," December 7, 1694. AGI EC 157. Hann, *Visitations*, 176.
84. Mariana Picazo Gurina, "Más Allá De Los Estereotipos: Nuevas Tendencias En El Estudio Del Género En Arqueología Clásica," *Arenal: Revista de Historia de las Mujeres* 24, no. 1 (2017): 5–31.
85. "Visitation of San Francisco de Oconi," December 2, 1694. Joaquín de Florencia, Visitation, 1694–1695. AGI EC 157. Hann, *Visitations*, 170.
86. "Visitation of San Juan Azpalaga," December 6, 1674, Visitation, 1694–1695. AGI EC 157. Hann, *Visitations*, 174.
87. Ibid. For earlier examples, see "Captain Juan Menendez Marquez, March 11, 1652"; and "Captain Luis Hernandez de Biana, March 11, 1652," P. K. Yonge Library of Florida History's microfilm 27F, reel 5.
88. "Visitation of San Francisco de Oconi," December 2, 1694. Joaquín de Florencia, Visitation, 1694–1695. AGI EC 157. Hann, *Visitations*, 170.
89. Ibid. For earlier discussions of Native women shaping male mobility, see "Florida matters," 1602 AGI SD Legajo 2533, accessed from the John Tate Lanning Collection. "Relación del viaje que hizo el Señor Pedro de Ibarra gobernador y Capitan general de la Florida," 1604, in Manuel Serrano y Sanz, *Documentos Historicos De La Florida y La Luisiana* (Madrid: Librería General de Victoriano Suárez, 1912), 164–193. Mary Ross, "The Restoration of the Spanish Missions in Georgia, 1598–1606," *Georgia Historical Quarterly* 10, no. 3 (1926): 171–199.
90. "Visitation of San Francisco de Oconi," December 2, 1694. Joaquín de Florencia, Visitation, 1694–1695. AGI EC 157. Hann, *Visitations*, 170.
91. For women's voices in colonial documents, see Jenny Sharpe, *Ghosts of Slavery: A Literary Archaeology of Black Women's Lives* (Minneapolis: University of Minnesota Press, 2003), 21. Katherine McKittrick, *Demonic Grounds: Black Women and the Cartographies of Struggle* (Minneapolis: University of Minnesota Press, 2006), 37–63.

Chapter Three. The Wars Women Were Already Fighting

1. For Spanish naming practices, see Silke Jansen, "Spanish Anthroponomy from an Ecological Linguistic Perspective: The Antilles Society in the Early Sixteenth Century," in *Linguistic Ecology and Language Contact*, ed.

Peter Mühlhäusler, Ralph Ludwig, and Steve Pagel (Cambridge: Cambridge University Press, 2019), 147–176.

2. "Criminial Case," AGI EC, Legajo 156A, folios 169–199.
3. "Confession of María Jacoba," October 10, 1678, AGI EC, Legajo 156A, folios 169–199. Amy Turner Bushnell, "Ruling 'the Republic of Indians' in Seventeenth-Century Florida," in *Powhatan's Mantle*, ed. Gregory A. Waselkov, Peter H. Wood, and Tom Hatley (Lincoln: University of Nebraska, 1989), 195–214.
4. For more on Calesa, see William Boyer III, "Mission, Negotiation, and Belief: The Role of the Acuera Chiefdom in Colonial Seventeenth-Century Florida," in *Indigenous Landscapes and Spanish Missions: New Perspectives from Archaeology and Ethnohistory*, ed. Lee M. Panich and Tsim D. Schneider (Phoenix: University of Arizona Press, 2014), 41–56.
5. "Juan del Pueyo," November 8, 1678. Criminial Case, AGI EC, Legajo 156A, folios 169–199. John H. Hann, "Heathen Acuera, Murder, and a Potano Cimarrona: The St. Johns River and the Alachua Prairie in the 1670s," *Florida Historical Quarterly* 70, no. 4 (1992): 451–474, quote 466. John H. Hann, *A History of the Timucua Indians and Mission* (Gainesville: University Press of Florida, 1996), 240.
6. "Testimony of Martín of San Francisco de Potano," October 6, 1678, AGI EC, Legajo 156A, folios 169–199.
7. For early uses of *cimarron* in Florida, see the epic poem "La Florida," by Alonso Gregorio de Escobedo published between 1598 and 1615, edition by Alexandra E. Sununu (New York: Academia Norteamericana de la Lengua Española, 2015), 304. John H. Hann, "Heathen Acuera," 451, footnote 2.
8. "Criminial Case," AGI EC, Legajo 156A, folios 169–199. John H. Hann, "Heathen Acuera," 451–474. John H. Hann, "Translation of Governor Rebolledo's 1657 [Visitation]: Visitation of Three Florida Provinces and Related Documents," *Florida Archaeology* 2 (1986), 104.
9. For intersections of gender and race, see Franco Barchiesi and Shona N. Jackson, "Introduction: The Antiblackness of Slavery and Abolition: Beyond the Political Economy of Capitalist Work," *International Labor and Working-Class History* 96 (2019): 1–16. For how race and gender worked together in other parts of Spanish America, see Sherwin K. Bryant, *Rivers of Gold, Lives of Bondage: Governing Through Slavery in Colonial Quito* (Chapel Hill: University of North Carolina Press, 2014); and *Imperial Subjects: Race and Identity in Colonial Latin America*, ed. Andrew B. Fisher and Matthew D. O'Hara (Durham: Duke University Press, 2009).
10. Ann Twinam, "Purchasing Whiteness: Conversations on the Essence of Pardo-ness and Mulatto-ness at the End of Empire," in *Imperial Subjects: Race and Identity in Colonial Latin America*, ed. Andrew B. Fisher and Matthew D. O'Hara (Durham: Duke University Press, 2009), 140–165.

11. For gender and antiblackness, see Iyko Day, "Being or Nothingness: Indigeneity, Antiblackness, and Settler Colonial Critique," *Critical Ethnic Studies* 1, no. 2 (2015): 102–121. Franco Barchiesi and Shona N. Jackson, "Introduction: The Antiblackness of Slavery and Abolition: Beyond the Political Economy of Capitalist Work," *International Labor and Working-Class History* 96 (2019): 1–16. Elizabeth L. Sweet, "Anti-Blackness/Nativeness and Erasure in Mexico: Black Feminist Geographies and Latin American Decolonial Dialogues for U.S. Urban Planning," *Journal of Race, Ethnicity, and the City* 2, no. 1 (2021): 78–92.
12. Jane Landers, "Spanish Sanctuary: Fugitives in Florida, 1687–1790," *Florida Historical Quarterly* 62, no. 3 (January 1984): 297–314, footnote 3. Jessica Marie Johnson, *Wicked Flesh: Black Women, Intimacy, and Freedom in the Atlantic World* (Philadelphia: University of Pennsylvania Press, 2020): 1.
13. "Carta del Gobernador" August 16, 1689. The letter explains the events in 1687. AGI, SD 227B, folios 406–407.
14. For developments in South Carolina, see Peter Wood, *Black Majority: Negroes in Colonial South Carolina from 1670 Through the Stono Rebellion* (New York: W. W. Norton & Company, 1974). S. Max Edelson, *Plantation Enterprise in Colonial South Carolina* (Cambridge: Harvard University Press, 2006).
15. Jane Landers, "Founding Mothers: Female Rebels in Colonial New Granada and Spanish Florida," *Journal of African American History* 98, no. 1 (2013): 7–23, 12.
16. Javier Á. Cancio-Donlebún Ballvé, "The King of Spain's Slaves in St. Augustine, Florida (1580–1618)," *Estudios del Observatorio/Observatorio Studies* 74: 1–81.
17. For these categorizations in Spanish America, see R. Douglas Cope, *The Limits of Racial Domination: Plebeian Society in Colonial Mexico City, 1660–1720* (Madison: University of Wisconsin Press, 1994), 50–59; Andrew B. Fisher and Matthew D. O'Hara, "Introduction: Racial Identities and Their Interpreters in Colonial Latin America," in *Imperial Subjects: Race and Identity in Colonial Latin America* (Durham: Duke University Press, 2009), 8–11. Aaron Althouse, "Contested Mestizos, Alleged Mulattos: Racial Identity and Caste Hierarchy in Eighteenth-Century Pátzcuaro, Mexico," *The Americas* 62, no. 2 (2005): 151–175. George Reid Andrews, *Afro-Latin America, 1800–2000* (Oxford: Oxford University Press, 2004).
18. "Pedro Ybarra to Crown," January 4, 1608, AGI SD 224. Jane Landers, "Cimarrón and Citizen: African Ethnicity, Corporate Identity, and the Evolution of Free Black Towns in the Spanish Circum-Caribbean," in *Slaves, Subjects, and Subversives: Blacks in Colonial Latin America*, ed. Jane Landers and Barry Robinson (Albuquerque: University of New Mexico Press, 2006), 111–145.

19. “Letter to the Crown,” January 30, 1682. AGI SD 226, folio 87. Bushnell, *Situado y Sabana: Spain’s Support System for the Presidio and Mission Provinces of Florida.* Anthropological Papers of the American Museum of Natural History, vol. 3 (1994), 91. For Black experience with Catholic institutions in Spanish America, see Herman L. Bennett, *Colonial Blackness: A History of Afro-Mexico* (Bloomington: Indiana University Press, 2009), 23–57.
20. Luis Rafael Arana, “Military Organization in Florida, 1671–1702,” in *The Military and Militia in Colonial Spanish America* (St. Augustine: Department of Military Affairs, Florida National Guard, n.d.), 11–22. Jane Landers, “The Geopolitics of Seventeenth-Century Florida,” *Florida Historical Quarterly* 92, no. 3 (2014): 480–490. See Luis Rafael Arana, “Military Manpower in Florida, 1670–1703,” *El Escribano* 8, no. 2 (1971): 40–63.
21. Landers, “The Geopolitics of Seventeenth-Century Florida,” 487.
22. Luis Rafael Arana, “Grammont’s Landing at Little Matanzas Inlet, 1686,” *El Escribano* (July 1972): 107–113. Luis Rafael Arana, “Pirates March on St. Augustine, 1683,” *El Escribano* 36 (1999): 64–72; and J. Leitch Wright, Jr., “Andrew Ranson: Seventeenth Century Pirate?” *Florida Historical Quarterly* 39, no. 2 (1960): 135–144.
23. Johnson, *Wicked Flesh*, 136, 134–137. For new work on the demography of San Agustín see Rachel L. Sanderson, “Baptism and Legitimacy in La Florida,” paper presented at the Graduate Student Workshop: New and Emerging Studies of the Spanish Colonial Borderlands, March 2022, Huntington Library and Archive.
24. Jane Landers, *Black Society in Spanish Florida* (Urbana: University of Illinois Press, 1999), Appendix 1 and 19–21; Paul E. Hoffman, *Florida’s Frontiers* (Bloomington: Indiana University Press, 2002), 158. For Black slaves owned by Native chiefs in Florida, see Hann, *A History of the Timucua Indians and Missions* (Gainesville: University Press of Florida, 1996), 114, 171. For the interplay of race, gender, and class see Marisa J. Fuentes, *Dispossessed Lives: Enslaved Women, Violence, and the Archive* (Philadelphia: University of Pennsylvania Press, 2016), 75–80. Christine Walker, “As Though She ‘Was a Virtuous Woman’: Colonial Changes to Gender Roles, Marital Practices, and Family Formation in Atlantic Jamaica, c. 1720–c. 1760,” *Journal of Colonialism and Colonial History* 21, 2 (2020). Jennifer M. Spear, *Race, Sex, and Social Order in Early New Orleans* (Baltimore: Johns Hopkins University Press, 2009), 50–51.
25. Jennifer L. Morgan, *Reckoning with Slavery: Gender, Kinship, and Capitalism in the Early Black Atlantic* (Durham: Duke University Press, 2021), 49.
26. “Governor Quiroga y Losada to King,” June 8, 1690, folio 16 AGI SD 227B. Margaret E. Boyle, *Unruly Women: Performance, Penitence, and Punishment in Early Modern Spain* (Toronto: University of Toronto Press, 2014), 19–42, especially 21. Nancy E. Van Deusen, *Between the Sacred and*

the Worldly: The Institutional and Cultural Practice of Recogimiento in Colonial Lima (Stanford: Stanford University Press, 2001), xii; Asunción Lavrín, *Sexuality and Marriage in Colonial Latin America* (Lincoln: University of Nebraska Press, 1992), 11. Allyson Poska, "Elusive Virtue: Rethinking the Role of Chastity in Early Modern Spain," *Journal of Early Modern History* 8, nos. 1–2 (2004): 135–146.

27. "Governor Quiroga y Losada to King," June 8, 1690, folio 16 AGI SD 227B.
28. Ibid.
29. Fuentes, *Dispossessed Lives*, 45.
30. Governor Quiroga y Losada to King, June 8, 1690, folio 16 AGI SD 227B.
31. "Royal Cédula," November 7, 1693, AGI SD 839. J. G. Dunlop, "William Dunlop's Mission to St. Augustine in 1688," *South Carolina Historical and Genealogical Magazine* 34, no. 1 (1933): 1–30.
32. For records accounting for clothing and food given to enslaved people, see "Accounts," September 1598–October 1601, AGI, Contaduría 951.
33. Susan R. Parker, "Life in St. Augustine at the Turn of the Eighteenth Century," *El Escribano* 39 (2002): 55–64. Susan R. Parker, "In My Mother's House: Dowry Property and Female Inheritance Patterns in Spanish Florida," in *Signposts: New Directions in Southern Legal History*, ed. Sally E. Hadden and Patricia Hagler Minter (Athens: University of Georgia Press, 2013), 26–46. Diana Reigelsperger, "Interethnic Relations and Settlement on the Spanish Florida Frontier, 1668–1763" (PhD diss., University of Florida, 2013), 191–193, 226–242.
34. Marriage of García and María, July 8, 1674, Marriages 1632–1720. Box 4. Digitization of the Archives of the Diocese of St. Augustine (DADS). For another example, see baptism of Manuel, son of Cosme Joseph Catalan (pardo) and María (negra). Baptism 1632–1694. Box 3. DADS.
35. Marriage of Juan and Isabel, February 17, 1675. Ibid. Marriage of Juan and Francisca, June 30, 1675. Ibid. Marriage of Phelipe and María Micaela, April 15, 1692. Ibid. See Baptism of Augstina, China. January 11, 1690. Baptism 1632–1694. Box 3. Ibid. For a good discussion on marriages and compadrazgo on the edges of the Spanish empire, see Paul Conrad, *The Apache Diaspora: Four Centuries of Displacement and Survival* (Philadelphia: University of Pennsylvania, 2021), 65–74.
36. Johnson, *Wicked Flesh*, 5. There are some exceptions: Bernarda, a parda, was born out of a union of Diego de Espinosa and Marta de Salas, a parda libre. October 26, 1690. Baptism 1632–1694. Box 3. DADS. For women's networks see Jessica Marie Johnson, "Death Rites as Birthrights in Atlantic New Orleans: Kinship and Race in the Case of María Teresa v. Perine Dauphine," *Slavery & Abolition* 36, no. 2 (2015): 233–256. Erin Trahey, "Among Her Kinswomen: Legacies of Free Women of Color in Jamaica," *William and Mary Quarterly* 76, no. 2 (2019): 257–288. Christine

Walker, *Jamaica Ladies: Female Slaveholders and the Creation of Britain's Atlantic Empire* (Chapel Hill: University of North Carolina Press and Omohundro Institute of Early American History and Culture, 2020), 214–224.

37. Baptism of María Gertrudis, natural daughter of María Gertrudis, negra. Baptism 1632–1694. Box 3. DADS. Baptism of Lorena, daughter of María, negra, "unknown father." Baptism 1632–1694. Box 3. Ibid. For thinking through these sources, see Ann Twinam, *Public Lives, Private Secrets: Gender, Honor, Sexuality, and Illegitimacy in Colonial Spanish America* (Stanford: Stanford University Press, 1999), 60–65. For illegitimacy, see Muriel Nazzari, "An Urgent Need to Conceal: The System of Honor and Shame in Colonial Brazil," in *The Faces of Honor: Sex, Shame, and Violence in Colonial Latin America*, ed. Lyman L. Johnson and Sonya Lipsett-Rivera (Albuquerque: University of New Mexico Press, 1998), 103–126.
38. Baptism of María, daughter of Theresa, April 1, 1687. Baptism 1632–1694. Box 3. DADS. See also Baptism of María Manuela, November 20, 1687. Ibid.
39. Susan Migden Socolow, *The Women of Colonial Latin America*, 2nd ed. (New York: Cambridge University Press, 2015), 140–156, quote from 154.
40. Juan Ignacio Arnaud Rabinal, Alberto Bernárdez Alvarez, Pedro Miguel Martín Escudero, and Felipe del Pozo Redondo, "Estructura De La Población De Una Sociedad De Frontera: La Florida Española, 1600–1763," *Revista Complutense de Historia de América* 17 (1991): 93–120. John R. Dunkle, "Population Change as an Element in the Historical Geography of St. Augustine," *Florida Historical Quarterly* 37, no. 1 (1958): 3–32.
41. Christopher Beats, "African Religious Integration in Florida During the First Spanish Period" (MA thesis, University of Central Florida, 2007), 60–70; for a list of "White Children with Black Sponsors," see 96–97. For women's support networks in later periods, see Chrissy Lutz and Dawn Herd-Clark, " 'No One Was on Their Own': Sociability Among Rural African American Women in Middle Georgia During the Interwar Years," *Agricultural History* 93, no. 3 (2019): 437–451.
42. Jane Landers, "Gracia Real De Santa Teresa De Mose: A Free Black Town in Spanish Colonial Florida," *American Historical Review* 95, no. 1 (1990): 9–30.
43. For racial relations in the Spanish world, see Magali M. Carrera, *Imagining Identity in New Spain: Race, Lineage, and the Colonial Body in Portraiture and Casta Paintings* (Austin: University of Texas Press, 2003), 11–15. Andrew B. Fisher and Matthew D. O'Hara, "Introduction: Racial Identities and Their Interpretations in Colonial Latin America," in *Imperial Subjects: Race and Identity in Colonial Latin America*, ed. Andrew B. Fisher and Matthew D. O'Hara (Durham: Duke University Press, 2009), 1–38. For thinking about antiblackness in the Spanish colonies, see Shona N. Jack-

son, *Creole Indigeneity: Between Myth and Nation in the Caribbean* (Minneapolis: University of Minnesota Press, 2012).

44. "Jesus María Letter," Cacique Don Manuel, December 9, 1651, AGI EC 155B, folios 380–385.
45. George Aaron Broadwell and Alejandra Dubcovsky, "Chief Manuel's 1651 Timucua Letter: The Oldest Letter in a Native Language of the United States," *Proceedings of the American Philosophical Society* 164, no. 4 (2020). George Aaron Broadwell, "Honorific Marking in the Timucua Language," paper presented to the Florida Anthropological Society, May 2016.
46. "Carta del gobernador de la Florida Juan Márquez Cabrera," January 25, 1682. AGI SD 226. John H. Hann, "Cloak and Dagger in Apalachicole Province in Early 1686," *Florida Historical Quarterly* 78, no. 1 (1999): 74–93. Jason B. Palmer, "Forgotten Sacrifice: Native American Involvement in the Construction of the Castillo de San Marcos," *Florida Historical Quarterly* 80, no. 4 (2002): 437–454.
47. For labor conditions in and around the fort, see "Report from the Franciscans about labor conditions," May 2, 1673. AGI 235. Accessed from John Tate Lanning Collection, Collection #267. St. Louis Mercantile Library, University of St. Louis, Missouri.
48. Ibid. Jason B. Palmer, "Forgotten Sacrifice: Native American Involvement in the Construction of the Castillo De San Marcos," *Florida Historical Quarterly* 80, no. 4 (2002): 437–454. Amy Turner Bushnell, *The King's Coffer: Proprietors of the Spanish Florida Treasury, 1565–1702* (Gainesville: University Presses of Florida, 1981), 19. Luis Rafael Arana, "A Bitter Pill for the Widow Cendoya," in *Defenses and Defenders at St. Augustine: A Collection of Writings by Luis Rafael Arana* (St. Augustine, Fla.: St. Augustine Historical Society, 1999), 37–49.
49. Landers, *Black Society in Spanish Florida*, 12–23. Irene A. Wright, "Dispatches of Spanish Officials Bearing on the Free Negro Settlement of Gracia Real De Santa Teresa De Mose, Florida," *Journal of Negro History* 9, no. 2 (1924): 144–195. Patrick Riordan, "Finding Freedom in Florida: Native Peoples, African Americans, and Colonists, 1670–1816," *Florida Historical Quarterly* 75, no. 1 (1996): 25–44.
50. "Confezion of Juan Méndez," December 27, 1688, AGI SD 227 folio 158.
51. Ira Berlin, *Many Thousands Gone: The First Two Centuries of Slavery in North America* (Cambridge: Belknap Press of Harvard University, 1998), 116–121.
52. "Confezion of Juan Méndez," December 27, 1688, AGI SD 227 folio 158.
53. Kathleen A. Deagan, "Mestizaje in Colonial St. Augustine," *Ethnohistory* 20, no. 1 (1973): 55–65. Barbara L. Voss, "Gender, Race, and Labor in the Archaeology of the Spanish Colonial Americas," *Current Anthropology* 49, no. 5 (2008): 861–893. For a good overview of these debates, see Rebecca Anne Goetz, "Rethinking the 'Unthinking Decision': Old Questions and

New Problems in the History of Slavery and Race in the Colonial South," *Journal of Southern History* 75, no. 3 (2009): 599–612. For the role of women slave owners, see Stephanie E. Jones-Rogers, *They Were Her Property: White Women as Slave Owners in the American South* (New Haven: Yale University Press, 2019), 205.

54. For "how central enslaved black bodies were to the production of urban and domestic spaces," see Fuentes, *Dispossessed Lives*, 37–45. Shauna J. Sweeney, "Market Marronage: Fugitive Women and the Internal Marketing System in Jamaica, 1781–1834," *William and Mary Quarterly* 76, no. 2 (2019): 197–222.
55. The house is identified as belonging to "the heirs of Don Pedro Benedit Horruytiner." Albert Manucy, *The Houses of St. Augustine, 1565–1821* (Gainesville: University Press of Florida, 1992), 60, 122–124. Susan Richbourg Parker, "St. Augustine in the Seventeenth-Century: Capital of La Florida," *Florida Historical Quarterly* 92, no. 3 (2014): 554–576.
56. "Cartas de los Gobernadores de Florida," August 16, 1688, AGI SD 227 folios 149–150.
57. "Testimony of Adrian," December 26, 1688, AGI SD 227 folio 155. "Testimony Lorenzo Iguale," December 27, 1688, AGI SD 227 folio 156.
58. There were two different men identified as Juan de la Cruz: one was identified as a pardo owned by de los Ángeles, and one was described as a "Mexican mulatto" owned by the heir of Benedit Horruytiner. Both gave testimonies. The former had witnessed the initial report of the crime; the latter was in the kitchen when the supposed murderer sought refuge. Marcos, the other enslaved person mentioned in the records, did not give testimony, but he is mentioned in the testimony of Lorenzo Iguale.
59. "Declarazión, Juan de la Cruz," December 26, 1688, AGI SD 227 folio 155. "Testimony Lorenzo Iguale," December 23, 1688, AGI SD 227 folios 151–152.
60. "Declarazión, Juan de la Cruz," December 26, 1688, AGI SD 227 folio 155. "Testimony Lorenzo Iguale," December 23, 1688, AGI SD 227 folios 151–152.
61. The trial of Andrés and Ajalap appears in EC 157A AGI, reprinted by John H. Hann, "Apalachee Counterfeiters in St. Augustine," *Florida Historical Quarterly* 67, no. 1 (1988): 52–68.
62. Ibid.
63. For more on women operating stores in the eighteenth century, see Janine Lanza, "Women Minding the Store in Eighteenth-Century France," *Early Modern Women* 10, no. 1 (2015): 131–140; Kim Todt, "A Venture of Her Own: Early American Women in Business," *Early Modern Women* 10, no. 1 (2015): 152–163; Yolanda Gamboa, "Female Agency and Daily Life in Early Colonial Florida's Ciudad Letrada," in *Perspectives on Early Modern Women in Iberia and the Americas: Studies in Law, Society, Art, and Literature in Honor of Anne J. Cruz*, ed. Adrienne Martin María Cristina

Quintero (New York: Escribana Books, 2015), 150–166; and Jane Landers, "African and African American Women and Their Pursuit of Rights Through Eighteenth-Century Spanish Texts," in *Haunted Bodies: Gender and Southern Texts*, ed. Anne Goodwyn Jones and Susan V. Donaldson (Charlottesville: University of Virginia Press, 1998): 56–78.

64. Kathleen Deagan, "San Agustín: First Urban Enclave in the United States," *North American Archaeologist* 3, no. 3 (1982): 183–205.
65. Hann, "Apalachee Counterfeiters in St. Augustine," 54.
66. For the role of Black women in the colonial economy, see Jessica Blake, "Black Tradeswomen and the Making of a Taste Culture in Lower Louisiana," *Early American Studies: An Interdisciplinary Journal* 19, no. 4 (2021): 735–768; Jane E. Mangan, *Trading Roles: Gender, Ethnicity, and the Urban Economy in Colonial Potosí* (Durham: Duke University Press, 2005), 134–160; and Philip D. Morgan, *Slave Counterpoint: Black Culture in the Eighteenth-Century Chesapeake and Lowcountry* (Chapel Hill: University of North Carolina Press, 1998), 358–376.
67. Hann, "Apalachee Counterfeiters in St. Augustine," 55–56. For women's shopping practices, see Ellen Hartigan-O'Connor, *The Ties That Buy: Women and Commerce in Revolutionary America* (Philadelphia: University of Pennsylvania Press, 2009).
68. For an overview of women and labor in Latin America, see Susan Migden Socolow, *The Women of Colonial Latin America* (New York: Cambridge University Press, 2015), 120–139. For the role and place of Black women in early colonial Spanish societies, see Danielle Terrazas Williams, "Finer Things: African-Descended Women, Sumptuary Laws, and Governance in Early Spanish America," *Journal of Women's History* 33, no. 3 (2021): 11–35.
69. For gender and labor, see Jennifer L. Morgan, *Laboring Women: Reproduction and Gender in New World Slavery* (Philadelphia: University of Pennsylvania Press, 2004), 150–165.
70. Hann, "Apalachee Counterfeiters in St. Augustine," 55–56.
71. Hann, "Apalachee Counterfeiters in St. Augustine," 56.
72. Pilar Pérez Cantó, "Las españolas en la vida colonial," *Historia de Las Mujeres en España y America Latina II: La Edad Moderna*, ed. Morant Deusa (Madrid: Ediciones Cátedra, 2005): 525–554. Serena R. Zabin, *Dangerous Economies: Status and Commerce in Imperial New York* (Philadelphia: University of Pennsylvania Press, 2009): 16–21. Eleanor Hubbard, *City Women: Money, Sex, and the Social Order in Early Modern London* (Oxford: Oxford University Press, 2012): 26–35.
73. Her story and experiences bear many similarities to the murdered "Yndia Chacata" from chapter 1, AGI EC 157. John Hann, *Visitations and Revolts in Florida, 1657–1695*, in *Florida Archaeology* 7 (1993), 275–276.
74. "To the Governor from Manuel de Solana," San Luis, October 21, 1702, AGI SD 858, folio 785. Angela Wanhalla argues that "as historical

subjects, Indigenous women tend to be associated with forms of involuntary movement; their mobility across imperial and colonial space is often equated with violence, coercion and abandonment"; "Indigenous Women, Marriage, and Colonial Mobility," in *Indigenous Mobilities: Across and Beyond the Antipodes*, edited by Rachel Standfield (Acton: Australian National University Press, 2018), 209–232.

75. "To the Governor from Maunel de Solana," San Luis, October 21, 1702, AGI SD 858, folio 785. For the gendered political power of eavesdropping, see Aisha K. Finch, *Rethinking Slave Rebellion in Cuba: La Escalera and the Insurgencies of 1841–1844* (Chapel Hill: University of North Carolina Press, 2015), 156–158.
76. Brooke Bauer, *Becoming Catawba* (Tuscaloosa: University of Alabama Press, forthcoming), chapter 2.
77. "Report of Christian Yndia Chacata," in Manuel Solana's letter to the governor, October 21, 1702. San Luis. AGI SD 858, folio 785.
78. Ibid.; emphasis mine.
79. Thomas Nairne, *Nairne's Muskhogean Journals: The 1708 Expedition to the Mississippi River*, ed. Alexander Moore (Jackson: University Press of Mississippi, 1988), 43.
80. Manuel Solana's letter to the Governor, October 21, 1702. San Luis. AGI SD 858, folio 785. She was not wrong; after the failed siege, many members of South Carolina's Assembly accused Moore of simply trying to "assault, kill, destroy, and take captive as many Indians as they possibly could." "Representation and Address by Several Members of This Assembly," June 26, 1703, cited in William J. Rivers, *A Sketch of the History of South Carolina to the Close of the Proprietary Government by the Revolution of 1719. With an Appendix Containing Many Valuable Records Hitherto Unpublished* (Charleston: McCarter & Co., 1856), 456. For a longer discussion of gender and territoriality, see Robert Sack, "Human Territoriality: A Theory," *Annals of the Association of American Geographers* 73, no. 1 (March 1983), 55–74. Doreen Massey, *Space, Place, and Gender* (Minneapolis: University of Minnesota Press, 1994), 179. Marcela Tovar-Restrepo and Clara Irazábal, "Indigenous Women and Violence in Colombia: Agency, Autonomy, and Territoriality," *Latin American Perspectives* 41, no. 1 (2014): 39–58. Juliana Barr, "Geographies of Power: Mapping Indian Borders in the 'Borderlands' of the Early Southwest," *William and Mary Quarterly* 68, no. 1 (2011): 5–46.
81. "Report of Christian Yndia Chacata," in Manuel Solana's letter to the governor, October 21, 1702. San Luis. AGI SD 858, folio 785.
82. Andrew Johnson and Thomas Blake Earle, "Atlantic, Environmental, and Southern: Towards a Confluence," *Atlantic Environments and the American South* (Athens: University of Georgia Press: 2019), 1–19.
83. "Manuel Solana to the Governor," October 21, 1702. San Luis. AGI SD 858, folio 785. For how to read and hear Native voices, see Sarah Deer,

"Heeding the Voice of Native Women: Toward an Ethic of Decolonization," *North Dakota Law Review* 81 (2005): 807–822. Karen Anderson, *Chain Her by One Foot: The Subjugation of Women in Seventeenth-Century New France* (New York: Routledge, 1991). Anna Brickhouse, "Mistranslation, Unsettlement, La Navidad," *PMLA* 128, no. 4 (2013): 938–946. Aisha Finch, "Black Feminist Knowledge Production, Archival Recuperation, and Slave Resistance Movements," *Women and Social Movements in the United States, 1600–2000*, vol. 23, no. 2 (2019): online.

Chapter Four. Women Besieged and Besieging

1. "Auto," December 24, 1702. AGI SD 858 folio 121.
2. For a later order on how to read ship signs, see "Señas, 1738." AGI SD 2593. Cited from Reel 44, Stetson Collection, PKY.
3. Jane Landers, "African and African American Women and Their Pursuit of Rights through Eighteenth-Century Spanish Texts," in *Haunted Bodies: Gender and Southern Texts*, ed. Anne Goodwyn Jones and Susan V. Donaldson (Charlottesville: University of Virginia Press, 1998), 56–78. Sophie White, *Voices of the Enslaved: Love, Labor, and Longing in French Louisiana* (Chapel Hill: University of North Carolina Press and Omohundro Institute of Early American History and Culture, 2019), 216–226.
4. "Francisco de Córcoles y Martínez to the King," April 9, 1711. AGI SD 843 Hann Collection, PKY. "Juan de Ayala y Escobar (interim governor) to the King, Florida," April 18, 1717, SD 843. Hann Collection, PKY. For an overview of the Native people in the Castillo, see Censuses of St. Augustine Native American Villages, 1711, 1717, 1726, 1728, 1736, 1737, 1738, 1739, in John E. Worth, *The Timucuan Chiefdoms of Spanish Florida*, vol. 2, *Resistance and Destruction* (Gainesville: University Press of Florida, 1998), 147–158.
5. For Native women in early slaving raids, see "Testimonio de Antonio Argüelles," in Governor Manuel de Cendoya to the Queen, October 31, 1671, AGI 839, accessed in Stetson Collection, Reel 13, PKY. For the consequences of slaving raids closer to the 1702 siege, see "Auto," October 27, 1702. San Luis. AGI SD 858 folio 783, and "Manuel Solana to Governor Zúñiga y Cerda," November 13, 1702, San Luís. AGI SD 858. Reel 27. Stetson Collection. PKY.
6. Rebecca Tsosie, "Changing Women: The Cross-Currents of American Indian Feminine Identity," *American Indian Culture and Research Journal* 12, no. 1 (1988): 1–37. Denise K. Lajimodiere, "Ogimah Ikwe: Native Women and Their Path to Leadership," *Wicazo Sa Review* 26, no. 2 (2011): 57–82. Brooke Bauer, *Becoming Catawba* (Tuscaloosa: University of Alabama Press, forthcoming), chapter 2.

7. Irene A. Wright, "Dispatches of Spanish Officials Bearing on the Free Negro Settlement of Gracia Real De Santa Teresa De Mose, Florida," *Journal of Negro History* 9, no. 2 (April 1924): 144–195. Jane Landers, "Spanish Sanctuary: Fugitives in Florida, 1687–1790," *Florida Historical Quarterly* 62, no. 3 (January 1984): 297–314.
8. "Auto," December 26, 1702. AGI SD 858 folio 121. On silence see Mark Slouka, "Listening for Silence: Notes on the Aural Life," in *Audio Culture: Readings in Modern Music*, ed. Christoph Cox and Daniel Warner (New York: Continuum, 2004), 40–46. Sophie Rosenfeld, "On Being Heard: A Case for Paying Attention to the Historical Ear," *American Historical Review* 116, no. 2 (2011): 316–334, especially 323–324.
9. For soundscapes, see R. Murray Schafer, *The Tuning of the World* (New York: Random House Inc., 1977). Peter A. Coates, "The Strange Stillness of the Past: Toward an Environmental History of Sound and Noise," *Environmental History* 10, no. 4 (October 2005): 636–665. Mark Smith, *Sensing the Past: Seeing, Hearing, Smelling, Tasting, and Touching in History* (Berkeley: University of California Press, 2007): 41–58. For rumors and sounds in colonial Virginia, see Matthew Kruer, *Time of Anarchy: Indigenous Power and the Crisis of Colonialism in Early America* (Cambridge: Harvard University Press, 2021), 51–77.
10. "Auto," December 26, 1702. AGI SD 858 folio 121.
11. The only comprehensive study of this siege comes from Charles W. Arnade, *The Siege of St. Augustine in 1702* (Gainesville: University of Florida Press, 1959). Sherry Johnson, "Maintaining the Home Front: Widows, Wives, and War in Late Eighteenth-Century Cuba," in *Gender, War, and Politics: War, Culture, and Society, 1750–1850*, ed. Karen Hagemann, Gisela Mettele, and Jane Rendall (London: Palgrave Macmillan, 2010): 206–224.
12. The 1702 siege of San Agustín is a well-documented confrontation. There are thousands of pages of correspondence, council meetings minutes, spy reports, military plans, and related materials detailing this military engagement. In the Spanish archive, a single *legajo* (bundle)—Santo Domingo, 858—helps to gather many of these varied sources. There is also a robust source base for thinking through English perspectives and experiences, but this chapter remains firmly rooted in the women inside the fort.
13. "Auto," November 6, 1702, AGI SD 858 folio 799. "Junta the Guerra," January 3, 1703, AGI SD 858 folio 908. Michelle LeMaster, "War, Masculinity, and Alliances on the Carolina Frontiers," in *Creating and Contesting Carolina: Proprietary Era Histories*, ed. Michelle LeMaster and Bradford Wood (Columbia: University of South Carolina Press, 2013), 164–185. For women and war in early America, see Ann M. Little, *Abraham in Arms: War and Gender in Colonial New England* (Philadelphia: University of Pennsylvania Press, 2007), and for larger discussion of gender

and political performance, see Betul Eksi and Elizabeth A. Wood, "Right-Wing Populism as Gendered Performance: Janus-faced Masculinity in the Leadership of Vladimir Putin and Recep T. Erdogan," *Theory & Society* 48, no. 5 (2019): 733–751.

14. The literature on Deerfield is vast; for two good examples, see Evan Haefeli and Kevin Sweeney, *Captors and Captives: The 1704 French and Indian Raid on Deerfield*, Native Americans of the Northeast (Amherst: University of Massachusetts Press, 2003), 3; and John Demos, *The Unredeemed Captive: A Family Story from Early America* (New York: Knopf, 1994).
15. For a good chronology of all the fronts of Queen's Anne War, see David Marley, *Wars of the Americas: A Chronology of Armed Conflict in the Western Hemisphere, 1492 to the Present* (Santa Barbara: ABC-CLIO, 2008): 2202–2243.
16. The southern fronts of Queen Anne's War are woefully understudied. The last overview comes from 1919: Verner W. Crane, "The Southern Frontier in Queen Anne's War," *American Historical Review* 24 (1919): 379–395.
17. For overviews on the long history of Spanish-Anglo rivalry in the area, see J. Leitch Wright, *Anglo-Spanish Rivalry in North America* (Athens: University of Georgia Press, 1971). Fred Lamar Pearson, Jr., "Anglo-Spanish Rivalry in the Chattahoochee Basin and West Florida, 1685 1704," *South Carolina Historical Magazine* 79, no. 1 (1978). Steven J. Oatis, *A Colonial Complex: South Carolina's Frontiers in the Era of the Yamasee War, 1680–1730* (Lincoln: University of Nebraska Press, 2004). Timothy Paul Grady, *Anglo-Spanish Rivalry in Colonial South-East America, 1650–1725* (London: Pickering & Chatto, 2010). For Yamasee movements, see Keith Ashley, "Yamasee Migration into the Mocama and Timucua Mission Provinces of Florida, 1667–1683: An Archaeological Perspective," in *The Yamasee Indians: From Florida to South Carolina*, ed. Denise I. Bossy (Lincoln: University of Nebraska Press, 2018), 55–79. Alan Gallay, *The Indian Slave Trade: The Rise of the English Empire in the American South, 1670–1717* (New Haven: Yale University Press, 2003), 40–69. For the 1686 attack see J. G. Dunlop, "Spanish Depredations, 1686," *South Carolina Historical and Genealogical Magazine* 30, no. 2 (1929): 81–89. For the 1702 Apalachee-Apalachicola confrontation, see "Acto," October 27, 1702. San Luis. AGI SD 858 folio 783 and "Manuel Solana to Governor Zúñiga y Cerda," November 13, 1702, San Luís. AGI SD 858. Reel 27. Stetson Collection. PKY.
18. "Representation and Address by Several Members of This Assembly," June 26, 1703, cited in William J. Rivers, *A Sketch of the History of South Carolina to the Close of the Proprietary Government by the Revolution of 1719. With an Appendix Containing Many Valuable Records Hitherto Unpublished* (Charleston: McCarter & Co: 1856), 456. Journals of the Commons

House of Assembly of South Carolina, 1702, James Moore, September 10, 1702. Printed for the Historical Commission of South Carolina and edited by A. S. Salley (Columbia: The State Company, 1932), 102–106. For an earlier discussion, see Journals of the Commons House of Assembly of South Carolina, 1701, James Moore, August 26, 1701. Printed for the Historical Commission of South Carolina and edited by A. S. Salley (Columbia: The State Company, 1926), 20. For an overview of the siege, see Arnade, *The Siege of St. Augustine in 1702*. There was also a special issue of *El Escribano* devoted to the 1702 siege: "Firestorm and Ashes: The Siege of 1702," *El Escribano* 39 (2002).

19. Daniel Hughes, "A Case of Multiple Identities in La Florida: A Statistical Approach to Nascent Cosmopolitanism," *Historical Archaeology* 46, no. 1 (2012): 8–27.
20. "Deposition of John Bee," April 26, 1738, in *Copy of several examinations, depositions and letter etc. in support of the representation to the Lords for Trade and Plantations*. The National Archives, Kew, CO 5/384, October 28, 1703–May 25, 1738.
21. "Carta del Teniente de Guale," December 5, 1702. AGI SD 858 folio 708. For the expected movement of women, see January 3, 1703, folio 409 AGI SD 840. For an overview of Guale, see John E. Worth, *The Struggle for the Georgia Coast: An 18th-Century Spanish Retrospective on Guale and Mocama* (New York: American Museum of Natural History, 1995), 9–55. Rebecca Saunders, *Stability and Change in Guale Indian Pottery, A.D. 1300–1702* (Tuscaloosa: University of Alabama Press, 2000): 169–182.
22. For the shifting names and locations of Guale towns, see Worth, *Struggle for the Georgia Coast*, 190–199.
23. Jerald T. Milanich, "Gone, But Never Forgotten: Mission Santa Catalina on Amelia Island and the 1702 Raid," *El Escribano* 39 (2002): 1–15.
24. "Carta del Teniente de Guale," November 5, 1702. AGI SD 858, folio 798. Arnade, *The Siege of St. Augustine in 1702*, 14–19. Amy Turner Bushnell, *Situado y Sabana: Spain's Support System for the Presidio and Mission Provinces of Florida*, Anthropological Papers of the American Museum of Natural History, vol. 3 (1994), 161. Worth, *Struggle for the Georgia Coast*, 50. For earlier Guale movements: "Declaration of Niquisalla," March 22, 1685, St. Augustine, Georgia Department of Archives and History (GDAH), Mary Ross Papers (MRP), Folder 88, 1445–50; "Auto of Governor Cabrera," March 22, 1685, GDAH, MRP, Folder 88, 1442–1444; "Antonio Matheos to Juan Márquez Cabrera," May 21, 1686, in John H. Hann, "Cloak and Dagger in Apalachicole," *Florida Historical Quarterly* 78, no. 1 (1999): 88–93. Ashley, "Yamasee Migration into the Mocama and Timucua Mission Provinces of Florida, 1667–1683," 55–79. For post-1702 Guale movements, see Susan Richbourg Parker, "Chief Francisco Jospogue: Reconstructing the Paths of a Guale-Yamasee Indian

Lineage Through the Spanish Record," in *The Yamasee Indians: From Florida to South Carolina*, ed. Denise I. Bossy (Lincoln: University of Nebraska Press), 281–307.

25. "Auto," San Agustín, November 5, 1702, AGI SD 858 folio 789.
26. "Auto [concerning the resettlement of Santa Catalina]," October 19, 1680. AGI EC 156A. Cited in Worth, *Struggle for the Georgia Coast*, 33.
27. For the centrality of Native women in discussions of sovereignty, see Katrina Jagodinsky, *Legal Codes and Talking Trees: Indigenous Women's Sovereignty in the Sonoran and Puget Sound Borderlands, 1854–1946* (New Haven: Yale University Press, 2016), 9–11.
28. "Carta del Teniente de Guale," November 4, 1702. AGI SD 858 folio 708. For earlier mentions of women coming for aid, see Worth, *Struggle for the Georgia Coast*, 24. For colonial violence against Native women, see Audra Simpson, *Mohawk Interruptus: Political Life Across the Borders of Settler States* (Durham: Duke University Press, 2014), 156.
29. "Captain Francisco Fuentes de Galarza (San Juan del Puerto, Guale) to Zúñiga y Cerda," November 4, 1702, AGI SD 858 folio 708.
30. Thomas Nairne, *Nairne's Muskhogean Journals: The 1708 Expedition to the Mississippi River*, ed. Alexander Moore (Jackson: University Press of Mississippi, 1988), 43. James Adair, *History of the American Indians* (1775), ed. Kathryn H. Braund (Tuscaloosa: University of Alabama Press, 2005), 197–200. Bauer, *Becoming Catawba*, chapter 2.
31. For women leaders participating in military conflict, see "Petition from Juan and Agustín, Timucua Indians," July 6, 1636, AGI SD 27B, accessed Jeannette Thurber Connor Collection, Reel 2, PKY. Testimony of Manuel Calderón, May 7, 1660. AGI Contaduría 964. Part of the Residencia of Diego de Rebolledo, folios 182–194. For a transcription of this testimony and many others see John Worth, "The Timucua Missions of Spanish Florida and the Rebellion of 1656" (PhD diss., University of Florida, 1992), 356–480.
32. "Auto," November 5, 1702, San Agustín, AGI SD 858 folio 789. South Carolina records provide almost no information on these captured individuals, but there are hints of the Spanish prisoners on April 28, 1704. Journal of the South Carolina Commons House of Assembly, 1702–6 (Green's Transcription). South Carolina Department of Archive and History (SCDAH), 235.
33. Marriage of Captain Francisco Fuentes and Francisca Guerreo, January 1686. Marriages 1632–1720. Box 4. Digitization of the Archives of the Diocese of St. Augustine (DADS).
34. "Testimony of Don Pedro de Rivera," Residencia de José Zúñiga y Cerda, February 11, 1707. AGI SD 858 folio 667.
35. Susanah Shaw Romney, " 'With & Alongside His Housewife': Claiming Ground in New Netherland and the Early Modern Dutch Empire," *William and Mary Quarterly* 73, no. 2 (2016): 187–224, quote on 191.

36. For a larger discussion of women, pregnancy, and war, see Patricia Crawford, "The Construction and Experience of Maternity in Seventeenth-Century England," in *Women as Mothers in Preindustrial England: Essays in Memory of Dorothy McLaren* (London: Routledge, 1990), 4–15; and Ashley Erin Wiedenbeck, "The Natural Mother: Motherhood, Patriarchy, and Power in Seventeenth-Century England" (PhD diss., Arizona State University 2015), 5–87. For discussion of how motherhood was seen and perceived, see Nora Doyle, *Maternal Bodies: Redefining Motherhood in Early America* (Chapel Hill: University of North Carolina Press, 2018), 15–52.
37. Journal of the Commons House of Assembly of South Carolina For 1703. Printed for the Historical Commission of South Carolina and edited by A. S. Salley (Columbia: The State Company, 1934), 5.
38. For discussions of intersectionality in wartime, see Eilish Rooney, "Intersectionality: Working in Conflict," in *The Oxford Handbook of Gender and Conflict*, ed. Fionnuala Ní Aoláin, Naomi R. Cahn, Dina Francesca Haynes, and Nahla Valji (New York: Oxford University Press, 2018), 328–342; and Valerie Traub, "History in the Present Tense: Feminist Theories, Spatialized Epistemologies, and Early Modern Embodiment," in *Mapping Gendered Routes and Spaces in the Early Modern World*, ed. Merry E. Wiesner (Burlington, Vt.: Ashgate, 2015), 15–53. For a larger discussion of intersectionality, see Kimberle Crenshaw, "Mapping the Margins: Intersectionality, Identity Politics, and Violence Against Women of Color," *Stanford Law Review* 43, no. 6 (1991): 1241–1299.
39. Journal of the Commons House of Assembly of South Carolina For 1703. Printed for the Historical Commission of South Carolina and edited by A. S. Salley (Columbia: The State Company, 1934), 5. For the productive and reproductive power of slave women, see Jennifer L. Morgan, *Laboring Women: Reproduction and Gender in New World Slavery* (Philadelphia: University of Pennsylvania Press, 2004), 166.
40. For the relationship between gender and war: Gina Martino, *Women at War in the Borderlands of the Early American Northeast* (Chapel Hill: University of North Carolina Press, 2018). Mary Beth Norton, "Eighteenth-Century American Women in Peace and War: The Case of the Loyalists," *William and Mary Quarterly* 33, no. 3 (1976): 386–409. Barton C. Hacker, "Women and Military Institutions in Early Modern Europe: A Reconnaissance," *Signs* 6, no. 4 (1981): 643–671. Cynthia Enloe, *Nimo's War, Emma's War: Making Feminist Sense of the Iraq War* (Berkeley: University of California Press, 2010). Thavolia Glymph, *The Women's Fight: The Civil War's Battles for Home, Freedom, and Nation*, Littlefield History of the Civil War Era (Chapel Hill: University of North Carolina Press, 2020). Robin May Schott, "Gender and 'Postmodern War,'" *Hypatia* 11, no. 4, Women and Violence (1996): 19–29, quote on 20.
41. Greta Lefleur, "Sex and 'Unsex': Histories of Gender Trouble in Eighteenth-Century North America," *Early American Studies* 12, no. 3 (2014): 469–499, especially footnote 3.

42. "Auto," November 6, 1702, AGI SD 858, folio 799. Junta de Guerra, January 3, 1703. AGI SD 858 folios 909–910. Michelle LeMaster, "War, Masculinity, and Alliances on the Carolina Frontiers," 164–185.
43. "Report from the Governor," November 5, 1702, AGI SD 858 folios 796–797. For a parallel in a later period, see Catherine Davies, "Colonial Dependence and Sexual Difference: Reading for Gender in the Writings of Simón Bolívar (1783–1830)," *Feminist Review* 79 (2005).
44. Rooney, "Intersectionality: Working in Conflict," 336. For more on memory and sieges, see Alexandra Wachter, " 'This Did Not Happen': Survivors of the Siege of Leningrad (1941–1944) and the 'Truth About the Blockade,' " in *Civilians Under Siege from Sarajevo to Troy*, ed. Alex Dowdall and John Horne (London: Palgrave Macmillan, 2018), 37–60.
45. "Auto," November 11, 1702. AGI SD 858 folios 854–855. For the longer history of the defensive and offensive role of San Agustín, see "Reales Cédulas Duplicadas," June 20, 1671. Expediente 263, AGN vol. 26, 248. For the role of gender in sieges, see Lauren Duval, "Mastering Charleston: Property and Patriarchy in British-Occupied Charleston, 1780–82," *William and Mary Quarterly* 75, no. 4 (2018): 589–622.
46. "Auto," November 5, 1702. AGI SD 858 folio 789. Journal of the Commons House of Assembly of South Carolina For 1703. Printed for the Historical Commission of South Carolina and edited by A. S. Salley (Columbia: The State Company, 1934), 5.
47. "Order by Governor Zúñiga y Cerda," November 10, 1702. AGI SD 858 folio 791.
48. "Report from the Governor," November 5, 1702, AGI SD 858 folios 796–798.
49. On the importance of familial and/or intimate relationships to colonial rule, see Susan Sleeper-Smith, *Indian Women and French Men: Rethinking Cultural Encounter in the Western Great Lakes*, Native Americans of the Northeast (Amherst: University of Massachusetts Press, 2001); Ann Laura Stoler, *Carnal Knowledge and Imperial Power: Race and the Intimate in Colonial Rule* (Berkeley: University of California Press, 2002); Durba Ghosh, *Sex and the Family in Colonial India: The Making of Empire* (Cambridge: Cambridge University Press, 2006); Sarah M. S. Pearsall, *Atlantic Families: Lives and Letters in the Later Eighteenth Century* (Oxford: Oxford University Press, 2008); Jennifer M. Spear, *Race, Sex, and Social Order in Early New Orleans* (Baltimore: Johns Hopkins University Press, 2009); and Susanah Shaw Romney, *New Netherland Connections: Intimate Networks and Atlantic Ties in Seventeenth-Century America* (Chapel Hill: University of North Carolina Press, 2014).
50. "Report from the Governor," November 5, 1702, AGI SD 858 folios 796–798, especially 797. "From Robert Daniel and James [Moore]" Correspondence, The National Archives, Kew, CO 5/382 Part 1 1702/11/09.

http://www.colonialamerica.amdigital.co.uk/Documents/Details/CO_5_382_Part1_005.

51. Jane G. Landers, "Female Conflict and Its Resolution in Eighteenth-Century St. Augustine," *The Americas* 54, no. 1 (1998): 557–574, especially 562–566. Terri L. Rolfson, "Women and the Labour of Laundry in the English Eighteenth Century" (MA thesis, Alberta University 2021).
52. Albert C. Manucy, *The Building of the Castillo De San Marcos,* National Park Service Interpretive Series (Washington, D.C.: U.S. Department of the Interior, National Park Service, 1955), 27–28.
53. "Auto," November 10, 1702, AGI SD 858 folios 849–850.
54. Elizabeth J. Reitz and Margaret Scarry, "Reconstructing Historic Subsistence with an Example from Sixteenth-century Spanish Florida," *Society for Historical Archaeology* (1985), 92. Elizabeth J. Reitz and Stephen L. Cumbaa, "Diet and Foodways of Eighteenth-century Spanish St. Augustine," in *Spanish St. Augustine: The Archaeology of a Colonial Creole Community,* ed. K. Deagan (New York: Academic Press, 1983): 151–185. John Jay TePaske, *The Governorship of Spanish Florida, 1700–1763* (Durham: Duke University Press, 1964), 77–82.
55. Elizabeth J. Reitz, "Animal Use and Culture Change in Spanish Florida," in *Animal Use and Culture Change,* ed. Kathleen Ryan and Pam Crabtree, MASCA Research Papers in *Science and Archaeology* 8 (1991): 62–77. Elizabeth J. Reitz, "Vertebrate Fauna from Seventeenth-Century St. Augustine," *Southeastern Archaeology* 11, no. 2 (1992): 79–94. (I thank Dr. Tanya Peres for these references.) Barbara L. Voss, "Gender, Race, and Labor in the Archaeology of the Spanish Colonial Americas," *Current Anthropology* 49, no. 5 (2008): 861–893, 866–867. Elizabeth J. Reitz, "The Spanish Colonial Experience and Domestic Animals," *Historical Archaeology* 26 (1992): 84–91. Elizabeth J. Reitz, "Zooarchaeological Analysis of a Free African Community: Gracia Real de Santa Teresa de Mose," *Historical Archaeology* 28 (1994): 23–40.
56. Juneisy Quintana Hawkins, "Anglo-Spanish Food Trade in the Colonial American Southeast, 1704–1763," paper presented at the Graduate Student Workshop: New and Emerging Studies of the Spanish Colonial Borderlands, March 2019, Huntington Library and Archive.
57. "María and Gertrudis Diaz Mejía," December 12, 1708, folio 298, AGI SD 848.
58. Mark F. Boyd, "The Siege of St. Augustine in 1702: A Report to the King of Spain by the Governor of East Florida," *Florida Historical Quarterly* 26, no. 4 (1948): 347; emphasis mine.
59. "Auto," November 9, 1702. Enrique Primo de Rivera, AGI SD 858 folios 838–839.
60. Ibid.
61. "Enrique Primo de Rivera," August 26, 1681. AGI SD 843. AGI SD 834. Theodore G. Corbett, "Population Structure in Hispanic St. Augustine,

1629–1763," *Florida Historical Quarterly* 54, no. 3 (1976): 263–284. Jane Landers, "Black Floridians and the Siege of 1702," *El Escribano* 39 (2002): 80–86. Jane Landers, "Africans and Native Americans on the Spanish Florida Frontier," in *Beyond Black and Red: African-Native Relations in Colonial Latin America*, ed. Matthew Restall (Albuquerque: University of New Mexico Press, 2005): 53–80. Jane Landers, *Black Society in Spanish Florida* (Urbana: University of Illinois Press, 1999), 21–28.

62. "Expediente 108," June 23, 1703. AGN Reales Cédulas Originales, Vol. 31, 320.
63. Ibid. For an even longer discussion on the need to light forts, see "Expediente 113," February 10, 1708. AGN Reales Cédulas Originales, vol. 31, 323. For a detailed description of the fort's rooms, see John H. Hann, "Translation of Alonso de Leturiondo's Memorial to the King of Spain," *Florida Archaeology* 2 (1986): 169–170.
64. "Auto," November 6, 1702, AGI SD 858 folios 799–800.
65. "Juan Saturnino de Abaurrea to King," September 29, 1704, AGI SD 858. Accessed through St. Augustine Historical Society, Florida, Reel 29. For more on Capitan Don Juan Saturnino de Abaurrea, see Worth, *Struggle for the Georgia Coast*, 31–33, 42, 127–145.
66. Baptism of Juana, 8 January 1703, born 7 November 1702. Baptism of Francisco, mulatto son of Juan de los Gasdos, slave of Adjutant Gerónimo Regidor, and Marta María, November 18, 1702, Cathedral Parish Records (CPR). Baptisms, dated November 1702–April 1703, CPR. Susan Richbourg Parker, "The Castillo Years, 1668–1763," in *Oldest City: The History of Saint Augustine*, ed. Susan Richbourg Parker (St. Augustine Historical Society, 2019), 76–101, quote on 87. Susan R. Parker, "Life in St. Augustine at the Turn of the Eighteenth Century," *El Escribano* 39 (2002): 55–64.
67. "Real Cédula, Oct 2. 1593," reissued on July 12, 1709. AGI SD 841, folio 670. For the centrality of European women in frontier regions, see Spear, *Race, Sex, and Social Order in Early New Orleans*, 42–51.
68. It was not the first time in the 137-year history of San Agustín that women sought refuge in the fort, but the 1702 siege saw all women relocate within the Castillo and stay for much longer than ever before. Manucy, *The Building of the Castillo De San Marcos*, 22. J. Leitch Wright, Jr., "Andrew Ranson: Seventeenth Century Pirate?" *Florida Historical Quarterly* 39, no. 2 (1960): 135–144. Gina M. Martino, *Women at War in the Borderlands of the Early American Northeast* (Chapel Hill: University of North Carolina Press, 2018), 57–58.
69. Bonnie G. McEwan, "The Archaeology of Women in the Spanish New World," *Historical Archaeology* 25, no. 4 (1991): 33–41. Charmian Mansell, "Beyond the Home: Space and Agency in the Experiences of Female Service in Early Modern England," *Gender & History* (2020), 9.
70. For the discussions of women as innocent and noncombatants in military conflict, see Stephanie McCurry, *Women's War: Fighting and Surviving the*

American Civil War (Cambridge: Belknap Press of Harvard University, 2019), 61. Laura Sjoberg and Jessica Peet, "A(nother) Dark Side of the Protection Racket," *International Feminist Journal of Politics* 13, no. 2 (2011): 163–182.

71. Ann M. Little, "The Shared Language of Gender in Colonial North American Warfare," in *The Routledge History of Gender, War, and the U.S. Military*, ed. Kara Dixon Vuic (Abingdon-on-Thames: Taylor & Francis, 2018): 11–23. Matthew Kruer, "Bloody Minds and Peoples Undone: Emotion, Family, and Political Order in the Susquehannock-Virginia War," *William and Mary Quarterly* 74, no. 3 (2017): 401–436.

72. For a longer and earlier description of the fort's inner structure, see John H. Hann, "Translation of Alonso de Leturiondo's Memorial to the King of Spain," *Florida Archaeology* 2 (1986): 169–170. Robert Hellman, "Firearm Technology and Supply in Spanish Florida" (MA thesis, Florida State University, 2001).

73. "Auto," November 9, 1702. Enrique Primo de Rivera, AGI SD 858 folios 838–839. Arnade, *The Siege of St. Augustine in 1702*, 22–29.

74. Early in the siege, the Spanish captured several English prisoners. Zúñiga y Cerda asked repeatedly about the amount and type of weaponry in Moore's army. Interrogation of Prisoners John Noble and Joseph William, November 9, 1702. AGSI SD 858 folio 823.

75. Alejandra Dubcovsky, *Informed Power: Communication in the Early American South* (Cambridge: Harvard University Press, 2016). For Florida's connections to the Spanish empire: "Expediente 286," October 20, 1671. AGN Reales Cédulas, vol. 26, 264; Expediente 332, November 24, 1671. AGN Reales Cédulas Duplicadas, vol. 26, 318.

76. Boyd, "The Siege of St. Augustine in 1702: A Report to the King of Spain by the Governor of East Florida," 345–352, quote on 349.

77. "Deposition of John Bee," April 26, 1738. The National Archives, Kew, CO 5/384. Gregory A. Moore, "The 1702 Siege of St. Augustine: English Miscalculation or Spanish Good Fortune?" *El Escribano* 39 (2002): 16–28. Parker, "Life in St. Augustine at the Turn of the Eighteenth Century," 55–64.

78. Boyd, "The Siege of St. Augustine in 1702: A Report to the King of Spain by the Governor of East Florida." For sounds in war, see J. Martin Daughtry, *Listening to War: Sound, Music, Trauma, and Survival in Wartime Iraq* (Oxford: Oxford University Press, 2015), 163. For an overview of the literature and issues concerning sonic history, see Richard Cullen Rath, "Hearing American History," *Journal of American History* 95, no. 2 (2008): 417–431; Sophia Rosenfeld, "On Being Heard: A Case for Paying Attention to the Historical Ear," *American Historical Review* 116, no. 2 (April 2011): 316–334. Two important overviews are provided by Richard Cullen Rath, *How Early America Sounded* (Ithaca: Cornell University Press, 2003), and Peter Charles Hoffer, *Sensory Worlds in Early America* (Balti-

more: Johns Hopkins University Press, 2003). Kristin Dutcher Mann, *The Power of Song: Music and Dance in the Mission Communities of Northern New Spain, 1509–1810* (Palo Alto: Stanford University Press, 2010). For archaeoacoustics in the Southeast, see Sarah Eyerly, Mark Sciuchetti, Rachel Bani, and Laura Zabanal, "Reconstructing the Sonic History of Mission San Luis de Talimali," in *Unearthing the Missions of Spanish Florida*, ed. Tanya Peres and Rochelle Marrinan (Gainesville: University Press of Florida, 2021), 280–303.

79. Hoffer, *Sensory Worlds in Early America*, 50–72. Rath, *How Early America Sounded*; Martin Daughtry, "Thanatosonics: Ontologies of Acoustic Violence," *Social Text 119* 32, no. 2 (2014): 25–51. James E. K. Parker, "Sonic Lawfare: On the Jurisprudence of Weaponised Sound," *Sound Studies* 5, no. 1 (2019): 72–96.
80. For women, sound, and war in other contexts: Lauren Curtis, "War Music: Soundscape and Song in Vergil," *Aeneid* 9, no. 63 (2017): 37–62.
81. "Auto," November 10, 1702, AGI SD 858 folios 847–848.
82. Ibid.
83. Ibid. For more on the tensions caused by women in public spaces, see Deborah L. Rotman, "Separate Spheres? Beyond the Dichotomies of Domesticity," *Current Anthropology* 47, no. 4 (2006): 666–674. Romina Zamora, "Lo Doméstico y Lo Público. Los Espacios De Sociabilidad De La Ciudad De San Miguel De Tucumán a Fines Del Siglo Xviii Y Comienzos Del Siglo XIX," *Nuevo Mundo, Mundos Nuevos [en línea]* (2010). Jaqueline Vassallo, "¿Historia De Las Mujeres O Historia De Género? Una Aproximación Al Estudio De Las Mujeres En La Ciudad De Córdoba a Fines Del Siglo Xviiii," *Revista Dos Puntas* V, no. 11 (2015): 153–178. Elizabeth Maddock Dillon, *The Gender of Freedom: Fictions of Liberalism and the Literary Public Sphere* (Stanford: Stanford University Press, 2004), 11–48.
84. Jim Sykes, "Ontologies of Acoustic Endurance: Rethinking Wartime Sound and Listening," *Sound Studies* 4, no. 1 (2018): 35–60, especially 44.
85. "Juan Clemente de Horruytiner," December 12, AGI SD 858 folio 887. For the tensions of having women in military presidios or settings, see Elizabeth S. Peña and Erik R. Seeman, "Desire and Distrust: The Paradox of Women at Old Fort Niagara," *New York History* 85, no. 1 (2004): 5–21. Lauren Duval, "Mastering Charleston: Property and Patriarchy in British-Occupied Charleston," 589–622. For how women's voices were galvanized in moments of conflict, see Kruer, *Time of Anarchy*, 68–73.
86. Carl D. Halbirt, "The Archaeology of the Cubo Line: St. Augustine's First Line of Defense," *Florida Anthropologist* 46 (1993): 105–127. Halbirt, "La Ciudad de San Augustín: A European Fighting Presidio in Eighteenth-Century La Florida," *Historical Archaeology* 38, no. 3 (2004): 33–46.

87. "Francisco Romo de Urisa," November 16, 1702, AGI SD 858 folio 858. For other Native spies during the siege, see "Declaración de Yndio Manuel Agramon," November 9, 1702 AGI SD 858 folios 831–832. As Spanish spies: "Auto," November 9, 1702, AGI SD 858 folios 842–844.
88. "Royal Cédula Relating to the Indians of Florida," March 15, 1702. AGI SD 836. Stetson Collection, PKY Reel 28. See also Alejandra Dubcovsky, "Defying Indian Slavery: Apalachee Voices and Spanish Sources in the Eighteenth-Century Southeast," *William and Mary Quarterly* 75, no. 2 (2018): 295–322.
89. Steven C. Hahn, *The Invention of the Creek Nation, 1670–1763* (Lincoln: University of Nebraska Press, 2004), 61. Mark F. Boyd, "Further Consideration of the Apalachee Missions," *The Americas* 9, no. 4 (1953): 469.
90. "Auto [Juan Lorenzo]," December 14, 1702. AGI SD 858 folios 888–889. Arnade, *The Siege of St. Augustine in 1702*, 51–52.
91. "Auto [Juan Lorenzo]," December 14, 1702. AGI SD 858 folios 888 –889. For women serving as symbols and mediators of peace: Barr, *Peace Came in the Form of a Woman: Indians and Spaniards in the Texas Borderlands* (Chapel Hill: University of North Carolina Press, 2007), 164–181.
92. "Juan Lorenzo," December 14, 1702. AGI SD 858 folios 888–889. Snyder, *Slavery in Indian Country: The Changing Face of Captivity* (Cambridge: Harvard University Press, 2010), 96. For more on Yamasees see Amy Turner Bushnell, "Living at Liberty: The Ungovernable Yamasees of Spanish Florida," in *The Yamasee Indians: From Florida to South Carolina*, ed. Denise I. Bossy (Lincoln: University of Nebraska Press, 2018), 27–54.
93. Ashley, "Yamasee Migration into the Mocama and Timucua Mission Provinces of Florida, 1667–1683," 55–79.
94. "Juan Pueyo," Visitation of Guale and Mocama, 1695, in Hann, *Visitations*, 227. Bushnell, *Situado y Sabana*, 175–176, 192.
95. "Juan Pueyo," Visitation of Guale and Mocama, 1695, in Hann, *Visitations*, 227.
96. "Juan Lorenzo," December 14, 1702. AGI SD 858 folios 888–889. Bushnell, *Situado y Sabana*, 175–176, 192.
97. Ibid. For Yamasee political developments, see Denise I. Bossy, "Spiritual Diplomacy, the Yamasees, and the Society for the Propagation of the Gospel Reinterpreting Prince George's Eighteenth-Century Voyage to England," *Early American Studies* 12, no. 2 (2014): 366–401.
98. "Auto [Juan Lorenzo]," December 14, 1702. AGI SD 858 folios 890–891.
99. Lynn Stephen and Shannon Speed, "Introduction," in *Indigenous Women and Violence: Feminist Activist Research in Heightened States of Injustice*, ed. Lynn Stephen and Shannon Speed (Tucson: University of Arizona Press, 2021), 3–26, quote on 20.
100. Aisha K. Finch, *Rethinking Slave Rebellion in Cuba: La Escalera and the Insurgencies of 1841–1844* (Chapel Hill: University of North Carolina Press, 2015): 141–167. Ayana Omilade Flewellen, "African Diasporic

Choices: Locating the Lived Experiences of Afro-Crucians in the Archival and Archaeological Record," *Nordisk Tidsskrift for Informationsvidenskab Og Kulturformidling* 8, no. 2 (2019): 54–74. Sophie White, *Voices of the Enslaved: Love, Labor, and Longing in French Louisiana* (Chapel Hill: University of North Carolina Press and Omohundro Institute of Early American History and Culture, 2019): 1–26.

101. Boyd, "The Siege of St. Augustine in 1702: A Report to the King of Spain by the Governor of East Florida," 347; emphasis mine.
102. "Auto," December 25, 1702. AGI SD 858 folios 894–95.
103. "Auto," December 24, 1702. AGI SD 858 folios 892–93.
104. Ibid.
105. Ibid.
106. Ibid.
107. Ibid.
108. "Auto," December 26, 1702. AGI SD 858 folio 121. For a later order on how to read ship signs: "Señas, 1738," AGI SD 2593. Cited from Reel 44, Stetson Collection, PKY.
109. "The Present State of Affairs in Carolina, by John Ash, 1706," in *Narratives of Early Carolina, 1650–1708*, ed. A. S. Salley, Jr. (New York: Charles Scribner's Sons, 1911), 265–276, quote on 272–273. Journal of the Commons House of Assembly of South Carolina, ed. A. S. Salley, Jr., and printed for the Historical Commission of South Carolina (Columbia: The State Company, 1934), 88, 127.
110. "Auto," December 31, 1702. AGI SD 858 folio 901.
111. "Declaration of Sebastián López de Toledo," January 4, 1703, AGI SD 858 folio 937.
112. "Auto," December 31, 1702. AGI SD 858 folio 901.
113. "Letter from General Berroa of Havana," December 31, 1702. AGI SD 858 folios 907–908.
114. Boyd, "The Siege of St. Augustine in 1702: A Report to the King of Spain by the Governor of East Florida," 349–350.
115. "Auto Suplicario," January 9, 1703. AGI SD 858 folio 933.
116. Ibid.
117. Boyd, "The Siege of St. Augustine in 1702: A Report to the King of Spain by the Governor of East Florida," 351.
118. "Junta de Guerra," January 3, 1703. AGI SD 858 folios 909–910.
119. Ibid.

Chapter Five. Narrating War and Loss

1. "Doña Francisca Ponce de León y Doña Juana Ponce de León," November 12, 1706, folio 69 AGI SD 841.
2. "Fray Claudio de Florencia to Governor Zúñiga y Cerda," [May?] 15, 1703, AGI SD 858.

3. "Doña Francisca Ponce de León y Doña Juana Ponce de León," November 12, 1706, folio 69 AGI SD 841.
4. Ibid; emphasis mine. For women petitioners, see Bianca Premo, "Before the Law: Women's Petitions in the Eighteenth-Century Spanish Empire," *Comparative Studies in Society and History* 53, no. 2 (2011): 261–289. For women's successful use of the law, see Silvia Marina Arrom, *The Women of Mexico City, 1790–1857* (Stanford: Stanford University Press, 1985), 79–98. Pilar Gonzalbo Aizpuru, "Las mujeres novohispanas y las contradicciones de una sociedad patriarcal," in *Las mujeres en la construcción de las sociedades iberoamericanas*, ed. Pilar Gonzalbo Aizpuru and Berta Ares Queija (Mexico City: El Colegio de México, 2004): 121–141. Lisa Sousa, "Women and Crime in Colonial Oaxaca: Evidence of Complementary Gender Roles in Mixtec and Zapotec Societies," in *Indian Women of Early Mexico*, ed. Susan Schroeder, Stephanie Wood, and Robert Haskett (Norman: University of Oklahoma Press, 1997), 199–221. Mónica Díaz and Rocío Quispe-Agnoli, *Women's Negotiations and Textual Agency in Latin America, 1500–1799*. Women and Gender in the Early Modern World (London: Routledge, 2017). Kimberly Gauderman, *Women's Lives in Colonial Quito: Gender, Law, and Economy in Spanish America* (Austin: University of Texas Press, 2003).
5. For the connection between elevating women of European descent and downgrading Black voices, see Natalie Zacek, *Settler Society in the English Leeward Islands, 1670–1776* (Cambridge: Cambridge University Press, 2010), 171. Judith Butler, *Gender Trouble: Feminism and the Subversion of Identity* (New York: Routledge, 1990), 170–178. Hilary McD. Beckles, "White Women and Slavery in the Caribbean," *History Workshop*, no. 36 (1993): 66–68. For silences in the archive, Jeffrey A. Erbig, Jr., and Sergio Latini, "Across Archival Limits: Colonial Records, Changing Ethnonyms, and Geographies of Knowledge," *Ethnohistory* 66, no. 2 (2019): 249–273. Valeria Añón, "Los usos del archivo: Reflexiones situadas sobre literatura y discurso colonial," *Indisciplinar la investigación: Archivo, trabajo de campo y escritura*, ed. Frida Gorbach and Mario Rufer (Mexico City: Siglo XXI, 2016), 251–274. Brian Connolly and Marisa Fuentes, "Introduction: From Archives of Slavery to Liberated Futures?" *History of the Present* 6, no. 2 (Fall 2016): 105–116.
6. For petitions and identity formation in Latin America, see Adrian Masters, "A Thousand Invisible Architects: Vassals, the Petition and Response System, and the Creation of Spanish Imperial Caste Legislation," *Hispanic American Historical Review* 98, no. 3 (2008): 377–406. Karen B. Graubart, "Pesa Más La Libertad: Slavery, Legal Claims, and the History of Afro-Latin American Ideas," *William and Mary Quarterly* 78, no. 3 (2021): 427–458.
7. Díaz Vara Calderón, "A 17th Century Letter of Gabriel Díaz Vara Calderón, Bishop of Cuba, Describing the Indians and Indian Missions of

Florida," ed. Lucy L. Wenhold, Smithsonian Miscellaneous Collections, vol. 95, no. 16 (Washington, D.C.: Smithsonian Institution Press, 1936). Albert C. Manucy, *The Houses of St. Augustine, 1565–1821* (Gainesville: University Press of Florida, 1992), 7. Luis Arnal Simón, *Arquitectura y urbanismo del septentrión novohispano: Fundaciones en la Florida y el Seno mexicano, siglos XVI al XVIII* (Universidad Nacional Autónoma de México, Facultad de Arquitectura, 2006), 19–48. For the condition of the city, see "Letter March 5, 1702," cited in Expediente 116. Reales Cédulas Originales, Volumen 31. AGN. "Letter April 20, 1703," Expediente 82, Reales Cédulas Originales, Volumen 31. AGN.

8. *Jonathan Dickinson's Journal; or, God's Protecting Providence. Being the Narrative of a Journey from Port Royal in Jamaica to Philadelphia between August 23, 1696 and April 1, 1697*, 6th ed. (London: James Phillips, 1787): 101–112.

9. "Auto Destroyed Homes," folios 691–702 Roll 10, AGI SD 841. These patterns grew over time. The property lists during the evacuation of Florida after the Seven Years' War revealed not only a continuation of women-owned property but also a variety in the type and size of property owned. While Maríana Horruytiner sold her property for over five hundred pesos, Lorenza Sanchez requested only ten pesos for her home. Doña Agustina Rexidor demanded a large sum because she owned several homes, while Geronomia Garcia and Doña Manuela Diaz asked for a more modest amount for land titles under their names. "Cuaderno de recivos," No. 1 Year 1764, AGI CUBA 372. For women's negotiations for property in other contexts, see Aske Laursen Brock and Misha Ewen, "Women's Public Lives: Navigating the East India Company, Parliament, and Courts in Early Modern England," *Gender & History* 33, no. 1 (2020): 3–23.

10. "Royal Cédula, Governor of Florida Don Laureano de Torres y Ayala," January 26, 1696, folio 376 AGI SD 835, Reel 24 accessed in St. Augustine Historical Society. For other women owning critical properties, see description of Doña Luisa de Los Ángeles y Arguelles, in John H. Hann, "Translation of Alonso de Leturiondo's Memorial to the King of Spain," *Florida Archaeology* 2 (1986): 201.

11. Verne E. Chatelain, *The Defenses of Spanish Florida, 1565 to 1763* (Washington, D.C.: Carnegie Institution of Washington, 1941): 64–75. John R. Dunkle, "Population Change as an Element in the Historical Geography of St. Augustine," *Florida Historical Quarterly* 37, no. 1 (1958): 3–32. Theodore G. Corbett, "Population Structure in Hispanic San Agustín, 1629–1763," *Florida Historical Quarterly* 54, no. 3 (1976): 263–284, 270. Kathryn L. Ness, *Setting the Table: Ceramics, Dining, and Cultural Exchange in Andalucía and La Florida* (Gainesville: University Press of Florida, 2016), 18.

12. "[On Soldiers]," October 30, 1669, vol. 26, Expediente 169, folio 167. Indiferente Virreinal Caja 4438, AGN. The presence of these soldiers in no

way diminishes the Native labor and contributions to the Castillo de San Marcos; Jason B. Palmer, "Forgotten Sacrifice: Native American Involvement in the Construction of the Castillo de San Marcos," *Florida Historical Quarterly* 80, no. 4 (2002): 437–454. For an earlier example of plazas in San Agustín, see "Governor to the Crown," June 28, 1683, AGI SD 226, folios 611–612.

13. Amy Bushnell, *The King's Coffer: Proprietors of the Spanish Florida Treasury, 1565–1702* (Gainesville: University Presses of Florida, 1981), 21. Asunción Lavrin and Edith Couturier, "Dowries and Wills: A View of Women's Socioeconomic Role in Colonial Guadalajara and Puebla, 1640–1790," *Hispanic American Historical Review* 59, no. 2 (1979): 280–304, 290. For more on dowries, see Edith Couturier, "Women and the Family in Eighteenth-Century Mexico: Law and Practice," *Journal of Family History* 10 (1985): 294–304. Danielle Terrazas Williams, " 'My Conscience Is Free and Clear': African-Descended Women, Status, and Slave Owning in Mid-Colonial Mexico," *The Americas* 75, no. 3 (2018): 525–554, especially 536. For women's efforts to control their own inheritances in the English model, see Christine Walker, *Jamaica Ladies: Female Slaveholders and the Creation of Britain's Atlantic Empire* (Chapel Hill: University of North Carolina Press and Omohundro Institute of Early American History and Culture, 2020), chapter 5.
14. Susan Richbourg Parker, "In My Mother's House: Dowry Property and Female Inheritance Patterns in Spanish Florida," in *Signposts: New Directions in Southern Legal History*, ed. Sally E. Hadden and Patricia Hagler Minter (Athens: University of Georgia Press, 2013), 19–44, especially 22–24.
15. Ibid. S. C. Bond, Jr., "Tradition and Change in First Spanish Period (1565–1763) St. Augustine Architecture: A Search for Colonial Identity" (PhD diss., State University of New York, Albany, 1995), 168–174. For another example of a dowry reclaimed in Florida, see "Petición hecha por Thomas Menéndez Marquez Contador, Oficial de la Real Caja del Presidio de la Florida, para que Ysabel de Cueba," September 28, 1698, Expediente 80, Indiferente Virreinal, Caja 5902 AGN.
16. Deborah A. Rosen, "Women and Property Across Colonial America: A Comparison of Legal Systems in New Mexico and New York," *William and Mary Quarterly* 60, no. 2 (2003): 355–381. Edith Couturier, "Women and the Family in Eighteenth-Century Mexico: Law and Practice," *Journal of Family History* 10, no. 3 (1985): 294–304. Joan R. Gundersen and Gwen Victor Gampe, "Married Women's Legal Status in Eighteenth-Century New York and Virginia," *William and Mary Quarterly* 39 (1982): 114–134. Asunción Lavrin and Edith Couturier, "Dowries and Wills: A View of Women's Socioeconomic Role in Colonial Guadalajara and Puebla, 1640–1790": "The inheritance system was bilateral, as children inherited both from the mother's and father's families. In a marriage,

both man and woman could retain separate properties and dispose of them as the law allowed" (286). Jose María Ots Capdequi, "Bosquejo historicó de los derechos de la mujer casada en la legislacion de Indias," *Revista General de Legislación y Jurisprudencia* 132 (1918): 162–182. For a comparison with the British model, see Carole Shammas, "Anglo-American Household Government in Comparative Perspective," *William and Mary Quarterly* 52, no. 1 (1995): 104–144.

17. Amy Turner Bushnell, " 'These People Are Not Conquered Like Those of New Spain': Florida's Reciprocal Colonial Compact," *Florida Historical Quarterly* 92, no. 3 (2014): 524–553. Jane Landers, "Gracia Real De Santa Teresa De Mose: A Free Black Town in Spanish Colonial Florida," *American Historical Review* 95, no. 1 (1990): 9–30. For this discussion in a slightly later period, see Nancy O. Gallman, "Reconstituting Power in an American Borderland: Political Change in Colonial East Florida," *Florida Historical Quarterly* 94, no. 2 (2015): 169–191.
18. For Native and Black in San Agustín, see Kathleen Deagan, "St. Augustine: First Urban Enclave in the United States," *North American Archaeologist* 3, no. 3 (1982); Kathleen Deagan, "Mestizaje in Colonial St. Augustine," *Ethnohistory* 20, no. 1 (1973). Barbara L. Voss, "Gender, Race, and Labor in the Archaeology of the Spanish Colonial Americas," *Current Anthropology* 49, no. 5 (2008): 861–893, 869. For Native women in European outposts, see Jennifer M. Spear, *Race, Sex, and Social Order in Early New Orleans* (Baltimore: Johns Hopkins University Press, 2009), 21–26.
19. María Elena Martínez, *Genealogical Fictions: Limpieza de Sangre, Religion, and Gender in Colonial Mexico* (Stanford: University of Stanford Press, 2008). Bianca Premo, "Familiar: Thinking Beyond Lineage and Across Race in Spanish Atlantic Family History," *William and Mary Quarterly* 70, no. 2 (2013): 295–316. Ann Twinam, *Purchasing Whiteness: Pardos, Mulattos, and the Quest for Social Mobility in the Spanish Indies* (Stanford: Stanford University Press, 2015), 1–4, 136–138.
20. "Auto Destroyed Homes," folios 691–702 Roll 10, AGI SD 841. Charles W. Arnade, *The Siege of St. Augustine in 1702* (Gainesville: University of Florida Press, 1959), 59–61. "Royal Cédula and petitions to leave," June 4, 1705, AGI SD 836, accessed in Reel 30, St. Augustine Historical Society.
21. Paul E. Hoffman, *Florida's Frontiers* (Bloomington: Indiana University Press, 2002), 174–206. For 1704 attacks, Alejandra Dubcovsky, " 'All of Us Will Have to Pay for These Activities': Colonial and Native Narratives of the 1704 Attack on Ayubale," *Native South* 10 (2017): 1–18. For the 1705 Timucua siege, see "Francisco de Florencia and Juan Pueyo to the Governor," August 13, 1706, folio 15, Roll 10 AGI SD 841. Jay Higginbotham, *Old Mobile: Fort Louis De La Louisiane, 1702–1711* (Mobile: Museum of the City of Mobile, 1977), 113–130. David Marley, *Wars of*

the Americas: A Chronology of Armed Conflict in the Western Hemisphere, 1492 to the Present (Santa Barbara: ABC-CLIO, 2008), 220–242.

22. Laura Sjoberg, "Theories of War," in *The Oxford Handbook of Gender and Conflict*, ed. Fionnuala Ní Aoláin, Naomi R. Cahn, Dina Francesca Haynes, and Nahla Valji (New York: Oxford University Press, 2018), 3–16. Mary Beth Norton, "Eighteenth-Century American Women in Peace and War: The Case of the Loyalists," *William and Mary Quarterly* 33, no. 3 (1976): 386–409. For women's role in conflict and its aftermath, see Elizabeth A. Wood, "The Trial of the New Woman: Citizens-in-Training in the New Soviet Republic," *Gender & History* 13, no. 3 (2001): 524–545.
23. "Claudio de Florencia to Governor Zúñiga y Cerda," [May?] 15, 1703, AGI SD 858. Junta de Guerra, May 22, 1703, folio 2. AGI SD 836.
24. Denise Bossy, "Godin & Co.: Charleston Merchants and the Indian Trade, 1674–1715," *South Carolina Historical Magazine* 114 (2013): 96–131, especially 129. See also Andrew B. Johnson, "Enslaved Native Americans and the Making of South Carolina" (PhD diss., Rice University, 2018), 171–218, 346–350. Honor Sachs, "Judith and Hannah: Eighteenth-Century Florida, South Carolina, and Virginia (US)," in *As If She Were Free: A Collective Biography of Women and Emancipation in the Americas*, ed. Erica L. Ball, Tatiana Seijas, and Terri L. Snyder (Cambridge: Cambridge University Press, 2020), 131–150.
25. William R. Gillaspie, "Survival of a Frontier Presidio: St. Augustine and the Subsidy and Private Contract Systems, 1680–1702," *Florida Historical Quarterly* 62, no. 3 (1984): 273–295. For women's successful use of the law, see Silvia Marina Arrom, *The Women of Mexico City, 1790–1857* (Stanford: Stanford University Press, 1985), 79–98; Pilar Gonzalbo Aizpuru, "Las mujeres novohispanas y las contradicciones de una sociedad patriarcal," in *Las mujeres en la construcción de las sociedades iberoamericanas*, ed. Pilar Gonzalbo Aizpuru and Berta Ares Queija (Mexico City: El Colegio de México, 2004): 121–14; Lisa Sousa, "Women and Crime in Colonial Oaxaca: Evidence of Complementary Gender Roles in Mixtec and Zapotec Societies," in *Indian Women of Early Mexico*, ed. Susan Schroeder et al. (Norman: University of Oklahoma Press, 1997): 199–21; Mónica Díaz and Rocío Quispe-Agnoli, *Women's Negotiations and Textual Agency in Latin America, 1500–1799*, Women and Gender in the Early Modern World (London: Routledge, 2017).
26. Silvia Marina Arrom, *The Women of Mexico City, 1790–1857* (Stanford: Stanford University Press, 1985): 58–65. Jane Landers, "Ana Gallum, Freed Slave and Property Owner (Florida, 1801)," in *Women in Colonial Latin America, 1526–1806: Texts and Contexts*, ed. Nora Jaffary and Jane Mangan (Indianapolis: Hackett Printing Company, 2018): 224–239, especially 225. James Daybel, *Women Letter-Writers in Tudor England* (Oxford: Oxford University Press, 2006), 61–90, especially 85. Lisa Vol-

lendorf, *The Lives of Women: A New History of Inquisitional Spain* (Nashville: Vanderbilt University Press, 2005), 53.

27. For more on these racial categories, see Ann Twinam, *Purchasing Whiteness: Pardos, Mulattos, and the Quest for Social Mobility in the Spanish Indies*; and Rebecca Earle, "The Pleasures of Taxonomy: Casta Paintings, Classification, and Colonialism," *William and Mary Quarterly* 73, no. 3 (2016): 427–466.
28. Marisa J. Fuentes, *Dispossessed Lives: Enslaved Women, Violence, and the Archive* (Philadelphia: University of Pennsylvania Press, 2016), 74. Jennifer L. Morgan, *Reckoning with Slavery: Gender, Kinship, and Capitalism in the Early Black Atlantic* (Durham: Duke University Press, 2021), 8–10. Cecily Jones, *Engendering Whiteness: White Women and Colonialism in Barbados and North Carolina, 1627–1865* (Manchester: Manchester University Press, 2007), 13–41.
29. Jennifer L. Morgan, *Laboring Women: Reproduction and Gender in New World Slavery* (Philadelphia: University of Pennsylvania Press, 2004), 69–106; Kathleen M. Brown, *Good Wives, Nasty Wenches, and Anxious Patriarchs: Gender, Race, and Power in Colonial Virginia* (Chapel Hill: University of North Carolina, 1996), 1–5. For representations of Black and Native grief: Sasha Turner, "The Nameless and the Forgotten: Maternal Grief, Sacred Protection, and the Archive of Slavery," *Slavery & Abolition* 38, no. 2 (2017): 232–250. Audra Simpson, *Mohawk Interruptus: Political Life Across the Borders of Settler States* (Durham: Duke University Press, 2014), 156.
30. Mention of law from October 2, 1593, Roll 11, folio 670 AGI SD 841. Kathryn Burns, "Forms of Authority: Women's Legal Representations in Mid-Colonial Cuzco," in *Women, Texts, and Authority in the Early Modern Spanish World*, ed. Marta V. Vicente and Luis R. Corteguera (Burlington, Vt.: Routledge, 2003), 149–163. Kathryn Burns, "Notaries, Truth, and Consequences," *American Historical Review* 110, no. 2 (2005): 350–379.
31. For petitions concerned with dowries, see "Royal Cédula in letter from January 22, 1691," AGI SD 836, accessed in Reel 23, St. Augustine Historical Society. Manuela Rodriguez's daughter tried to secure the money for herself; see "March 23, 1702," folio 305–306, AGI SD 840. See also: "Doña Francisca Ponce de Leon y Doña Juana Ponce de Leon," November 12, 1706, folio 69 AGI SD 840. "Cédula for Ysabel Hernádez," November 7, 1703, AGI SD 2529, accessed on Reel 30 in St. Augustine Historical Society
32. "Catalina Hernandez de la Cruz, viuda del Ayudante," May 15, 1701, folio 218, AGI SD 840 Roll 10.
33. Bianca Premo, "Felipa's Braid: Women, Culture, and the Law in Eighteenth-Century Oaxaca," *Ethnohistory* 61, no. 3 (2014): 497–523. Bianca Premo, "Before the Law: Women's Petitions in the Eighteenth-Century Spanish Empire," 261–289. On the patriarchal structure of Colonial Latin American law, see Charlene Villaseñor Black, "Gender and Representation in the Early Modern Hispanic World," in *Mapping Gendered Routes and Spaces in the Early*

Modern World, ed. Merry E. Wiesner (Burlington, Vt.: Ashgate, 2015): 75–97. Susan Kellogg, *Law and the Transformation of Aztec Culture, 1500–1700* (Norman: University of Oklahoma Press, 1995), especially xix. Margarita Ortega López, "Protestas de las mujeres castellanas contra el orden patriarcal privado durante el siglo XVIII," *Cuadernos de Historia Moderna* 19 (1997): 65–89. Sonya Lipsett-Rivera, "Marriage and Family Relations in Mexico During the Transition from Colony to Republic," in *State and Society in Spanish America During the Age of Revolution*, ed. Victor Uribe-Urán (Wilmington: Scholarly Resources, 2001), 121–148. For more critical approaches to patriarchy, see Allyson M. Poska, "The Case for Agentic Gender Norms for Women in Early Modern Europe," *Gender & History* 30, no. 2 (2018): 354–365; Thomas Black, *The Limits of Gender Domination: Women, the Law, and Political Crisis in Quito, 1765–1830* (Albuquerque: University of New Mexico Press, 2010): 1–11; Patricia Seed, *To Love, Honor, and Obey in Colonial Mexico* (Stanford: Stanford University Press, 1988), 227–235; Stephanie Spencer-Wood, "Feminist Theorizing of Patriarchal Colonialism, Power Dynamics, and Social Agency Materialized in Colonial Institutions," *International Journal of Historical Archaeology* 20, no. 3 (2016): 477–491.

34. For an example of a petition that took a long time to resolve, see "Governor Laureano de Torres y Ayala enclosing letter of Antonia Barbossa," February 18, 1698, AGI SD 228, accessed on Reel 25 in St. Augustine Historical Society. "María, Manuela, and Lorenza de Aspiolea," November 2, 1705, AGI SD 2529 accessed on Reel 30 in St. Augustine Historical Society.
35. Bianca Premo, "Before the Law: Women's Petitions in the Eighteenth-Century Spanish Empire," 266.
36. "María Mendoza widow of Ensign Diego de Argüelles," October 12, 1706, folio 133, AGI SD 841. For a discussion of women in war and peace in a different context, see Mary Beth Norton, "Eighteenth-Century American Women in Peace and War: The Case of the Loyalists," 386–409.
37. "Antonia de Argüelles," November 20, 1706, folio 149, Roll 11 AGI SD 841. "Juana Cordera Meriaz," January 10, 1709, folio 554, Roll 11 AGI SD 841.
38. For the evolution of women's reporting, recording, and demanding payment during wartime, see Myna Trustram, *Women of the Regiment: Marriage and the Victorian Army* (New York: Cambridge University Press, 1984), 8–15, 50–55; and Kristin A. Collins, " 'Petitions Without Number': Widows' Petitions and the Early Nineteenth-Century Origins of Public Marriage-Based Entitlements," *Law and History Review* 31, no. 1 (2013): 1–60.
39. "Petition by María de Pedroza," December 2, 1706, folio 137, AGI SD 841. "Letter of Support by Governor," December 2, 1706, folios 139–145 AGI SD 841.
40. "Antonia Grosso's petition," February 4, 1706, folio 541 AGI SD 840.

41. "Gertrudis de Uriza," November 2, 1708, folio 880, AGI SD 836. For other Spanish prisoners see "Comy Johnston to the Secry," July 5, 1710, Charles Town, South Carolina, in *Carolina Chronicle: The Papers of Gideon Johnston, 1707–1716*, ed. Frank J. Klingbert (Berkeley: University of California Press, 1946), 55.
42. "Gertrudis de Uriza," November 2, 1708, folio 880, AGI SD 836.
43. "Governor's support of Antonia Grosso's petition," February 6, 1706, folio 539, AGI SD 840. Arnade, *The Siege of St. Augustine in 1702*, 39–40.
44. For a brief mention of these petitions, see Diana Reigelsperger, "Interethnic Relations and Settlement on the Spanish Florida Frontier, 1668–1763" (PhD diss., University of Florida, 2013), 86–94.
45. "María and Gertrudis Diaz Mejía," December 12, 1708, folio 298, AGI SD 848.
46. Ibid.
47. "Doña Gertrudis de Argüelles," April 20, 1708, folio 439, AGI SD 833.
48. Ibid.
49. Martha Few, *Women Who Live Evil Lives: Gender, Religion, and the Politics of Power in Colonial Guatemala, 1650–1750* (Austin: University of Texas Press, 2002), 1–10, 50–70, 112. Kimberly Gauderman, *Women's Lives in Colonial Quito: Gender, Law, and Economy in Spanish America* (Austin: University of Texas Press, 2003). Gregorio Saldarriaga, "Redes y estrategias femeninas de inserción social en tierra de fronteratres mujeres desarraigadas en Antioquia (siglo XVII)," in *Las mujeres en la construcción de las sociedades iberoamericanas*, ed. Pilar Gonzalbo Aizpuru and Berta Ares Queija (Mexico City: El Colegio de México, 2004): 141–161. Nancy van Deusen, "Circuits of Knowledge Among Women in Early Seventeenth-Century Lima," in *Gender, Race, and Religion in the Colonization of the Americas*, ed. Nora E. Jaffary (London: Routledge, 2007), 137–150. Amanda E. Herbert, *Female Alliances: Gender, Identity, and Friendship in Early Modern Britain* (New Haven: Yale University Press, 2014), 1–21, especially 8. Brianna Leavitt-Alcántara, *Alone at the Altar: Single Women and Devotion in Guatemala, 1670–1870* (Stanford: Stanford University Press, 2018).
50. For discussions of public/private, see Ann Twinam, *Public Lives, Private Secrets: Gender, Honor, Sexuality, and Illegitimacy in Colonial Spanish America* (Stanford: Stanford University Press, 1999), 20–34. Ann Twinam, "Estrategias de Resistencia, manipulación de los espacios privado y público por mujeres latinoamericanas de la época colonial," in *Las mujeres en la construcción de las sociedades iberoamericanas*, ed. Pilar Gonzalbo Aizpuru and Berta Ares Queija (Mexico City: El Colegio de México, 2004), 251–269. For a later period, see Bárbara Reyes, *Private Women, Public Lives: Gender and the Missions of the Californias* (Austin: University of Texas Press, 2009), 1–16.

51. "Doña María de Argüelles y Canizares," April 14, 1711, folio 56 AGI SD 843. For other examples: "Catalina Hernandez de la Cruz viuda del Ayudante," May 15, 1701, folio 218, Roll 10, AGI SD 840; "María de Mendoza," November 30, 1706, folio 131, Roll 11 AGI SD 841; "Doña Manuela Benedit Horruytiner," March 7, 1707, folio 244, Roll 11 AGI SD 841.
52. "Muxer María de Pedroza," December 2, 1706, folio 137, AGI SD 841.
53. The Spanish Crown was careful with its purse. There were several women reprimanded for making false petitions. These petitions were not unauthentic since the women *had* lost their husbands and fathers. But there was often a discrepancy on the date and details surrounding their deaths. Their requests were sometimes desperate efforts to secure claims long ignored by the crown and other times careful ploys to obtain a larger sum of money. The point, however, is that they tended to get caught. "Two widows," April 13, 1711, folio 49, Roll 12 AGI SD 843.
54. For some examples see "Don Joseph de Zúñiga y Cerda to Crown," August 9, 1715, folio 757 AGI SD 836; "Governor Zúñiga y Cerda Memorial for Helena de Aldeco," September 25, 1705, folios 798–799 AGI SD 836; "Governor Zúñiga y Cerda memorial for Doña Gertrudis de Urisa," November 20, 1708, folio 881, AGI SD 836.
55. For women's petitions that support existing structures of power, see Bianca Premo, "Before the Law: Women's Petitions in the Eighteenth-Century Spanish Empire." Stephanie McCurry, *Confederate Reckoning: Power and Politics in the Civil War South* (Cambridge: Harvard University Press, 2012), 4.
56. There are least two petitions from her: "Doña María de Argüelles y Canizares," April 14, 1711, folio 56, AGI SD 843, and again "Doña María de Argüelles y Canizares," February 3, 1715, folio 331 AGI SD 843.
57. "Helena de Aldeco," September 25, 1705, folios 798–799, AGI SD 836.
58. "Helena de Aldeco," September 25, 1705, folio 804, AGI SD 836. For how women created identities through exclusion, see Ann Twinam, *Public Lives, Private Secrets: Gender, Honor, Sexuality, and Illegitimacy in Colonial Spanish America*.
59. "Agustina Rodriguez de Mesa," August 31, 1701, AGI SD 833 accessed on Reel 37 in St. Augustine Historical Society. "Dionisia Gonzales de Villa García," March 26, 1702, AGI SD 840 accessed on Reel 27 in St. Augustine Historical Society.
60. Iyko Day, "Being or Nothingness: Indigeneity, Antiblackness, and Settler Colonial Critique," *Critical Ethnic Studies* 1, no. 2 (2015): 102–121. Tiffany Lethabo King, *The Black Shoals: Offshore Formations of Black and Native Studies* (Durham: Duke University Press, 2019), 17–21.
61. *Plaza muerta* refers to a pension received due to injury or incapacity to work; it was also a paid military post or a paid position with no assigned duties.
62. "Governor Laureano de Torres y Ayala enclosing letter of Antonia Barbossa," February 18, 1698, AGI SD 228, accessed on Reel 25 in St. Augustine Historical Society.

63. "María, Manuela, and Lorenza de Aspiolea," November 2, 1705, AGI SD 2529 accessed on Reel 30 in St. Augustine Historical Society.
64. For another petition that spanned a decade, see "Luisa de Uriza y Sotomayor," n.d., folios 1100–1101, AGI SD 836.
65. "Gertrudis de Uriza," November 2, 1708, folio 880, AGI SD 836.
66. "Helena de Aldeco," September 25, 1705, folios 798–799, AGI SD 836.
67. "Doña María de la Rocha," October 4, 1704, AGI SD 848 accessed on Reel 29 in St. Augustine Historical Society
68. "Helena de Aldeco," September 25, 1705, folios 798–799, AGI SD 836. For another example, see "Doña Agustina," AGI SD 836, March 30, 1708, folio 970 AGI SD 836. For how language of sacrifice created opportunities, see Stephanie McCurry, *Confederate Reckoning: Power and Politics in the Civil War South*, 150.
69. "Widow Gertrudis de Uriza," October 3, 1702, folios 397–400, AGI SD 840.
70. Ibid. Doña Juana de Florencia made a similar argument in her petition, "Juana de Florencia," February 4, 1709, folios 662–664, AGI SD 841.
71. "Ana María de Argüelles," March 12, 1707, AGI SD 843 accessed on Reel 30 in St. Augustine Historical Society.
72. Ibid.
73. There are few extant petitions directly from men; most claims from men come from the itemized list of lost property made by Governor Zúñiga y Cerda. "Auto," January 1708, folios 691–702, Roll 11 AGI SD 841.
74. "Diego Caro," June 16, 1705, folios 766–767, AGI SD 836.
75. Ibid.
76. "Governor Zúñiga y Cerda Memorial for Helena de Aldeco," "Doña María de Argüelles y Canizares," April 14, 1711, folio 56, AGI SD 843. For another failed male petition, see "Don Manuel Quiñones," December 12, 1708, AGI SD (Audiencia de Santo Domingo), 836, folio 980.
77. AGI SD 841 folios 691–702. For a brief discussion of this source, see Charles Arnade, "The Avero Story: An Early Saint Augustine Family with Many Daughters and Many Houses," *Florida Historical Quarterly* 40, no. 1 (1961): 1–34, especially 1–3.
78. On integrated living arrangements in Spanish America, see R. Douglas Cope, *The Limits of Racial Domination: Plebeian Society in Colonial Mexico City, 1660–1720* (Madison: University of Wisconsin Press, 1994). Premo, "Familiar: Thinking Beyond Lineage," 300–302. Yolanda Gamboa, "Mujeres Españolas Y Vida Cotidiana En El San Agustín Colonial," *Puente Atlántico del siglo XXI. Boletín interdisciplinar de la Asociación de Licenciados y Doctores Españoles en Estados Unidos (ALDEEU)* (2003): 7–9. For Native women and property ownership, see Miriam Melton-Villanueva, "Cacicas, Escribanos, and Landholders: Indigenous Women's Late Colonial Mexican Texts, 1703–1832," *Ethnohistory* 65, no. 2 (2018): 297–322.

79. "The concept of genealogy is central both because it alludes to the process of historicizing race and because in the early modern Hispanic world it was ubiquitous and consequential." Martínez, *Genealogical Fictions*, 3. For creation of narratives of war, see Belinda Linn Rincón, *Bodies at War: Genealogies of Militarism in Chicana Literature and Culture* (Tucson: University of Arizona Press, 2017), 6–8, 17–20. Miriam Cooke, *Women and the War Story* (Berkeley: University of California Press, 1996), 1–12. Susan Jeffords, *The Remasculinization of America: Gender and the Vietnam War* (Bloomington: Indiana University Press, 1989).
80. AGI SD 858 [983].
81. "Marriage of Joseph Carabina, negro slave." January 28, 1703. Marriages, 1632–1720. Box 4. Digitization of the Archives of the Diocese of St. Augustine (DADS).
82. Brown, *Good Wives, Nasty Wenches, and Anxious Patriarchs: Gender, Race, and Power in Colonial Virginia*, 41–105.

Chapter Six. The War That Never Ends

1. Bonnie G. McEwan, "Colonialism on the Spanish Florida Frontier: Mission San Luis, 1656–1704," *Florida Historical Quarterly* 92, no. 3 (2014): 591–625.
2. Baptism of Juana de Florencia, December 11, 1662, in the *Baptisms and Burials 17th Century and the Archive of Ecclesiastical Records of the St. Augustine Diocese.* Slave Societies Digital Archive. Marriage of Jacinto Roque Pérez and Juana de Florencia, November 19, 1675. Marriages, 1632–1720. Box 4. Digitization of the Archives of the Diocese of St. Augustine (DADS).
3. "Joseph de Zúñiga y Cerda to Jacinto Roque," November 5, 1700, AGI SD 858, folio 250. "Don Patricio, Cacique of Ivitachuco, and Don Andrés, Cacique of San Luis, to the King," February 12, 1699, in *Here They Once Stood: The Tragic End of the Apalachee Missions*, ed. Mark F. Boyd, Hale G. Smith, and John W. Griffin (Gainesville: University of Florida Press, 1951), 24–26. Jacinto Roque, in Alonso Solana 1687, Autos and Inquiry, AGI ES 156 Cuaderno E, folio 31. "Juana's 1709 Petition," AGI SD 841 folios 623–661. Bonnie G. McEwan, "San Luis De Talimali: The Archaeology of Spanish-Indian Relations at a Florida Mission." *Historical Archaeology* 25, no. 3 (1991): 37. John H. Hann, *Apalachee: The Land Between the Rivers* (Gainesville: University Press of Florida, 1988), 13–17. Amy Bushnell, "The Menéndez Marquéz Cattle Barony at La Chua and the Determinants of Economic Expansion in Seventeenth-Century Florida," *Florida Historical Quarterly* 56, no. 4 (April 1978): 407–431; John F. Scarry, "The Apalachee Chiefdom: A Mississippian Society on the Fringe of the Mississippi World," in *The Forgotten Centuries: Indians and Europeans in the American South, 1521–1704*, ed. Charles M. Hudson and Carmen Chaves Tesser (Athens: University of Georgia Press, 1994), 156–178; Patrick

Johnson, "Apalachee Identity on the Gulf Coast Frontier," *Native South* 6: 110–141.

4. "Manuel Solana to Governor Zúñiga y Cerda," November 13, 1702. AGI SD 858. "Manuel Solana to Don Francisco Martinéz," November 11, 1702. AGI México 618. "Don Juan de Velasco to Viceroy Duke of Alburquerque," San Juan de Ulua, January 21, 1703. AGI México 618. "Duque of Albuquerque," May 18, 1704, folio 47 AGI Mexico 618. "Juana's 1709 Petition," AGI SD 841 folios 623–661. John H. Hann and Bonnie G. McEwan, *The Apalachee Indians and Mission San Luis* (Gainesville: University Press of Florida, 1998), 53–63.
5. For attacks on Apalachee, see Hann, *Apalachee*, 264–283; Gallay, *The Indian Slave Trade: The Rise of the English Empire in the American South, 1670–1717* (New Haven: Yale University Press, 2003), 145–180; Christina Snyder, *Slavery in Indian Country: The Changing Face of Captivity in Early America* (Cambridge: Harvard University Press, 2010), 70–78. Alejandra Dubcovsky, "Defying Indian Slavery: Apalachee Voices and Spanish Sources in the Eighteenth-Century Southeast," *William and Mary Quarterly* 75, no. 2 (2018): 295–322.
6. James Moore, "An Account of What the Army Did, under the Command of Col. Moore, in His Expedition Last Winter, against the Spaniards and the Spanish Indians," in *Historical Collections*, ed. B. R. Carroll (New York: Harper & Brothers, 1836), 576. "Zúñiga y Cerda to the King," October 6, 1704, folios 287–289 and "Zúñiga y Cerda chiefs of Ivitachuco and San Luís and other chiefs," April 24, 1704, AGI SD 858.
7. "Fray Claudio de Florencia's Questions," San Agustín, AGI SD 841, folios 626–630.
8. For a longer discussion on gender and racialization, see Joshua Piker, "Indians and Race in Early America: A Review Essay," *History Compass* 3, no. 1 (2005). Sharon Block, *Rape and Sexual Power in Early America* (Chapel Hill: University of North Carolina Press, 2006), 246.
9. "Don Patricio, Cacique of Ivitachuco, and Don Andrés, Cacique of San Luis, to the King." February 12, 1699, in Boyd et al., *Here They Once Stood*, 24–26. Jacinto Roque, in Alonso Solana 1687, Autos and Inquiry, AGI ES 156 Cuaderno E, folio 31. "Juana's 1709 Petition," AGI SD 841 folios 623–661.
10. John H. Hann and Bonnie G. McEwan. *The Apalachee Indians and Mission San Luis* (Gainesville: University Press of Florida, 1998), 54–63. Ronald Childers, "Apalachee: The Final Days," unpublished manuscript. Hann Collection, PKY.
11. "Visitation, 1694–1695." AGI EC 157. John Hann, *Visitations and Revolts in Florida, 1657–1695*, in *Florida Archaeology* 7 (1993), 120. Hann and McEwan. *The Apalachee Indians and Mission San Luis*, 177–183. Bonnie McEwan, "Hispanic Life on Seventeenth-Century Florida Frontier," 255–267. Bonnie G. McEwan and John H. Hann, "Reconstructing a

Spanish Mission: San Luis de Talimali," *OAH Magazine of History* 14, no. 4 (2000): 16–19.

12. "Auto sobre el abasto," November 29, 1700. AGI SD 858, folios 831–835. For more on cattle in early Florida, see Jason Herbert, "Beast of Many Names: Cattle, Conflict, and the Transformation of Indigenous Florida, 1519–1858" (PhD diss., University of Minnesota, 2022).
13. "Joseph de Zúñiga y Cerda to Jacinto Roque," November 5, 1700, AGI SD 858, folio 250. "Don Patricio, Cacique of Ivitachuco, and Don Andrés, Cacique of San Luis, to the King." February 12, 1699, in Boyd et al., *Here They Once Stood*, 24–26. Jacinto Roque, in Alonso Solana 1687, Autos and Inquiry, AGI ES 156 Cuaderno E, folio 31.
14. Baptism of Juana de Florencia, December 11, 1662, Box 4. DADS.
15. "Francisca de Leyba y Artiaga, wife of Capitán Matheo Luis de Florencia," January 29, 1671, AGI SD 234. Pilar Gonzalbo Aizpuru, "Hacia Una Historia De La Vida Privada En La Nueva España," *Historia Mexicana* 42, no. 2 (1992): 353–377.
16. Claudio de Florencia had been born in Florida, but all his siblings and his parents, Matheo Luis de Florencia and Luisa de Los Ángeles, had arrived from Seville. Pedro, Claudio's younger son and Juana's father, was not present during the attack. Pedro named one of his sons Claudio. "Fray Claudio de Florencia's Testimony," July 1709, AGI SD 841. Folio 630.
17. Aubrey Lauersdorf, "An Apalachee Revolt? Reconceptualizing Violence in Seventeenth-Century Apalachee," *Florida Historical Quarterly* 100, no. 1 (2021): 23–51. Hann, *Apalachee*, 14–22. Amy Turner Bushnell, " 'That Demonic Game': The Campaign to Stop Indian *Pelota* Playing in Spanish America, 1675–1684," *The Americas* 35, no. 1 (1978): 1–19.
18. "Testimony of Nicolás Mendes," July 8, 1709, AGI SD 841, folios 644–649; "Testimony of Juan Ruíz Mexía, July 8, 1709," AGI SD 841, folios 631–635.
19. "Testimony of Nicolás Mendes," July 8, 1709, AGI SD 841, folios 644–649.
20. "Testimony of Alonso Naranjo," July 8, 1709, AGI SD 841, folios 641–644.
21. "Fray Claudio de Florencia's Testimony," July 1709, AGI SD 841. Folio 630. For the impact and implications of these experiences and narratives, see Noam Lupu and Leonid Peisakhin, "The Legacy of Political Violence Across Generations," *American Journal of Political Science* 61, no. 4 (2017): 836–851. Francisco Villamil, "Mobilizing Memories: The Social Conditions of the Long-term Impact of Victimization," *Journal of Peace Research* 58 (2020): 399–416.
22. "Juan Francisco's Testimony," July 8, 1709, AGI SD 841. Folio 630.
23. Aubrey Lauersdorf, "An Apalachee Revolt? Reconceptualizing Violence in Seventeenth-Century Apalachee," 23–52. Hann, *Apalachee*, 14–22.
24. Doña Juana married young, even for the time. "Marriage of Jacinto Roque Pérez and Juana de Florencia," November 19, 1675. Marriages, 1632–1720, Box 4. DADS. "For example, in the eighteenth century most

women in Mexico City married for the first time between the ages of 17 and 27, with the average age of marriage being 20.5 years"; see Susan Migden Socolow, *The Women of Colonial Latin America*, 2nd ed. (Cambridge: Cambridge University Press, 2000), 67. Marriage patterns in colonial Spanish America tended to be endogamous. Juana and Jacinto's marriage was no different: they were both from the highest echelons of Florida society: "Petition of Jazinto Roque Pérez." 1689, Expediente 033, Indiferente Virreinal Caja 4842, AGN. Carmen Castañeda, "La formación de la pareja y el matrimonio," in *Familias novohispanas: Siglos XVI al XIX*, ed. Pilar Gonzalbo Aizpuru (México: El Colegio de México, 1991), 73–90. Ramón A. Gutiérrez, "Honor Ideology, Marriage Negotiation, and Class-Gender Domination in New Mexico, 1690–1846," *Latin American Perspectives* 12 (Winter 1985): 81–104.

25. "Testimony of Capitan Don Francisco Romo de Urisa," July 10, 1709, AGI SD 841, folios 656–659. For Florencia's political power, see "Pablo Hita y Salazar to King," June 15, 1675, Casa de Contratación, 3309, AGI. *Florencia Visita*, EC 157 Cuaderno 4, AGI. For trade connections, "Thomas Menéndez Marquez and Joaquín de Florencia to Governor Laureano de Torres," April 15, 1697, AGI SD 228. Amy Turner Bushnell, "The Menéndez Marquéz Cattle Barony at La Chua and the Determinants of Economic Expansion in Seventeenth-Century Florida," *Florida Historical Quarterly* 56, no. 4 (1978): 407–431, especially 424–425.

26. "Francisco de la Guerra y Vega to Pedro de Florencia," January 10, 1667, Expediente 017, Indiferente de Guerra Caja, 4101, AGN. "Fray Claudio de Florencia's Testimony," July 1709, AGI SD 841. Folio 630.

27. Claudio de Florencia hints at the closeness of the two, by describing Jacinto as "the deceased husband and conjoined person of the said Doña Juana Cathalina de Florencia." "Fray Claudio de Florencia's Testimony," July 1709, AGI SD 841. Folio 624. Amy Turner Bushnell, *The King's Coffer: Proprietors of the Spanish Florida Treasury, 1565–1702* (Gainesville: University Presses of Florida, 1981), 17.

28. Susan Migden Socolow, *The Women of Colonial Latin America*, 72, 92. Silvia Marina Arrom, "Historia de la Mujer y de la Familia Latinoamericanas," *Historia Mexicana* 2 (1992): 379–418.

29. "Governor Quiroga y Losada to King sending Families to Apalachee," April 1, 1688, AGI SD 227. "Requesting the sending of twelve women," n.d. Petition included in "Doña Juana's 1709 Petition," AGI SD 841, folios 670–690. For similar arguments in different contexts, see Juliana Barr, *Peace Came in the Form of a Woman: Indians and Spaniards in the Texas Borderlands* (Chapel Hill: University of North Carolina Press, 2007), 121; Miroslava Chavez-Garcia, *Negotiating Conquest: Gender and Power in California, 1770s to 1880s* (Tucson: University of Arizona Press, 2004), xv; Sarah Deutsch, *No Separate Refuge: Culture, Class, and Gender on an Anglo-Hispanic Frontier in the American Southwest, 1880–1940* (New York: Oxford

University Press, 1987), 3–12; and Susanah Shaw Romney, "'With & Alongside His Housewife': Claiming Ground in New Netherland and the Early Modern Dutch Empire," *William and Mary Quarterly* 73, no. 2 (2016): 187–224.

30. "Zúñiga y Cerda to the King, March 30, 1704," AGI SD 833, folio 92; also in Boyd et al., *Here They Once Stood*, 48–50. José de Zúñiga y Cerda and D. Luis Chacón, *Primera y Breve Relación de la favorables noticias . . .* (Madrid, 1703), held at the John Carter Brown Library, Providence, R.I.
31. Hann, *Apalachee*, 272–273, 385–397. Dubcovsky, "Defying Indian Slavery," 295–322.
32. "Governor Zúñiga to King," Boyd et al., *Here They Once Stood*, 49. "General Inspection of Juan Francisco," July 8, 1709, AGI SD 841, folios 635–640.
33. Bonnie McEwan, "Hispanic Life on Seventeenth-Century Florida Frontier," 255–267. Bonnie G. McEwan and John H. Hann, "Reconstructing a Spanish Mission: San Luis de Talimali," *OAH Magazine of History* 14, no. 4 (2000): 16–19. Cathy Matson, "Women's Economies in North America Before 1820: Special Forum Introduction," *Early American Studies* 4, no. 2 (2006): 271–290.
34. "Fray Claudio de Florencia," San Agustín, July, 6, 1709 AGI SD 841, folios 626–630 [26–34]. "Testimony Juan Peñalosa," AGI SD 841, folio 655.
35. "Zúñiga y Cerda to the King, March 30, 1704," AGI SD 833, folio 92; Boyd et al., *Here They Once Stood*, 48–50. Dubcovsky, "All of Us Will Have to Pay for These Activities," 1–18.
36. For the earlier attack, see "Don Patricio, Cacique of Ivitachuco, and Don Andrés, Cacique of San Luis, to the King." February 12, 1699, in Boyd et al., *Here They Once Stood*, 24–26. Moore's Letter, *Boston-Newsletter*, May 1, 1704. Calvin B. Jones, "Colonial James Moore and the Destruction of The Apalachee Missions in 1704," *Bureau of Historical Sites and Properties* (1972): 25–33. Steven. J. Oatis, *A Colonial Complex: South Carolina's Frontiers in the Era of the Yamasee War, 1680–1730* (Lincoln: University of Nebraska Press, 2004): 42–61.
37. "Fray Claudio de Florencia," San Agustín, AGI SD 841, folios 623–630, quote on 629.
38. "Testimony of Juan Francisco," July 8, 1709, AGI SD 841, folios 635–640.
39. "Juana's 1709 Petition," AGI SD 841 folios 623–661.
40. "Governor Zúñiga y Cerda to the King," March 30, 1704. Florida. AGI SD 840. Hann Collection, PKY. Childers Docs Binder 1–9, PKY. "Extracts from the act of an inquiry into the deaths of the Fathers in Apalachee . . ." June 1705, AGI SD 864 folio 54 in Boyd et al., *Here They Once Stood*, 48–50. "Manuel Solana to Zúñiga y Cerda," June 10, 1704, AGI SD 858, CDB 1–10, Hann Collection, PKY.
41. For how Native nations worked through the slave trade, see *The Yamasee Indians: From Florida to South Carolina*, ed. Denise I. Bossy (Lincoln: University of Nebraska Press, 2018); Stephen Warren, *The Worlds the Shaw-*

nees Made: Migration and Violence in Early America (Chapel Hill: University of North Carolina Press, 2014). Miller Wright, "The Development of Slaving Societies in the Americas: Marginal Native and Colonial Slavers in São Paulo and Carolina, 1614–1715" (PhD thesis, Rice University, 2021).

42. "Manuel de Solana to Governor Zúñiga y Cerda, July 8, 1704, AGI SD 857, Boyd et al., *Here They Once Stood*, 54.
43. "Testimony of Nicolás Mendes," July 8, 1709. AGI SD 841, folios 644–649.
44. "Manuel Solana, Inventory," August 19, 1704. AGI, SD 858. John H. Hann, "Church Furnishings, Sacred Vessels, and Vestments Held by the Missions of Florida: Translation of Two Inventories," *Florida Archaeology* 2 (1986): 146–164.
45. "Zúñiga y Cerda to King," September 10, 1704, cited in Boyd et al., *Here They Once Stood*, 67.
46. "Testimony of Nicolás Mendes," July 8, 1709, AGI SD 841, folios 644–649. "Council of War," July 13, 1704. AGI SD 858. Boyd et al., *Here They Once Stood*, 56.
47. "The Departure of Apalachee," October 6, 1704, AGI SD 858, folio 1059.
48. "Jacinto Roque Pérez to Manuel Solana," April 10, 1704, AGI SD 858, folios 1044–1045. "February 10, 1708," Reales Cédulas Originales, volume 33, 325. Expediente 114. AGN.
49. "February 10, 1708," Reales Cédulas Originales, volume 33, 325. Expediente 114. AGN.
50. "March 15, 1706," Reales Cédulas Originales, volume 33. Pages 37–39, Expediente 9. AGN. Emphasis mine. See also "To the King," n.d. AGI SD 855 folio 53. For gendered notions of "peacekeeping," see Claire Duncanson, "Forces for Good? Narratives of Military Masculinity in Peacekeeping Operations," *International Feminist Journal of Politics* 11, no. 1 (2009): 63–80.
51. "Governor Francisco de Córcoles y Martínez to the King, St. Augustine," AGI SD 841, folios 623–625.
52. "Junta of October 16," 1706, AGI México 633.
53. "Franciscans to King," May 7, 1707, AGI SD 854, folio 61. Boyd et al., *Here They Once Stood*, 87.
54. "Royal officials to Viceroy," August 18, 1704. AGI SD 857, folios 13–14. Boyd et al., *Here They Once Stood*, 61.
55. "Testimony of Nicolás Mendes," July 8, 1709. AGI SD 841, folios 644–649.
56. "Fray Claudio de Florencia's Questions," San Agustín, AGI SD 841, folio 627.
57. "Juana's 1709 Petition," AGI SD 841 folios 623–661.
58. "Approval of Doña Juana de Florencia's Petition," March 23, 1715, AGI SD 837 folios 43–44.

59. "Fray Claudio de Florencia's Questions," San Agustín, AGI SD 841, folios 626–633. The eight witnesses were Capitan Juan Ruíz Mejía (Juana's nephew), Don Juan Francisco, Adjutant Alonso Naranjo, Squad Leader Nicolás Mendes, Captain Joaquín de Florencia (cousin of Juana's father), Juan de Peñalosa, and Captain Francisco Romo de Urisa (Interim Sergeant-Major and Juana's uncle), and Governor Francisco de Córcoles y Martínez.
60. "Testimony of Nicolás Mendes," July 8, 1709. AGI SD 841, folios 644–649; emphasis mine.
61. Ibid.
62. Ibid.
63. "Testimony of Juan Francisco, July 8, 1709. AGI SD 841, folios 635–639.
64. "Testimony of Alonso Naranjo," July 8, 1709. AGI SD 841, folios 641–644.
65. "Testimony of Joaquín de Florencia," July 9, 1709. AGI SD 843, folios 649–652. "Testimony of Capitan Don Francisco Romo de Urisa," July 10, 1709. AGI SD 841, folios 656–659. For crafting gender identity in petitions, see Matthew Goldmark, "Reading Habits: Catalina De Erauso and the Subjects of Early Modern Spanish Gender and Sexuality," *Colonial Latin American Review* 24, no. 2 (2015): 215–235. Patricia Seed, "Marriage Promises and the Value of a Woman's Testimony in Colonial Mexico," *Signs* 13, no. 2 (1988): 253–276.
66. "Fray Claudio de Florencia's Questions," San Agustín, AGI SD 841, folios 626–633.
67. "Testimony of Juan Ruíz Mexía, July 8, 1709," AGI SD 841, folios 631–635.
68. "Testimony of Juan Francisco, July 8, 1709," AGI SD 841, folios 635–639.
69. Juan Ignacio Arnaud Rabinal and Pedro Miguel Martín Escudero. "Plazas Muertas y Otras Gracias Reales En Florida: Una Sociedad Dependiente En El Siglo XVII," in *Aportaciones Militares a La Cultura, Arte Y Ciencia En El Siglo XVIII Hispanoamericano: Jornadas Nacionales De Historia Militar*, ed. Pedro Mora Piris (Sevilla: Cátedra General Castaños, Capitanía General de la Región Militar Sur, 1991), 65–69.
70. August 17, 1709. Reales Cédulas Originales. Volume 34, 155. Expediente 69. AGN.
71. "Testimony of Juan Francisco, July 8, 1709," AGI SD 841, folios 635–639.
72. "Testimony of Juan Ruíz Mexía, July 8, 1709," AGI SD 841, folios 631–635.
73. For disappearance and erasure, see Jean M. O'Brien, *Firsting and Lasting: Writing Indians Out of Existence in New England* (Minneapolis: University of Minnesota Press, 2010), 55–105; Christine DeLucia, "The Memory Frontier: Uncommon Pursuits of Past and Place in the Northeast after King Philip's War," *Journal of American History* 98, no. 4 (March 2012): 975–997.
74. "Manuel Solana to Zúñiga y Cerda," June 10, 1704, AGI SD 858, CDB 1–10, Hann Collection, PKY "Manuel Solana to Zúñiga y Cerda," July 8, 1704, AGI SD 858 CDB 1–10, Hann Collection, PKY. Dubcovsky, "Defying Indian Slavery," 295–322.

75. Mishuana Goeman, *Mark My Words: Native Women Mapping Our Nations* (Minneapolis: University of Minnesota Press, 2013), 2–12. For collective biographies, see Erica Ball, Tatiana Seijas, and Terri L. Snyder, "Introduction," in *As If She Were Free: A Collective Biography of Women and Emancipation in the Americas*, ed. Erica L. Ball, Tatiana Seijas, and Terri L. Snyder (Cambridge: Cambridge University Press, 2020), 1–23. Alison Booth, *How to Make It as a Woman: Collective Biographical History from Victoria to the Present* (Chicago: University of Chicago Press, 2004).
76. "Autos and Inquiry," 1687 AGI ES 156 Cuaderno E, folio 31. Juan Márquez Cabrera a Su Magestad," April 15, 1686 AGI 856 in the Lanning Papers no. 702. "Testimony of Jacinto Roque," Alonso Solana 1687, AGI ES 156 Cuaderno E, folios 32–33. John H. Hann, *The Native American World Beyond Apalachee: West Florida and the Chattahoochee Valley* (Gainesville: University Press of Florida, 2006), 106, 129.
77. "Autos and Inquiry," Alonso Solana 1687, AGI ES 156 Cuaderno E, folios 22–23. "Juan Márquez Cabrera a Su Magestad," April 15, 1686, AGI 856 in the Lanning Papers no. 702.
78. "Cédula Real," October 30, 1669. Indiferente Virreinal, Caja 4438, volume 26, Expediente 169, FS. 167. Archivo General de la Nación (AGN). Theodore G. Corbett, "Population Structure in Hispanic San Agustín, 1629–1763," *Florida Historical Quarterly* 54, no. 3 (1976): 263–284, 270.
79. For more on Lieutenant Governor Matheos, "Letter of Antonio Matheos," in Folder 4, Bolton Papers, Bancroft Library. "Antonio Matheos to Márquez Cabrera," February 8, 1686, AGI SD 839, in Lanning Papers no. 702. Thomas Jefferson Library, University of Missouri, St. Louis. John H. Hann, "Cloak and Dagger in Apalachicole Province in Early 1686," *Florida Historical Quarterly* 78, no. 1 (1999): 74–93. Fred Lamar Pearson, Jr., "Anglo-Spanish Rivalry in the Chattahoochee Basin and West Florida, 1685–1704," *South Carolina Historical Magazine* 79, no. 1 (1978). Dubcovsky, *Informed Power*, chapter 5.
80. "Testimony of Jacinto Roque," Alonso Solana 1687, AGI ES 156 Cuaderno E, folios 32–33.
81. "Testimony of Antonio Matheos," in Alonso Solana 1687, AGI ES 156 Cuaderno E, folios 52–59. Bonnie G. McEwan, "The Apalachee Indians of Northwest Florida," in *Indians of the Greater Southeast: Historical Archaeology and Ethnohistory*, ed. Bonnie G. McEwan (Gainesville: University Press of Florida, 2000): 57–84.
82. "Autos and Inquiry," Alonso Solana 1687, AGI ES 156 Cuaderno E, folios 22–23. "Juan Márquez Cabrera a Su Magestad," April 15, 1686, AGI 856 in the Lanning Papers no. 702. "Testimony of Jacinto Roque," Alonso Solana 1687, AGI ES 156 Cuaderno E, folio 32–33.
83. Jennifer Baszile, "Apalachee Testimony in Florida: A View of Slavery from the Spanish Archives," in *Indian Slavery in Colonial America*, ed. Alan Gallay (Lincoln: University of Nebraska Press, 2009), 185–206.

84. "Testimony of Antonio Matheos," in Alonso Solana 1687, AGI ES 156 Cuaderno E, folio 52–59.
85. "Matheo Chuba in San Luis," in Alonso Solana 1687, Autos and Inquiry Made, AGI ES legajo, 156, Cuaderno E, folios 31–32.
86. "Testimony of Jacinto Roque," Alonso Solana 1687, AGI ES 156 Cuaderno E, folios 32–33.
87. "Matheo Chuba in San Luis," in Alonso Solana 1687, Autos and Inquiry, AGI ES legajo, 156, Cuaderno E, folios 31–32.
88. Ibid.
89. Ibid.
90. "Don Patricio, Cacique of Ivitachuco, and Don Andrés, Cacique of San Luis, to the King," February 12, 1699, in Boyd et al., *Here They Once Stood.* Jacinto Roque, in Alonso Solana 1687, Autos and Inquiry, AGI ES 156 Cuaderno E, folio 31. For more on Native epistolary practices in the region, see George Aaron Broadwell and Alejandra Dubcovsky, "Chief Manuel's 1651 Timucua Letter: The Oldest Letter in a Native Language of the United States," *Proceedings of the American Philosophical Society* 164, no. 4 (2020).
91. "Don Patricio, Cacique of Ivitachuco, and Don Andrés, Cacique of San Luis, to the King," February 12, 1699, in Boyd et al., *Here They Once Stood.*
92. "Don Patricio, Cacique of Ivitachuco, and Don Andrés, Cacique of San Luis, to the King. February 12, 1699, in Boyd et al., *Here They Once Stood.* "Testimony of Jacinto Roque," in Alonso Solana 1687, Autos and Inquiry, AGI ES 156 Cuaderno E, folio 31.
93. The wife of Nicolás Suárez faced a similar charge; she kept two Native men for her service. She employed Icho Favian from Ivitachuco and Chuguta Antonio from Ayubale. Though both men were in theory paid for their services, she did not allow them to return home. Their wives petitioned for their return. AGI EC 157. Hann, *Visitations*, 170, 172. For other examples of enslavement see chapter 2 of this book.
94. AGI ES 153, 1721, [8–9].
95. AGI ES 153 B, folio 83. Timothy Paul Grady, *Anglo-Spanish Rivalry in Colonial South-East America, 1650–1725* (London: Pickering & Chatto, 2010), 108–112.
96. "Petition of Don Manuel Quiñones," December 12, 1708, AGI SD 836, folio 980. Quiñones's report was subsequently misfiled. Rather than being grouped with the 1701 Ayala *Visitation*, it lies with materials from the 1720s.
97. AGI ES 153, 1721 [8–9], emphasis mine. For women as "handmaidens of empire," see Christine Walker, *Jamaica Ladies: Female Slaveholders and the Creation of Britain's Atlantic Empire* (Chapel Hill: University of North Carolina Press and Omohundro Institute of Early American History and Culture, 2020), 5–24. Sarah Pearsall, *Atlantic Families: Lives and Letters in the Later Eighteenth Century* (Oxford: Oxford University Press, 2008).

98. AGI ES 153, 1721; [8–9]
99. Ibid.
100. Hann, *Apalachee*, 271–275. See "Variant Versions of Colonel James Moore's Letters About His Assault on Apalachee," in Hann, *Apalachee*, Appendix 12, 385–398. Document #3 Governor Joseph de Zúñiga y Zerda to the Caciques of Yvitachuco and leading men and caciques of the province, Florida, April 24, 1704. AGI SD 858 folios 275–276, Hann Collection, HC-Comps_2004. Amy Turner Bushnell, "Patricio De Hinachuba: Defender of the Word of God, the Crown of the King, and the Little Children of Ivitachuco," *American Indian Culture and Research Journal* 3, no. 3 (1979): 1–21.
101. "Governor Zúñiga y Zerda to the Caciques of Yvitachuco," April 24, 1704. AGI SD 858 folios 275–276.
102. Ibid.
103. Ibid.
104. Ibid.
105. Amy Turner Bushnell, "The Menéndez Marquéz Cattle Barony at La Chua and the Determinants of Economic Expansion in Seventeenth-Century Florida," 407–431. Justin B. Blanton, "The Role of Cattle Ranching in the 1656 Timucuan Rebellion: A Struggle for Land, Labor, and Chiefly Power," *Florida Historical Quarterly* 92, no. 4 (2014): 667–684.
106. Paul E. Hoffman, *Florida's Frontiers* (Bloomington: Indiana University Press, 2002), 180. John H. Hann, "Summary Guide to Spanish Florida Missions and Visitas, with Churches in the Sixteenth and Seventeenth Centuries," *The Americas* 66, no. 4 (1990): 513.
107. "Franciscans to King," May 7, 1707, AGI SD 854, folio 61, emphasis added. Boyd et al., *Here They Once Stood*, 87. Steven C. Hahn, *The Invention of the Creek Nation, 1670–1763* (Lincoln: University of Nebraska Press, 2004), 64.
108. "Francisco de Córcoles y Martínez about siege of Abosaya," January 30, 1706, AGI SD 858, folios 285–287.
109. Ibid.
110. "May 16, 1704," AGI Mexico 618, folio 57. "Manuel de Solana to Governor Zúñiga y Cerda," July 8, 1704, AGI SD 858, Boyd et al., *Here They Once Stood*, 55–56. "Autos of Governor Zúñiga y Cerda" July 12, 1704, AGI SD 857, folios 60–61, Boyd et al., *Here They Once Stood*, 54. Mississippi Provincial Archives 1701–1729: French Dominion, vol. 2 (Press of the Mississippi Department of Archives and History), 25.
111. Mississippi Provincial Archives 1701–1729: French Dominion, vol. 2 (Press of the Mississippi Department of Archives and History), 25.
112. James F. Brooks, "Life Proceeds from the Name: Indigenous People and the Predicament of Hybridity," in *Clearing a Path: Theorizing the Past in Native American Studies*, ed. Nancy Shoemaker (New York: Routledge, 2002), 181–205.

Epilogue

Epigraph. Selection from Anna Marie Sewell, "Washing the World," from prairiepomes.com 2013. https://www.poetryfoundation.org/poems/146970/washing-the-world, used with permission from the author.

1. Glenna Stumblingbear-Riddle, "Standing with Our Sisters: MMIWG2S," *American Psychological Association* (November 2018). https://www.apa.org/pi/oema/resources/communique/2018/11/standing-sisters Patricia Tjaden and Nancy Thoennes. "The Prevalence, Incidence, and Consequences of Violence Against Women," Findings from the National Violence Survey Against Women. National Institute of Justice and the Centers for Disease Control (2000). https://www.ncjrs.gov/pdffiles1/nij/183781.pdfa. For Latin American context, see Laura Raquel Valladares de la Cruz, "Mujeres Indígenas Entre Guerras: Viejas Y Nuevas Expresiones De La Violencia," *Encartes* 4, no. 4 (2019): 145–174.
2. Marcie Rendon, "Trigger Warning or Genocide Is Worse Than Racism," *About Place Journal* 6, no. 2 (2022).
3. Sarah Deer, *The Beginning and End of Rape: Confronting Sexual Violence in Native America* (Minneapolis: University of Minnesota Press, 2015). Joyce Green, ed., *Making Space for Indigenous Feminism*, 2nd ed. (Blackpoint, N.S.: Fernwood Publishing, 2017).
4. For a contemporary example, see Joaqlin Estus, "Instagram Apologizes, MMIWG Movement Erased Online," May 6, 2021, *Indian Country Today*, https://indiancountrytoday.com/news/mmiwg-movement-erased-online.

Index

Page numbers in *italics* denote figures.